STABILIZATION OF THE DOMESTIC
AND
INTERNATIONAL ECONOMY

CARNEGIE - ROCHESTER CONFERENCE SERIES ON PUBLIC POLICY

A supplementary series to the Journal of Monetary Economics

Editors

KARL BRUNNER
ALLAN H. MELTZER

Production Editor

GAIL McGUIRE

VOLUME 5

NORTH-HOLLAND PUBLISHING COMPANY
AMSTERDAM · NEW YORK · OXFORD

STABILIZATION OF
THE DOMESTIC AND
INTERNATIONAL ECONOMY

Editors

KARL BRUNNER

Graduate School of Management
The University of Rochester

ALLAN H. MELTZER

Carnegie-Mellon University

1977

NORTH-HOLLAND PUBLISHING COMPANY
AMSTERDAM · NEW YORK · OXFORD

ISBN North-Holland for this volume: 0 7204 0709 5

Publishers:

NORTH-HOLLAND PUBLISHING COMPANY
AMSTERDAM · NEW YORK · OXFORD

Distributors for the U.S.A. and Canada:

ELSEVIER NORTH-HOLLAND, INC.
52 VANDERBILT AVENUE
NEW YORK, N.Y. 10017

Library of Congress Cataloging in Publication Data

Main entry under title:

Stabilization of the domestic and international economy.

(Carnegie-Rochester conference series on public policy ; v. 5)
  1. Economic stabilization--Congresses.
2. Indexation (Economics)--Congresses.
3. Inflation (Finance)--Congresses. I. Brunner, Karl, 1916-   II. Meltzer, Allan H.
III. Series.
HB3730.S72   339.5   76-58908
ISBN 0-7204-0709-5

PRINTED IN THE NETHERLANDS

INTRODUCTION TO THE SERIES

The Carnegie-Rochester Conference on Public Policy was initiated several years ago through the efforts of the Center for Research in Government Policy and Business at the University of Rochester and the Center for the Study of Public Policy at Carnegie-Mellon University. This book is the fifth volume in the series which presents the papers prepared for the conferences, plus the comments of discussants and participants.

Policies depend not only on theories and evidence, but on the structure of policymaking bodies and the procedures by which policies are made, implemented, and changed. The conferences direct the attention of economists to major problems of economic policy and institutional arrangements. We hope that the papers and the conferences will encourage further research on policy and on the effects of national agencies and international institutions on the choice of policies.

The Carnegie-Rochester Conference is an open forum. Participants are united by their interest in the issues discussed and by their belief that analysis, evidence, and informed discussion have lasting effects on the public and its institutions.

This fifth volume of the series, offered as a supplement to the Journal of Monetary Economics, contains papers presented at the April 1974 and November 1975 conferences. The invited contributions by Robert E. Lucas, Jr. and Michael Parkin were originally presented at a June 1976 Conference on Growth without Inflation at the Institüt für Weltwirtschaft, Kiel, West Germany. Future volumes of the conference proceedings will be mailed to subscribers as a supplement to the journal. The editor of the journal will consider for publication comments on the papers published in the supplement.

We wish to acknowledge the unfailing assistance of Mrs. Jean Morris and Mrs. Jean Patterson in every aspect of the organization of the conferences from their beginning, and in the production of the papers for the series.

K. BRUNNER
A.H. MELTZER
Editors

CONTENTS

Karl Brunner and Allan H. Meltzer:
Stabilization of the Domestic and International
Economy 1

Robert E. Lucas, Jr.:
Understanding Business Cycles 7

Michael Parkin:
Inflation without Growth: A Long-Run Perspective
on Short-Run Stabilization Policies 31

Alan S. Blinder:
Indexing the Economy through Financial
Intermediation 69

Stanley Fischer:
Wage Indexation and Macroeconomic Stability 107

Edmund S. Phelps:
Indexation Issues: A Comment on the Blinder and
Fischer Papers 149
Guillermo A. Calvo and Edmund S. Phelps:
Appendix: Employment Contingent Wage Contracts 160

Michael Parkin:
Indexing the Economy through Financial
Intermediation: A Comment 169

Clifford W. Smith, Jr.:
On the Indexation of Contracts under Uncertainty:
A Comment on the Blinder Paper 173

Robert J. Gordon:
Structural Unemployment and the Productivity
of Women 181

Robert E. Hall:
    Structural Unemployment and the Productivity
    of Women: A Comment 231

André Farber, Richard Roll and Bruno Solnik:
    An Empirical Study of Risk under Fixed and
    Flexible Exchange 235

Jerome L. Stein:
    Social Welfare under Fixed and Flexible Exchange
    Rates: A Comment on the Farber, Roll and Solnik
    Paper 267

Richard James Sweeney and Thomas D. Willett:
    Eurodollars, Petrodollars, and World Liquidity and
    Inflation 277

Dale W. Henderson:
    Eurodollars, Petrodollars, and World Liquidity and
    Inflation: A Comment 311

STABILIZATION OF THE DOMESTIC AND INTERNATIONAL ECONOMY

Karl Brunner
University of Rochester

and

Allan H. Meltzer
Carnegie-Mellon University

The appropriate response to shorter-run movements in prices and employment and longer-run inflation remains in the forefront of economists' discussions of stabilization policy. Some argue that we should accept inflation and adjust financial policies to maintain inherited inflation for the indefinite future. Others find that longer-run welfare is best served with a gradual adjustment of financial policies to a noninflationary level. Some prefer fluctuating to fixed exchange rates; others hold that fluctuating exchange rates increase inflation. These intellectual and political disputes about stabilization policy are expected to continue.

The fifth volume of the Carnegie-Rochester Conference Series on Public Policy contains seven papers on domestic or international aspects of stabilization policy. The papers reexamine our approach to macro problems and question the adequacy of current explanations. Several papers and comments analyze the reasons for the existence and nonexistence of indexed contracts and the impact of wage indexation on stability of the economy. Other papers examine the welfare aspects of unemployment and explore the behavior of floating exchange rates and the role of the Eurodollar market.

The opening paper by Robert Lucas is of fundamental importance. "Understanding Business Cycles" questions the direction of the work initiated by the Keynesian revolution and emphasizes the potential usefulness of problems and programs formulated in the pre-Keynesian literature on the business cycle. "The most rapid progress toward a coherent and useful aggregate economic theory will result from the acceptance of the problem statement as advanced by the business cycle theorists, and not from further attempts to refine the jerry-built structures to which Keynesian macroeconomics has led us." Lucas then outlines in some detail an alternative approach to the analysis of an economy's macro behavior involving the systematic integration of "business cycle analysis" into economic theory. Such integration forms, according to Lucas, a necessary condition for a rational approach to stabilization policies.

The new approach differs from the current approach not only in the actions that it implies but also in its views of what policy can achieve and how policy should be formulated.

> Accompanying the redirection of scientific interest occasioned by the Keynesian Revolution was a sharp change in the nature of the contribution to policy which economists hoped to offer and which the public has come largely to accept. The effort to 'explain business cycles' had been directed at identifying institutional sources of instability, with the hope that, once understood, these sources could be removed or their influence mitigated by appropriate institutional changes. The process envisaged was the painfully slow one of public discussion and legislative reform; on the other side, there was the hope of long-term or 'permanent' institutional improvement. The abandonment of the effort to explain business cycles accompanied a belief that policy could effect immediate, or very short-term, movement of the economy from an undesirable current state, <u>however arrived at</u>, to a better state.

Michael Parkin, the author of the second paper, considers the problems associated with "Inflation without Growth: A Long-Run Perspective on Short-Run Stabilization Policies." The paper addresses the phenomenon of persistent inflation and sluggish growth. Two conflicting views are presented with very different implications for the choice of appropriate policies. A detailed examination of the competing explanations finds serious faults with the prevalent emphasis on sociological patterns and institutional factors. A subsequent section investigates the "sources of inflationary monetary policy."

Parkin discusses four hypotheses. The hypothesis judged to be most promising emphasizes the nature of the political process in democratic societies and the role of politicians engaged in advancing their individual prospects. Parkin argues that, in all the western democracies, we observe the consequences of this process for resource allocation in lower growth accompanied by an expanding system of wealth transfers.

Parkin's explanation of the sources of inflationary monetary policy and declining growth suggests that we will not return to stable prices. The adjustment of an economy to long-run inflation emerges as an unresolved problem. Alan S. Blinder's paper, "Indexing the Economy through Financial Intermediation," attempts "to unravel. . .[a]. . .mystery," by exploring the

2

reason for the comparatively infrequent emergence of indexed contracts. Blinder suggests that, "risk-averse firms would be happy to link factor payments to a price index which follows closely the movements of their own output prices, but shy away from contracts linking wages and interest to some broad price index whose movement might easily outstrip their selling prices. Conversely, workers and bondholders may be unwilling to bear the substantial risk of linking their factor payments to the prices of firms for which they work or to which they lend. . .they prefer linkage to a broad price index." Occurrence of indexation thus depends on contract conditions acceptable to both demanders and suppliers. Blinder suggests that, ". . .a new kind of financial intermediary can solve the problem." A mutual fund should be established holding bonds indexed in terms of specific output prices. The total return on the portfolio approximates an instrument indexed to a broadly based price index.

Stanley Fischer investigates another aspect of indexation. His paper, "Wage Indexation and Macroeconomic Stability," is motivated by two conflicting views about the effect of wage indexation on macro stability. The author develops three models of wage indexation. Each model ". . .suggests that whether wage indexing is stabilizing or not depends on the nature of the disturbances affecting the economy." Fischer also examines the role of monetary policy in indexed and non-indexed economies and explores the opportunities for stabilization in contexts exhibiting different patterns of disturbances.

Fischer's analysis is incomplete. He fails to ask why optimal contracts do not arise. If wage indexation is the appropriate response to monetary shocks but not to real shocks, society can achieve optimality by providing, ex ante, contracts that compensate workers or employers for any losses they have experienced as a result of nominal shocks. Contracts of this kind would be superior to complete indexation or non-indexation. To enter such a contract, both parties would require the ability to separate losses from real and nominal shocks after they have occurred.

The role of contracts and their properties is the subject of Edmund Phelps' comment on the Blinder and Fischer papers. Phelps is critical of the theory used to analyze indexation of wages. He proposes an alternative theory in which wage contracts provide for indexation in response to price level changes and changes in employment. In an appendix, co-authored with Guillermo Calvo, the appropriate response of wages and monetary policy to supply shocks is analyzed. The analysis shows that the appropriate response depends on the type of contracts assumed to prevail. As Phelps suggests at the end of his comment, we do not have a satisfactory answer to Keynes' problem of reducing real wages.

Michael Parkin and Clifford Smith direct their comments to Blinder's paper and particularly to his proposal for a new intermediary. Both offer some reasons why the benefits provided by the intermediary may be less than the costs of providing them.

Rising inflation has been accompanied by rising unemployment. The short-run Phillips trade-off seemed to erode and, in several countries, a positively sloped Phillips curve seemed to emerge. Whatever the interpretation of this change, the social costs and benefits of unemployment, or of programs designed to lower unemployment, require assessment. Robert J. Gordon's paper offers some analysis of "Structural Unemployment and the Productivity of Women." Robert Hall comments on Gordon's paper.

Gordon notes two major changes during recent decades affecting the analysis of labor markets. One change is general acceptance of the natural rate hypothesis. The other is the gradual recognition during the past ten years of a structural shift in unemployment. The shift appears as a relative increase of teenagers and women in the U.S. labor force and is reflected in the increase in the natural rate of unemployment from 4.1 percent in 1956 to 5.6 percent in 1974. The evaluation of policy issues depends on the welfare assessment of this structural change.

According to Gordon, welfare probably would have increased as a result of the changing composition of the labor force if the average unemployment rate of the various social groups had remained unchanged. The case for an adverse welfare effect depends on the fact that the unemployment rates of teenagers and women have increased relative to the rates for adult men. An elaborate conceptual framework, supplemented with tentative data, yields some estimates and a cautious judgment of the effect of shifts in employment. A principal conclusion of Gordon's study is that the social cost of the higher unemployment rates for teenagers and adult females than for adult males is "amazingly small." To reduce the unemployment rate for teenagers to the level reached in 1956 would require a substantial reduction in the minimum wage.

The last two papers in the volume bear on the international aspects of financial policies producing the inflation of recent years. Farber, Roll and Solnik investigate the comparative behavior of exchange rate systems. Their joint efforts produced "An Empirical Study of Risk under Fixed and Flexible Exchange."

For years many writers have argued that floating rates destabilize economies and that risk and uncertainty increase with floating. Farber, Roll and Solnik suspend judgment on the first question but analyze the second issue in detail. They show that the proper distinction for most countries in the 1960s and 1970s is not between fixed and fluctuating rates but between small, frequent adjustments and large, less frequent adjustments of par values.

By comparing the frequency distribution of changes in exchange rates under a fixed rate and a flexible rate regime, the authors demonstrate that a comparison of standard deviations does not adequately summarize the difference in exchange rate regimes. The shape of the distributions differs substantially in the two regimes and thus provides a basis for determining actual practices. Both empirical distributions seem non-normal for all countries.

The authors use the technique known as stochastic dominance to determine the regime most preferred by investors. The results are inconclusive. Risk-averse investors would have preferred a fixed rate system for Italy, and a flexible rate system for Brazil, Canada, and Spain. For thirteen other countries, the results are ambiguous.

Farber, Roll and Solnik then examine the relative risk associated with portfolios of fluctuating and fixed rate currencies when there is covariance between exchange rates. The authors trace the changes in efficient portfolios occurring in the two regimes. They find that the efficient frontier moved to the right under a flexible rate system. But, they also infer from their statistical work that the "price of risk" declined. An interpretation is offered to reconcile these observations.

Jerome Stein is critical of the use of portfolio analysis to draw conclusions about the welfare effects of exchange rate systems. He argues that the proper measure of welfare gained or lost from adopting fluctuating exchange rates can be made by comparing the (unanticipated) fluctuations in the economy with the opportunities for policy to lower the variance of real income.

The large variations in credit market conditions produced by inflation in 1973-74 added to the strains imposed on the international payments system by the OPEC policies that were pursued in late 1973 and 1974. There were reports of substantial apprehension about the ability of the Eurodollar market to adjust to the strains. This apprehension was reenforced by suggestions that the Eurocurrency market is an international money creating machine running out of control. Richard J. Sweeney and Thomas D. Willett consider some aspects of these issues in their paper, "Eurodollars, Petrodollars, and World Liquidity and Inflation."

The authors' detailed examination of the contribution of the Eurodollar market to inflation shows that additions to national money stock figures were comparatively modest and much smaller than the gross or net figures usually cited. They emphasize that the net liabilities supplied by the Eurocurrency institutions correspond more nearly to the M4 or M5 measures of the national money stock than to more usual definitions such as M1, or M2. Hence, Euro-dollars are a type of credit, not money. Sweeney and Willett also criticize various constructions of a world money stock and the inclusion of Eurodollars in such measures. They find serious fault with relations centered on the concept of an international reserve base. Dale Henderson's comment extends the argument and suggests that properly constructed domestic money stocks include only the deposits held by domestic wealth owners.

Much of the discussion of the world money stock has been based on less than careful analysis of the mechanisms by which Eurodollars affect domestic price levels. An uncritical acceptance of the notion that inflation is generated by naming some asset "money" and watching it grow, combined with careless reasoning about the Eurodollar market, generated misunderstanding about the role of the Eurodollar market. Sweeney and Willett consider and reject several of the arguments for regulating and controlling the Euromarkets, and Henderson extends and modifies their argument.

UNDERSTANDING BUSINESS CYCLES*

Robert E. Lucas, Jr.
University of Chicago

I.

Why is it that, in capitalist economies, aggregate variables undergo repeated fluctuations about trend, all of essentially the same character? Prior to Keynes' General Theory, the resolution of this question was regarded as one of the main outstanding challenges to economic research, and attempts to meet this challenge were called business cycle theory. Moreover, among the interwar business cycle theorists, there was wide agreement as to what it would mean to solve this problem. To cite Hayek, as a leading example:

> [T]he incorporation of cyclical phenomena into the system of economic equilibrium theory, with which they are in apparent contradiction, remains the crucial problem of Trade Cycle Theory;[1]

> By 'equilibrium theory' we here primarily understand the modern theory of the general interdependence of all economic quantities, which has been most perfectly expressed by the Lausanne School of theoretical economics.[2]

A primary consequence of the Keynesian Revolution was the redirection of research effort away from this question onto the apparently simpler question of the determination of output at a point in time, taking history as given.[3] A secondary consequence of this Revolution, due more to Tinbergen than to Keynes, was a rapid increase in the level of precision and explicitness with which aggregate economic theories were formulated. As a result, Keynesian macro-

---

*Paper prepared for the Kiel Conference on Growth without Inflation, June 22-23, 1976; revised, August 1976. I would like to thank Gary Becker, Jacob Frenkel, Don Patinkin, Thomas Sargent, and Jose Scheinkman for their comments and suggestions.

[1]Hayek (1933), p. 33n.

[2]Hayek (1933), p. 42n.

[3]This redirection was conscious and explicit on Keynes' part. See, for example, the first sentence of his chapter on the trade cycle. "Since we claim to have shown in the preceding chapters what determines the volume of employment at any time, it follows, if we are right, that our theory must be capable of explaining the phenomena of the trade cycle " (1936), p. 313.

economics has benefited from several decades of methodological improvement whereas, from this technical point of view, the efforts of the business cycle theorists appear hopelessly outdated.

Yet from another point of view, they seem quite modern. The observation that macroeconomics is in need of a microeconomic foundation has become commonplace, and though there is much confusion about the nature of this need and about what it would mean to satisfy it, it is likely that many modern economists would have no difficulty accepting Hayek's statement of the problem as roughly equivalent to their own. Whether or not this is so, I wish in this essay to argue that it <u>should</u> be so, or that the most rapid progress toward a coherent and useful aggregate economic theory will result from the acceptance of the problem statement as advanced by the business cycle theorists, and not from further attempts to refine the jerry-built structures to which Keynesian macroeconomics has led us.

Honoring one's intellectual ancestors is a worthwhile aim in itself, but there is a more immediate reason for interpreting the contemporary search for a theoretically sound aggregative economics as a resumption of the work of pre-Keynesian theorists. Accompanying the redirection of scientific interest occasioned by the Keynesian Revolution was a sharp change in the nature of the contribution to policy which economists hoped to offer and which the public has come largely to accept. The effort to "explain business cycles" had been directed at identifying institutional sources of instability, with the hope that, once understood, these sources could be removed or their influence mitigated by appropriate institutional changes. The process envisaged was the painfully slow one of public discussion and legislative reform; on the other side, there was the hope of long-term or "permanent" institutional improvement. The abandonment of the effort to explain business cycles accompanied a belief that policy could effect immediate, or very short-term, movement of the economy from an undesirable current state, <u>however arrived at</u>, to a better state.

The belief that this latter objective is attainable, and that the attempt to come closer to achieving it is the only legitimate task of research in aggregate economics is so widespread that argument to the contrary is viewed as "destructive," a willful attempt to make life more difficult for one's colleagues who are only trying to improve the lot of mankind. Yet the situation is symmetric. If the business cycle theorists were correct, the short-term manipulation on which much of aggregative economics is now focused only diverts attention from discussion of stabilization policies which might actually be effective; such postponement is, moreover, accompanied by the steady and entirely understandable erosion in the belief on the part of noneconomists that

8

aggregative economics has anything useful to say.

In the next section, I will review some of the main qualitative features of the events we call business cycles, and then turn to the Keynesian response to these facts, to the progress made along the line Keynes and Tinbergen initiated, and finally to the severe limits to this progress which have now become apparent. The remainder of the essay will consider the prospects of accounting for cyclical phenomena by an economic theory, in the narrow sense in which Hayek and other business cycle theorists have used that term.

II.

Let me begin to sharpen the discussion by reviewing the main qualitative features of economic time series which we call "the business cycle." Technically, movements about trend in gross national product in any country can be well described by a stochastically disturbed difference equation of very low order. These movements do not exhibit uniformity of either period or amplitude, which is to say, they do not resemble the deterministic wave motions which sometimes arise in the natural sciences. Those regularities which are observed are in the co-movements among different aggregative time series.

The principal among these are the following.[4] (i) Output movements across broadly defined sectors move together. (In Mitchell's terminology, they exhibit high conformity; in modern time series language, they have high coherence.) (ii) Production of producer and consumer durables exhibits much greater amplitude than does the production of nondurables. (iii) Production and prices of agricultural goods and natural resources have lower than average conformity. (iv) Business profits show high conformity and much greater amplitude than other series. (v) Prices generally are procyclical. (vi) Short-term interest rates are procyclical; long-term rates slightly so. (vii) Monetary aggregates and velocity measures are procyclical.

---

[4] The features of economic time series listed here are, curiously, both "well known" and expensive to document in any careful and comprehensive way. A useful, substantively oriented introduction is given by Mitchell (1951), who summarizes mainly interwar, U.S. experience. The basic technical reference for these methods is Burns and Mitchell (1946). U.S. monetary experience is best displayed in Friedman and Schwartz (1963). An invaluable source for earlier British series is Gayer, Rostow, and Schwartz (1953), esp. Vol. II. The phenomena documented in these sources are, of course, much more widely observed. Most can be inferred, though with some difficulty, from the estimated structure of modern econometric models.

An important recent contribution is Sargent and Sims (1976), which summarizes postwar U.S. quarterly series in several suggestive ways, leading to a qualitative picture very close to that provided by Mitchell, but within an explicit stochastic framework, so that their results are replicatable and criticizable at a level at which Mitchell's are not.

There is, as far as I know, no need to qualify these observations by restricting them to particular countries or time periods: they appear to be regularities common to all decentralized market economies. Though there is absolutely no theoretical reason to anticipate it, one is led by the facts to conclude that, with respect to the qualitative behavior of co-movements among series, business cycles are all alike. To theoretically inclined economists, this conclusion should be attractive and challenging, for it suggests the possibility of a unified explanation of business cycles, grounded in the general laws governing market economies, rather than in political or institutional character-istics specific to particular countries or periods.

I have omitted the behavior of foreign trade statistics from the above catalogue of phenomena-to-be-explained, in part because, for a large economy like the U.S., trade statistics do not exhibit high enough conformity to be cyclically interesting. For a smaller country, to be sure, export movements would do much to "explain" cycles, but to focus on open-economy explanations would, I think, beg the more difficult and crucial question of the ultimate origins of cyclical movements.

Also omitted, but too striking a phenomenon to pass over without com-ment, is the general reduction in amplitude of all series in the twenty-five years following World War II. At this purely descriptive level, it is impossible to distinguish good luck from good policy. Nevertheless, so long a period of relative stability strongly suggests that there is nothing inherent in the workings of market economies which requires living with the level of instability we are now experiencing, or to which we were subject in the pre-World War II years. That is, attempts to document and account for regular cyclical movements need not be connected in any way to a presumption that such movements are an inevitable feature of capitalist economies.

III.

The implications of Keynesian macroeconomic models conform well to the time series features reviewed above. Early versions (for example, by Hicks, 1937, and Modigliani, 1944) fit well qualitatively; the econometric models which developed from this theory and from Tinbergen's largely independent early work[5] conform well quantitatively. These models located the primary

---

[5]For example, see Tinbergen (1939). This work was not explicitly Keynesian; indeed, it was conceived as an empirical complement to Haberler's review and synthesis of theoretical work on business cycles (1936). Keynes, on his part, was actively hostile toward Tinbergen's work. See Moggridge (1973), pp. 285-320. In referring to those who built in part on Tinbergen's work as "Keynesian" I am, then, contributing to the continuation of an historical injustice.

disturbances in investment behavior, linked via lags (in Tinbergen's U. S. model) to the highly volatile profit series. Movements in these high-amplitude series then induce general movements in output and employment. Since these disturbances were, in Hicks' terms, "IS shifts," they were consistent with procyclically moving interest rates and velocity. The assumption of rigid wages and prices was a good empirical first approximation. Later on, a wage-price sector (still later called a Phillips curve) was added to fit observed procyclical wage and price movements.[6]

In this description, movements in money play no important role in accounting for cycles. This feature certainly did not result directly from the theoretical models; Keynes, Hicks, and Modigliani all gave great emphasis to monetary forces. The de-emphasis on money was on empirical grounds: econometricians from Tinbergen on discovered that monetary factors did not seem very important empirically.[7]

The empirical success of these developments was measured in an original and historically apt way by Adelman and Adelman (1959) in their simulation of the Klein-Goldberger model of the U. S. economy. The Adelmans posed, in a precise way, the question of whether an observer armed with the methods of Burns and Mitchell (1946) could distinguish between a collection of economic series generated artificially by a computer programmed to follow the Klein-Goldberger equations and the analogous series generated by an actual economy. The answer, to the evident surprise of the Adelmans (and, one suspects, of Klein and Goldberger, who had in no way directed their efforts to meeting this criterion) was <u>no</u>.[8]

This achievement signaled a new standard for what it means to understand business cycles. One exhibits understanding of business cycles by constructing a <u>model</u> in the most literal sense: a fully articulated artificial economy which behaves through time so as to imitate closely the time series behavior of actual economics. The Keynesian macroeconomic models were the first to attain this level of explicitness and empirical accuracy; by doing so, they altered the meaning of the term "theory" to such an extent that the older business cycle theories could not really be viewed as "theories" at all.

These models are not, however, "equilibrium theories" in Hayek's sense. Indeed, Keynes chose to begin the <u>General Theory</u> with the declaration (for

---

[6] Klein and Goldberger (1955).

[7] Tinbergen (1939), pp. 183-185. Tinbergen, as did most subsequent macroeconometricians, used the significance of interest rates to test the importance of money.

[8] It is not correct that a search for "good fits" would have led to a model satisfying the Adelmans' criteria; think of fitting polynomials in time to "explain" each series over the sample period.

Chapter II is no more than this) that an equilibrium theory was unattainable: that unemployment was not explainable as a consequence of individual choices and that the failure of wages to move as predicted by the classical theory was to be treated as due to forces beyond the power of economic theory to illuminate.

Keynes wrote as though the "involuntary" nature of unemployment were verifiable by direct observation, as though one could somehow look at a market and verify directly whether it is in equilibrium or not. Nevertheless, there were serious empirical reasons behind this choice, for nowhere is the "apparent contradiction" between "cyclical phenomena" and "economic equilibrium" theory sharper than in labor market behavior. Why, in the face of moderately fluctuating nominal wages and prices, should households choose to supply labor at sharply irregular rates through time? Most business cycle theorists had avoided this crucial problem, and those who addressed it had not resolved it. Keynes saw that by simply sidestepping this problem with the unexplained postulate of rigid nominal prices, an otherwise classical model could be transformed into a model which did a fair job of accounting for observed time series.

This decision on the part of the most prestigious theorist of his day freed a generation of economists from the discipline imposed by equilibrium theory, and, as I have described, this freedom was rapidly and fruitfully exploited by macroeconometricians. Now in possession of detailed, quantitatively accurate replicas of the actual economy, economists appeared to have an inexpensive means to evaluate various proposed economic policy measures. It seemed legitimate to treat policy recommendations which emerged from this procedure as though they had been experimentally tested, even if such policies had never been attempted in any actual economy.

Yet the ability of a model to imitate actual behavior in the way tested by the Adelmans (1959) has almost nothing to do with its ability to make accurate conditional forecasts, to answer questions of the form: how would behavior have differed had certain policies been different in specified ways? This ability requires invariance of the structure of the model under policy variations of the type being studied. Invariance of parameters in an economic model is not, of course, a property which can be assured in advance, but it seems reasonable to hope that neither tastes nor technology vary systematically with variations in countercyclical policies. In contrast, agents' decision rules will in general change with changes in the environment. An equilibrium model is, by definition, constructed so as to predict how agents with stable tastes and technology will choose to respond to a new situation. Any disequilibrium model, constructed by simply codifying the decision rules which agents have found it useful to use over some previous sample period, without explaining why these rules were used, will be of no use in predicting the consequences of nontrivial policy changes.

The quantitative importance of this problem is, of course, a matter to be settled by examination of specific relationships in specific models. I have argued elsewhere[9] that it is of fatal importance in virtually all sectors of modern macroeconomic models, primarily because of the faulty treatment of expectations in these models. Rather than review these arguments in detail, let me cite the most graphic illustration: our experience during the recent "stagflation."

As recently as 1970, the major U. S. econometric models implied that expansionary monetary and fiscal policies leading to a sustained inflation of about 4 percent per annum would lead also to sustained unemployment rates of less than 4 percent, or about a full percentage point lower than unemployment has averaged during any long period of U. S. history.[10] These forecasts were widely endorsed by many economists not themselves closely involved in econometric forecasting. Earlier, Friedman (1968) and Phelps (1968) had argued, purely on the basis of the observation that equilibrium behavior is invariant under the units change represented by sustained inflation, that no sustained decrease in unemployment would result from sustained inflation. In this instance, the policy experiment in question was, most unfortunately, carried out, and its outcome is now too clear to require detailed review.

It is important that the lesson of this episode not be lost. The issue is much deeper than the addition of a few new variables to econometric Phillips curves (though this is the only revision in macroeconomic models which has followed from it), as Friedman made clear in his Presidential Address. Friedman's argument did not proceed on the basis of a specific aggregative model, with a better "wage-price sector" than the standard models. On the contrary, it was based on a general characteristic of economic equilibrium: the zero-degree homogeneity of demand and supply functions. Thus, without using any very specific model, and without claiming the ability to forecast in any detail the initial response of the economy to an inflation, one can, in the case of sustained inflation, reason that, if the unemployment rate prior to the inflation were an equilibrium (or "natural") rate, then the same rate will be an equilibrium once the inflation is underway.

The case of sustained inflation is a relatively simple one (though apparently not too simple, as it is still highly controversial). For other kinds of policy questions, one would need a more explicit model. How would the variance, and other moments, of real output change if a policy of 4 percent monetary growth were adopted? Under a balanced budget fiscal rule? Under flexible rather than fixed exchange rates? One can generate numerical answers

---

[9] Lucas (1976).

[10] Hirsch (1972), de Menil and Enzler (1972).

to questions of this sort from current macroeconomic models, but there is no reason for anyone to take these numbers seriously. On the other hand, neither can quantitative answers be obtained by purely theoretical reasoning. To obtain them, one needs an explicit, equilibrium account of the business cycle.

IV.

I have summarized, in section II, the main features of the cyclical behavior in quantities and prices. In section III, I have argued the practical necessity of accounting for these facts in equilibrium (that is, non-Keynesian) terms. That is, one would like a theory which accounts for the observed movements in quantities (employment, consumption, investment) as an optimizing response to observed movements in prices.

In the next section, I will describe the general point of view toward individual decision making to be taken in the remainder of the paper, and will explain, in particular, why the recurrent character of business cycles is of central importance. Given this general view, I shall consider in sections VI and VII the way in which relative price movements induce fluctuations in employment and investment. Sections VIII, IX, and X examine the conditions under which these same quantity responses may be triggered by movements in general, or nominal, prices. Not surprisingly, the source of general price movements is located, in section XI, in monetary changes.

V.

The view of the prototypical individual decision problem taken by modern capital theory is a useful point of departure for considering behavior over the cycle, though it is in some respects highly misleading. An agent begins a period with stocks of various kinds of capital accumulated in the past. He faces time paths of prices at which he can trade in the present and future. Based on his preferences over time paths of labor supplied and goods consumed, he formulates a plan. Under certainty, he is viewed as simply executing a single plan without revision; with uncertainty, he must draw up a contingency plan, saying how he will react to unforeseeable events.

Even to begin to think about decision problems of this general form, one needs to imagine a fairly precise view of the future in the mind of this agent. Where does he get this view, and how can an observer infer what it is? This aspect of the problem has received rather offhand treatment in traditional capital theory, and no treatment at all in traditional macroeconomics. Since it is absolutely crucial for understanding business cycles, we must pursue it here in some detail.

At a purely formal level, we know that a rational agent must formulate a subjective joint probability distribution over all unknown random variables which impinge on his present and future market opportunities. The link between this subjective view of the future and "reality" is a most complex philosophical question, but the way it is solved has little effect on the structure of the decision problem as seen by an individual agent. In particular, any distinction between types of randomness (such as Knight's (1921) distinction between "risk" and "uncertainty") is, at this level, meaningless.

Unfortunately, the general hypothesis that economic agents are Bayesian decision makers has, in many applications, little empirical content: without some way of inferring what an agent's subjective view of the future is, this hypothesis is of no help in understanding his behavior. Even psychotic behavior can be (and today, is) understood as "rational," given a sufficiently abnormal view of relevant probabilities. To practice economics, we need some way (short of psychoanalysis, one hopes) of understanding which decision problem agents are solving.

John Muth (1961) proposed to resolve this problem by identifying agents subjective probabilities with observed frequencies of the events to be forecast, or with "true" probabilities, calling the assumed coincidence of subjective and "true" probabilities rational expectations. Evidently, this hypothesis will not be of value in understanding psychotic behavior. Neither will it be applicable in situations in which one cannot guess which, if any, observable frequencies are relevant: situations which Knight[11] called "uncertainty." It will most likely be useful in situations in which the probabilities of interest concern a fairly well defined recurrent event, situations of "risk" in Knight's terminology. In situations of risk, the hypothesis of rational behavior on the part of agents will have usable content, so that behavior may be explainable in terms of economic theory. In such situations, expectations are rational in Muth's sense. In cases of uncertainty, economic reasoning will be of no value.

These considerations explain why business cycle theorists emphasized the recurrent character of the cycle, and why we must hope they were right in doing so. Insofar as business cycles can be viewed as repeated instances of essentially similar events, it will be reasonable to treat agents as reacting to cyclical changes as "risk," or to assume their expectations are rational, that they have fairly stable arrangements for collecting and processing information, and that they utilize this information in forecasting the future in a stable way, free of systematic and easily correctable biases.

---

[11]Knight (1921). I am interpreting the risk-uncertainty distinction as referring not to a classification of different types of individual decision problems but to the relationship between decision maker and observer.

VI.

In moving from these general considerations to more specific theory, it will be helpful to consider as an example a "representative" agent.[12] Imagine a single worker-producer, confronted each period with a given market price for a good which he then makes to order, at a fixed rate of output per hour. That is, he comes to his place of work, observes his current selling price, determines how many hours to work that day, sells his produce, then goes home to relax.

The good he receives in exchange for the effort is "money"; I shall not be concerned with the historical reasons for this arrangement, but simply take it for granted. This money, in turn, is spent on a wide variety of goods, different from day to day. Some purchases he makes on his way home, in an hour's break from work, or several days later. I assume for now that he holds no other securities. I assume also that this agent lives in a cycle-free world, in which the general or average level of prices does not change, though individual prices fluctuate from day to day.

Now let us postulate an increase of 10 percent in today's selling price, as compared to the average of past prices. How will this hypothetical producer respond? The answer given by economic theory must be: who knows? At this point, I have said nothing which would enable one to imagine what the producer thinks this price movement <u>means</u>. If he believes the price change signals a permanent change in his selling price, we know from much evidence that he will work no harder, and probably a little less hard. That is, we know that "long run" (very unfortunate terminology, since the "long-run" response to a permanent price change will be <u>immediate</u>) labor supply elasticities are zero or negative.

What if, at the opposite extreme, the price change is transitory (as would be the case if each period's price were an independent drawing from a fixed distribution)? The answer in this case amounts to knowing the rate at which the producer is willing to substitute labor today for labor tomorrow. If "leisure" is highly substitutable over time, he will work longer on high price days and close early on low price days. Less is known about actual labor supply responses to transitory price movements than about the "long-run" response, but what we do know indicates that leisure in one period is an excellent substitute for leisure in other, nearby periods. Systematic evidence at the aggregate level was obtained by Rapping and myself (1970); Ghez and Becker (1975) reached

---

[12] Many of the arguments in this and subsequent sections have been developed more explicitly elsewhere. The closest single parallel treatment is in Lucas (1975). See also Phelps, et al. (1970), Barro (1976), Sargent and Wallace (1975), Sargent (1976). In what follows, I will not document particular arguments, nor will I attempt to apportion credit (or blame) for ideas discussed.

16

the same conclusion at a disaggregative level. The small premiums required to induce workers to shift holidays and vacations (take Monday off instead of Saturday, two weeks in March rather than in August) point to the same conclusion, and this "casual" evidence is somewhat more impressive because of its probabilistic simplicity: holidays are known to be transitory. On the basis of this evidence, one would predict a highly elastic response to transitory price changes.

Before dealing with complications to this example, let us note its promise for business cycle theory. I have described a producer who responds to small price fluctuations with large fluctuations in output and employment: exactly what we observe over the cycle. The description rests on economically intelligible substitution effects, not on unintelligible "disequilibria." Yet let us go slowly: our aggregative observations refer to co-movements of output and prices generally; the example refers to relative price movements in a stationary environment.

Before facing this difficult issue, let us consider some variations on the example just considered. First, from a descriptive point of view, it often seems more realistic to think of demand information being conveyed to producers by quantity changes: new orders, inventory rundowns, and the like. There seems to be no compelling substantive reason to focus exclusively on prices as signals of current and future demand. At this verbal level, it seems to me harmless and accurate to use the terms price increase and sales increase interchangeably. Somewhat surprisingly, however, rigorous analysis of equilibrium determination when producers set prices is extremely difficult, and no examples relevant to business cycle behavior exist.

A second variation is easy to carry out. Rather than consider a worker-entrepreneur, one could separate these functions, introduce firms, and consider labor and product markets separately. In the present context, this would introduce a distinction between wages and prices, and raise the issue of risk-allocating arrangements between employers and workers.[13] It would also permit the study of possibly different information sets for firms and workers. None of these questions is without interest, but all are, in my opinion, peripheral for business cycle theory. Observed real wages are not constant over the cycle, but neither do they exhibit consistent pro- or countercyclical tendencies. This suggests that any attempt to assign systematic real wage movements a central role in an explanation of business cycles is doomed to failure. Accordingly, I will proceed as though the real wage were fixed, using the terms "wages" and "prices" interchangeably.

---

[13]One such arrangement is the practice of "laying off" workers. See Azariadis (1975).

Additional variations can be obtained by distinguishing among various uses of the worker-producer's time when he is not working. Many writers have attempted, for example, to interpret measured unemployment as time engaged in job search. Certainly, if one substitutes away from work one substitues into some other activity, and experience shows that one's belief in the importance of substitution is bolstered by some plausible illustrations. Nevertheless, there is little evidence that much time is spent in job search, that search is less costly when unemployed than when employed, or, for that matter, that measured unemployment measures any activity at all. Economically, the important issue is the magnitude of the elasticity of employment with respect to transitory wage and price movements, not the reasons why that elasticity is what it is.

Indeed, I suspect that the unwillingness to speak of workers in recession as enjoying "leisure" is more a testimony to the force of Keynes' insistence that unemployment is "involuntary" than a response to observed phenomena. One doesn't want to suggest that people like depressions! Of course, the hypothesis of a cleared labor market carries with it no such suggestion, any more than the observation that people go hungry in cleared food markets suggests that people enjoy hunger.

VII.

More complex variations on this example arise when capital of various kinds is introduced. Let us do this, retaining still the assumption of stability over time in the general level of prices.

Three possibilities of interest arise. First, suppose that current production can be stored as finished goods inventory. This possibility seems to work against the account of price-output co-movements sketched above. The producer will surely produce in low price periods for sale later when price is high, smoothing labor supply relative to the case where storage is precluded. On the industry level, however, this behavior also dampens price movements. The net result is likely to be a reduction in the elasticity of employment-production with respect to price, and an increase in the real sales-price elasticity.

As a second possibility, suppose the producer can use a part of his current production to acquire a machine which will raise his output-per-hour in all future periods. As a third, suppose he can take a course in school which will have the same effect. Since these two possibilities do not differ economically, they may be considered as one. In the example of purely transitory price movements, discussed earlier, it is clear that neither of these options will ever be exercised -- provided the producer was satisfied with his original stock of capital. By the time the new capital can be applied to production, the price movement which made it appear profitable will have vanished.

Current relative price movements will have their maximal effect on capital accumulation when, at the opposite extreme, they are regarded as permanent. In this case, however, as I have noted, employment will be insensitive to price movements. Thus, to observe investment and employment moving systematically in the direction of relative price movements, it must be the case that such movements are a _mix_ of transitory and permanent elements. In such a situation, the producer will find himself obliged to engage in what engineers call "signal processing": he observes a single variable (price) changing through time; these movements arise from movements in more fundamental variables (the transitory and permanent components of price) which cannot be observed directly; from these observed price movements, together with his knowledge of the relative importance of the two unobserved sources of price change, he imperfectly infers the movements in the two components. Based on his solution to this implied conditional probability calculation, he takes a decision. Not surprisingly, the decision turns out to be an average of the decisions appropriate to the two extremes.

To recapitulate, our hypothetical producer is taken to face stochastic price variability, which is describable as a mix of transitory and permanent components, both unobserved. His optimal response to price movements depends on two factors: the way he interprets the information contained in these changes, and his preferences concerning intertemporal substitution of leisure and consumption. Under assumptions consistent with rational behavior and available evidence, his response to an unforeseen price increase is a sizable increase in labor supplied, a decline in finished goods inventory, and an expansion in productive capital accumulation of all kinds. This behavior is symmetric; the responses to price decreases are the opposite.[14]

VIII.

It is time to think of situating this representative producer in an economy comprised of similar agents, though of course producing different goods and subject to different individual price movements. To do this, one must go behind price movements to the changes in technology and taste which underlie them. These changes are occurring all the time and, indeed, their

---

[14] What is happening to consumption expenditures as these employment and investment responses take place? In his critique of equilibrium business cycle models, Grossman (1973) argues that consumption must necessarily move in the opposite direction from labor supplied. Since this is not what is in fact observed over the cycle, it would indeed by a serious paradox if a negative correlation were a consequence of utility theory. One can derive it for special cases (see Lucas, 1972, Fig. 1) but this implication is certainly not a general fact for optimizing households; it does not, for example, follow from Rapping's and my (1970) theory or from that of Ghez and Becker (1975, ch. 4).

importance to individual agents dominates by far the relatively minor movements which constitute the business cycle. Yet these movements should, in general, lead to relative, not general price movements. A new technology, reducing costs of producing an old good or making possible the production of a new one, will draw resources into the good which benefits, and away from the production of other goods. Taste shifts in favor of the purchase of one good involve reduced expenditures on others. Moreover, in a complex modern economy, there will be a large number of such shifts in any given period, each small in importance relative to total output. There will be much "averaging out" of such effects across markets.

Cancellation of this sort is, I think, the most important reason why one cannot seek an explanation of the general movements we call business cycles in the mere presence, per se, of unpredictability of conditions in individual markets. Yet this argument is not entirely tight. It is surely possible for a large number of agents spontaneously to feel an urge to increase their work weeks and expand investments. More seriously, there have been many instances of shocks to supply which affect all, or many, sectors of the economy simultaneously. Such shocks will not cancel in the way I have described, and they will induce output fluctuations in the aggregate. They will not, however, lead to movements which fit the description sketched in section II: all supply shifts will lead to countercyclical price movements (other things being equal) in contrast to the procyclical movements we observe.

It is, then, possible to situate our hypothetical producer in a general equilibrium setting, in which his price and output fluctuate, yet aggregate levels do not. His responses to these relative prices movements will mimic the aggregate responses to general price movements which constitute the business cycle. We have then a coherent model, but not one which as yet accounts for the general phenomena to be explained. This model can, without difficulty, be modified to permit general, supply-induced output fluctuations, but these bear no resemblance to the modern business cycle.

Before leaving this world of stable aggregates, it is worth stressing that most of the risk which troubles and challenges economic agents would be present in such a setting. Will consumers take to a novel automobile design, or will it become a national joke? Will a dozen years of training in piano lead to the concert stage, or just a pleasurable hobby? Will this week's overtime wages help finance a child's education, or tide the family over next month's strike? By the time one has acquired the information necessary to resolve questions like these, it is too late; one way or the other, one is committed.

Compared to risks of this nature and magnitude, the question of whether the hours actually worked in the year ahead will be 1.03 times what one plans for now, or .97, seems a minor one, and seems so because it is. In aggregative economic theory, we are accustomed to think of business cycles as a kind of risk imposed on an otherwise stable environment. Such habits of thought reflect the transfer of abstractions useful for some purposes into contexts where they involve fatal distortions of reality.

IX.

Let us now drop the assumption of stability in average prices. From the point of view of the individual producer, this involves only a slight change in the nature of the signal processing problem which must be solved. Before, a given movement in his "own price" could mean a permanent relative price change or a transitory one. Now, it can also mean that all prices are changing, a situation which, if correctly diagnosed, would lead to no real response on the producer's part. Yet, for the same reason that permanent and transitory relative price movements cannot be sorted out with certainty at the time, neither can relative and general movements be distinguished. General price increases, exactly as will relative price increases, will induce movements in the same direction in employment and investment.

Unlike the responses to taste and technology changes described earlier, these responses to general price increases will not tend to cancel over markets. To be sure, some producers will observe declines in demand even during price expansions, but more will observe increases (this is what a general price increase means), and therefore more will be expanding in real terms than will be contracting. The net effect will be co-movements in prices, output, and investment at the aggregate level, just as is observed over the actual cycle.

It is essential to this argument that general price movements not be perceived as such as they are occurring. Within the context of the aggregative models ordinarily used, this assumption may seem implausible: how could traders not know the price of goods? In the reality of a multi-commodity world, however, no one would want to observe all prices every day, nor would many traders find published price indices particularly useful. An optimizing trader will process those prices of most importance to his decision problem most frequently and carefully, those of less importance less so, and most prices not at all. Of the many sources of risk of importance to him, the business cycle and aggregate behavior generally is, for most agents, of no special importance, and there is no reason for traders to specialize their own information systems for diagnosing general movements correctly.

By the same reasoning, one can see that sustained inflation will not affect agents' real decisions in the way that transitory price movements do. Nothing is easier than to spot and correct systematic <u>bias</u> in forecasts. Such corrections involve no changes in agents' information systems or in the costs of processing information. There may, of course, be some lag in diagnosing sustained inflation for what it is; about as often, agents will incorrectly perceive a transitory inflation as though it were sustained.

Changes in the degree of price variability will have more fundamental effects on agents' information processing behavior, because they affect the "weights" placed on price information in forecasting future prices. The general idea is that one trusts "noisy" price signals less.

X.

The aggregate or average response to general price movements becomes more complex as one considers investment as well as employment responses. Investment decisions will be distorted by general price movements, for the same reasons as will employment, and in the same direction as the responses induced by relative price movements.

Further complications follow, however, from the observation that current investment affects future <u>capacity</u>, and hence future prices. This effect can be seen to extend in time, perhaps even to amplify, the initial effects of general price movements.

To spell this out in more detail, imagine that some event occurs which would, if correctly perceived by all, induce an increase in prices generally. Sooner or later, then, this adjustment will occur. Initially, however, more traders than not perceive a relative price movement, possibly permanent, in their favor. As a result, employment and investment both increase. Through time, as price information diffuses through the economy, these traders will see they have been mistaken. In the meantime, however, the added capacity <u>retards</u> price increases generally, postponing the recognition of the initial shock. In this way, unsystematic or short-term shocks to prices can lead to much longer swings in prices.

In addition, there is a downturn automatically built in to this expansion of capacity. When recognition of general inflation does occur, investment will have to become less than normal for a time while capacity readjusts downward. There is no reason to expect this readjustment to come rapidly, or to be describable as a "crash," or "bust."

This scenario, like the earlier description of the employment response, depends crucially on the confusion on the part of agents between relative and general price movements. This is especially clear in the case of investment, since optimal investment policy has a great deal of "smoothing" built into it:

since investment is a long-term commitment, it will respond only to what seem to be relatively permanent relative price shifts.

This observation has led, on serious grounds, to skepticism as to the importance of accelerator effects in the business cycle. How can moderate cyclical movements in prices lead to the high-amplitude movements in durable goods purchases which are observed? Here again, one must insist on the minor contribution of economy-wide risk to the general risk situation faced by agents. For individual investment projects, rates of return are highly variable, often negative, and often measured in hundreds of percent. A quick, current response to what seems to others a weak "signal" is often the key to a successful investment. The agent who waits until the situation is clear to everyone is too late; someone else has already added the capacity to meet the high demand. What appears, at the aggregate level, to be a high-amplitude response pattern to low-amplitude shocks is, at the level at which decisions are made, a high-amplitude response to still higher amplitude movements in returns to individual investments.[15]

XI.

I began section II with a definition of business cycles as repeated fluctuations in employment, output, and the composition of output, associated with a certain typical pattern of co-movements in prices and other variables. Since in a competitive economy, employment and output of various kinds are chosen by agents in response to price movements, it seemed appropriate to begin by rationalizing the observed quantity movements as rational or optimal responses to observed price movements. This has been accomplished in the preceding five sections. I turn next to the sources of price movements.

For explaining secular movements in prices generally, secular movements in the quantity of money do extremely well. This fact is as well established as any we know in aggregative economics, and is not sensitive to how one measures either prices or the quantity of money.[16] There is no serious doubt as to the direction of effect in this relationship; no one argues that the anticipation of

---

[15]"Austrian" or "monetary-over-investment" business cycle theory (see Haberler, 1936, or Hayek, 1933) was based on this same idea of mistaken investment decisions triggered by spurious price signals. However, the price which this theory emphasized was the rate of interest, rather than product prices as stressed here. Given the cyclical amplitude of interest rates, the investment-interest elasticity needed to account for the observed amplitude in investment is much too high to be consistent with other evidence.

[16]Friedman and Schwartz (1963).

sixteenth-century inflation sent Columbus to the New World to locate the gold to finance it. This evidence has no direct connection to business cycles, since it refers to averages over much longer periods, but the indirect connections are too strong to be ignored: we have accounted for the pattern of co-movements among real variables over the cycle as responses to general price movements; we know that, in the "long run," general price movements arise primarily from changes in the quantity of money. Moreover, cyclical movements in money are large enough to be quantitatively interesting. All these arguments point to a monetary shock as the force triggering the real business cycle.

The direct evidence on short-term correlations between money, output, and prices is much more difficult to read. Certain extreme episodes appear to indicate that depressions and recoveries are money-induced.[17] In general, however, the link between money and these and other variables is agreed to be subject, in Friedman's terms, to "long and variable lags."

Paradoxically, this weakness in the short-term evidence linking money to economic activity, and in particular to prices, is encouraging from the point of view of monetary business cycle theory. To see why, recall the theoretical link between general price movements and economic activity as sketched above. This connection rested on the hypothesis that the signal processing problem of identifying general price movements from observations of a few individual prices was too difficult to be solved perfectly by agents. Now suppose it were true that one could describe short-term general price movements by a simple, fixed function of lagged movements in some published monetary aggregate. Then, far from being difficult, the signal processing problem to be solved by agents would be trivial; they could simply observe current monetary aggregates, calculate the predicted current and future price movements they imply, and correct their behavior for these units changes perfectly. The result would be a very tight relationship between money and prices, over even very short periods, and no relationship at all between these movements and changes in real variables.

These remarks do not, of course, explain why monetary effects work with long and variable lags. On this question little is known. It seems likely that the answer lies in the observation that a monetary expansion can occur in a variety of ways, depending on the way the money is "injected" into the system, with different price response implications depending on which way is selected. This would suggest that one should describe the monetary "state" of the economy as being determined by some unobservable monetary aggregate, loosely related to observed aggregates over short periods but closely related secularly.

---

[17] Again, see Friedman and Schwartz (1963).

XII

Let me recapitulate the main features of the business cycle theory sketched in the preceding sections. We began by imagining an economy with fluctuating tastes and technology, implying continually changing <u>relative</u> prices, and studied the co-movements in quantities and prices which would emerge if agents behaved in their own interest and utilized their incomplete information effectively. We then superimposed on this economy sizable, unsystematic movements in a monetary aggregate, adding an additional source of "noise" to individual price movements. The result is to generate a pattern of co-movements among aggregate series which appears to match the observations summarized in section II.

In retrospect, this account seems rather embarrassingly simple: one wonders why it seems to be necessary to undo a Revolution to arrive at it. Yet one must be careful not to overstate what has, in fact, been arrived at. I think it is fairly clear that there is nothing in the behavior of observed economic time series which precludes ordering them in equilibrium terms, and enough theoretical examples exist to lend confidence to the hope that this can be done in an explicit and rigorous way. To date, however, no equilibrium model has been developed which meets these standards and which, at the same time, could pass the test posed by the Adelmans (1959). My own guess would be that success in this sense is five, but not twenty-five years off.[18]

The implications for economic policy of a successful business cycle theory of the sort outlined here are, I think, easy to guess at even when the theory itself is in a preliminary state. Indeed, much of the above is simply an attempt to understand and make more explicit the implicit model underlying the policy proposals of Henry Simons, Milton Friedman, and other critics of activist aggregative policy. By seeking an equilibrium account of business cycles, one accepts <u>in advance</u> rather severe limitations on the scope of governmental countercyclical policy which might be rationalized by the theory. Insofar as fluctuations are induced by gratuitous monetary instability, serving no social purpose, then increased monetary stability promises to reduce aggregate, real variability and increase welfare. There is no doubt, however, that <u>some</u> real variability would remain even under the smoothest monetary and fiscal policies. There is no <u>prima facie</u> case that this residual variability would be better dealt

---

[18]Proceeding further out on this limb, it is likely that such a "successful" model will be a close descendant of Sargent's (1976).

with by centralized, governmental policies than by individual, decentralized responses.[19]

In view of this lack of novelty in the realm of policy, it seems a fair question to ask: why do we need the theory? The general answer, I think, is that in a democratic society it is not enough to believe oneself to be right; one must be able to explain <u>why</u> one is right. We live in a society in which the unemployment rate fluctuates between, say, 3 and 10 percent. It follows that both situations are attainable, and it is clear that most people are happier at three than at ten. It is also clear that government policies have much to do with which of these situations prevails at any particular time. What could be more natural, then, than to view the task of aggregative economics as that of discovering which policies will lead to the more desirable situation, and then advocating their adoption? This was the promise of Keynesian economics, and even now, when the scientific emptiness of this promise is most evident, its appeal is understandable to all who share the hope that social science offers more than elegant rationalization of the existing state of affairs.

The economically literate public has had some forty years to become comfortable with two related ideas: that market economies are inherently subject to violent fluctuations which can only be eliminated by flexible and forceful governmental responses; and that economists are in possession of a body of scientifically tested knowledge enabling them to determine, at any time, what these responses should be. It is doubtful if many who are not professionally committed hold, today, to the latter of these beliefs. This in itself settles little in the dispute as to whether the role of government in stabilization policy should be to reduce its own disruptive part or actively to offset private sector instability. As long as the business cycle remains "in apparent contradiction" to economic theory, both positions appear tenable. There seems to be no way to determine how business cycles are to be dealt with short of understanding what they are and how they occur.

---

[19]That is to say, active countercyclical policy would require the same kind of cost-benefit defense used in evaluating other types of government policies. See Phelps (1972), and also Prescott's review (1975).

REFERENCES

1. Adelman, I., and Adelman, F. L., "The Dynamic Properties of the Klein-Goldberger Model," Econometrica, 27, No. 4, (October 1959), 596-625.

2. Azariadis, C., "Implicit Contracts and Underemployment Equilibria," Journal of Political Economy, 83, No. 6, (December 1975), 1183-1202.

3. Barro, R. J., "Rational Expectations and the Role of Monetary Policy," Journal of Monetary Economics, 2, No. 1, (January 1976), 1-32.

4. Burns, A. F., and Mitchell, W. C. Measuring Business Cycles. New York: National Bureau of Economic Research, 1946.

5. Friedman, M., "The Role of Monetary Policy," Presidential Address to the American Economic Association, American Economic Review, 58, No. 1, (March 1968), 1-17.

6. Friedman, M., and Schwartz, A. J. A Monetary History of the United States, 1867-1960. Princeton: Princeton University Press for the National Bureau of Economic Research, 1963.

7. Gayer, A. D., Rostow, W. W., and Schwartz, A. J. The Growth and Fluctuation of the British Economy, 1790-1850. Oxford: The Clarendon Press, 1953.

8. Ghez, G. R., and Becker, G. S. The Allocation of Time and Goods Over the Life Cycle. New York: National Bureau of Economic Research, 1975.

9. Grossman, H. I., "Aggregate Demand, Job Search, and Employment," Journal of Political Economy, 81, No. 6, (November/December 1973), 1353-1369.

10. Haberler, G. Prosperity and Depression. Geneva: League of Nations, 1936.

11. Hayek, F. A. von. Monetary Theory and the Trade Cycle. London: Jonathan Cape, 1933.

12. Hicks, J. R., "Mr. Keynes and the 'Classics': A Suggested Interpretation," Econometrica, 5, (1937), 147-159.

13. Hirsch, A. A., "Price Simulations with the OBE Econometric Model," in The Econometrics of Price Determination Conference. (ed. O. Eckstein), Washington, D. C.: Board of Governors of the Federal Reserve System and Social Science Council, 1972.

14. Keynes, J. M. The General Theory of Employment, Interest and Money. London: Macmillan, 1936.

15. Klein, L. A., and Goldberger, A. S. An Econometric Model of the United States, 1929-52. Amsterdam: North Holland, 1955.

16. Knight, F. H. Risk, Uncertainty and Profit. Boston: Houghton Mifflin, 1921.

17. Lucas, R. E., Jr., "Expectations and the Neutrality of Money," Journal of Economic Theory, 4, No. 2, (April 1972), 103-123.

18. _____ , "An Equilibrium Model of the Business Cycle," Journal of Political Economy, 83, No. 6, (December 1975), 1113-1144.

19. _____ , "Econometric Policy Evaluations: A Critique," in The Phillips Curve and Labor Markets, (eds. K. Brunner and A. H. Meltzer), Carnegie-Rochester Conference Series on Public Policy, 1, Amsterdam: North Holland, 1976, 19-46.

20. Lucas, R. E., Jr., and Rapping, L. A., "Real Wages, Employment, and Inflation," in Microeconomic Foundations of Employment and Inflation Theory, (eds. E. S. Phelps, et al.), New York: Norton, 1970.

21. de Menil, G., and Enzler, J. J., "Price and Wages in the FR-MIT Econometric Model," in The Econometrics of Price Determination Conference, (ed. O. Eckstein), Washington, D. C.: Board of Governors of the Federal Reserve System and Social Science Council, 1972.

22. Mitchell, W. C. What Happens During Business Cycles. New York: National Bureau of Economic Research, 1951.

23. Modigliani, F., "Liquidity Preference and the Theory of Interest and Money," Econometrica, 12, No. 1, (January 1944), 45-88.

24. Moggridge, D. (ed.) The Collected Writings of John Maynard Keynes, Vol. XIV. London: Macmillan, 1973.

25. Muth, J., "Rational Expectations and the Theory of Price Movements," Econometrica, 29, No. 3, (July 1961), 315-335.

26. Phelps, E.S., "Money Wage Dynamics and Labor Market Equilibrium," Journal of Political Economy, 76, No. 4, II, (July/August 1968), 687-711.

27. _____. Inflation Policy and Unemployment Theory: The Cost-Benefit Approach to Monetary Planning. London: Macmillan, 1972.

28. Phelps, E. S., et al. Microeconomic Foundations of Employment and Inflation Theory. New York: Norton, 1970.

29. Prescott, E. C., "Efficiency of the Natural Rate," Journal of Political Economy, 83, No. 6, (December 1975), 1229-1236.

30. Sargent, T. J., "A Classical Macroeconometric Model for the United States," Journal of Political Economy, 84, No. 2, (April 1976), 207-237.

31. Sargent, T. J., and Sims, C. A., "Business Cycle Modeling Without Pretending to Have Too Much A Priori Economic Theory," University of Michigan working paper, March 1976. ·

32. Sargent, T. J., and Wallace, N., " 'Rational' Expectations, the Optimal Monetary Instrument, and the Optimal Money Supply Rule," Journal of Political Economy, 83, No. 2, (April 1975), 241-254.

33. Tinbergen, J. Business Cycles in the United States of America, 1919-32. Geneva: League of Nations, 1939.

INFLATION WITHOUT GROWTH: A LONG-RUN PERSPECTIVE
ON SHORT-RUN STABILIZATION POLICIES

Michael Parkin*

Professor of Economics

University of Western Ontario

There is widespread agreement that the recent economic performance of the western world has been unsatisfactory. Inflation rates have become too high and unpredictable while growth[1] and capital accumulation rates have become too low and unemployment has become excessive. The rate of inflation in the boom of 1973-74 was higher, in most countries, than it had been since the turbulent interwar years, and the recession from which the world economy is now recovering was the deepest since the Great Depression. Also, the rate of capital accumulation has been lower throughout the latest cycle than during any other postwar cycle.

While there is widespread agreement on the seriousness and unsatisfactory nature of the recent trends in inflation, output, capital accumulation, and employment, there is strong disagreement[2] on what should be done about it. The popular view, embraced by the press, by most governments, and by international organizations such as the OECD, is that inflation has become a problem because of a major change in attitudes, especially on the part of organized labor. In particular, a greater concern with both equity and real income growth has led to demands for a faster growth rate in money wages. These, in turn, with sluggish productivity growth and (relatively) constant profit margins, have led to a faster rate of inflation. Growth rates of real output have been unsatisfactorily low because of a failure of the market economy to deal adequately with intertemporal allocation. Uncertainty about the future leads entrepreneurs to invest too little and households to save too little. On this view, the solution to the problems of excessive inflation and sluggish growth are

---

*
An earlier draft of this paper was presented at the Conference on "Growth without Inflation: Microeconomic and Monetary Aspects" at the Institut für Weltwirtschaft, Kiel, West Germany, June 22-23, 1976. I am grateful to Robin Bade, Peter Howitt, David Laidler, Michael Sumner, and the Conference participants for comments on and criticisms of that draft, and to Richard Smith of the University of Manchester Inflation Research Programme, "Inflation: Its Causes, Consequences and Cures," for research assistance.

[1]It is not clear that trend growth rates have slackened off in the 1970s, although they may have. It is necessary to wait and see how far the 1976 recovery goes before that can be determined.

[2]It is interesting to note that this contrasts with a widely held view of only a decade ago. Thus, Solow (1965, p. 146) writes, ". . .I think that most economists feel that short-run macroeconomic theory is pretty well in hand. . . .The basic outlines of the dominant theory have not changed in years. All that is left is the trivial job of filling in the empty boxes. . . ."

simple and direct. Inflation has to be checked by direct controls on wages. Prices also need to be controlled directly but only so as to make wage controls acceptable to organized labor. Growth can only be improved by greater direct state intervention either in the form of investment subsidies or of direct state involvement in industry (such as, for example, the United Kingdom's National Enterprise Board).[3] Monetary and fiscal policy, on this view, should continue to be assigned the job of aiming for full employment by discretionary adjustments in interest rates, tax rates, and government spending levels. Further, since one of the primary sources of inflationary pressure is a feeling of unfairness concerning the distribution of income, fiscal policy should also be used to mitigate that pressure by engineering massive redistributions in favor of the "weaker members of society." Additionally, since frustration with real income levels is also a source of inflationary pressure, monetary and fiscal policy should be used to achieve a high overall level of resource utilization and economic activity.

This popular view of the causes and cures of the world's current economic ills stands in sharp contrast to the diagnosis and prescription which emerge from the theoretical and empirical research in economics which has been undertaken over the past 200 (and more) years. In this alternative view, the inflation acceleration of the late 1960s and early 1970s was caused (in a proximate sense) by a rise in the rate of growth of the world money supply. That money supply growth arose as a consequence of a monetary policy, the centerpiece of which was the pegging of nominal interest rates, and of a fiscal policy which saw both the scale of public spending and the size of deficits rise substantially. The poor growth performance has been a consequence of these monetary and fiscal policies. First, there has been an increase in uncertainty concerning future inflation rates which makes it less attractive to enter into long-term loan contracts denominated in money terms. Also, because profits and interest income are taxed in nominal terms, real after-tax profits and interest yields have become low or even negative. The solution which follows from this analysis is less obvious and harder to appreciate than the popular cure. Its first prescription is that interest rate levels should cease to form the centerpiece of monetary policy and, instead, that the money supply should be placed on an announced steady growth path consistent with gradually reducing and subsequently stabilizing the rate of inflation. Secondly, fiscal policy should be directed at supplying the optimal quantity of public goods and at redistribution. How much each of these activities should be indulged in is not a settled matter.

---

[3]This is a public sector agency with wide powers to invest in and to reorganize private corporations.

However, it should be recognized that, at full employment, public spending "crowds out" private spending; there is a trade-off, therefore, between private consumption and its rate of growth on the one hand, and public consumption on the other. Thirdly, if positive rates of inflation are going to persist for some time, their distortionary effects, especially through the tax system, need to be minimized by a permissive attitude toward indexation in private contracts and through the indexing of the tax laws.

The primary aim of this paper is to spell out the above diagnosis and prescription more fully and to argue that they are fundamentally correct, and that the popular view, embedded in much current policy, is both wrong and dangerous.

It must be recognized that much of the recent increase in public spending and deficits has arisen from large increases in redistributive transfer payments. The belief that redistribution is just is also widespread. A secondary aim of this paper will be, therefore, to examine the recent literature (mainly theoretical) on distributive justice in order to establish some guidelines for redistribution while, at the same time, avoiding the open-ended commitment to bale out every unsound activity that appears on the scene.

The paper makes prescriptions for policy based on an analysis of the likely effects of alternative policies. It does not make predictions as to what policy will be. I recognize that this is the easier problem to solve. The real problem is that of understanding how political systems behave sufficiently well so as to design a constitution and a set of political institutions which can pursue those monetary and fiscal policies which are consistent with stability and efficiency. However, a prior problem is the resolution of the professional argument concerning what those appropriate policies are.

I want to emphasize that the main message of this paper is not that David Hume had all the right answers to all the important monetary questions and Adam Smith to the real questions,[4] and that the research and events of the past 200 years have confirmed this. It is accepted that, throughout the nineteenth and early twentieth centuries, the swings in economic activity were too great, and that there was too much poverty. The interventions designed to eradicate these problems—large-scale redistribution through taxation and social security programs and discretionary monetary and fiscal stabilization programs--have had some success in achieving their objectives. However, they have been shown to have had serious adverse side effects. Rather, the main message is that there are alternative means of dealing with redistribution and price and output

---

[4]The distinction is important, for Adam Smith was the originator of the real bills doctrine. I am indebted to David Laidler for this point.

stability which do not have adverse side effects and which are superior to those currently in use for achieving their primary objectives.

In part I the competing explanations of the inflation explosion are examined, and the supremacy of the monetary explanation and the inadequacy of the wage-push sociological explanation established. Since there already exists a large body of survey literature on the vast primary literature on this topic, this section draws heavily on and presents a compression of those surveys.[5] Part II analyzes the sources of inflationary money supply growth and argues that this is primarily the result of the combination of low interest rate policies in the face of rising public spending. In part III, the effects of inflation in combination with tax laws appropriate for a stable price level are examined. In principle, there are many such effects, but the focus here is on the intertemporal allocation of resources and the rate of capital accumulation. Part IV faces the problem that there is a popular clamor for large-scale redistribution which has been the major source of growth in public spending, and reviews the recent theoretical literature on this topic for guidance on how redistribution may best be achieved while wreaking the least possible damage to allocative efficiency and inflationary finance. Part V summarizes the main conclusions.

I. COMPETING EXPLANATIONS OF THE INFLATION EXPLOSION

As a prelude to examining the two main groups of competing explanations of the inflation explosion, it will be helpful to establish the facts which need to be explained. In Chart 1, the world[6] average inflation rate is presented along with an indication of its dispersion as measured by the range and the standard deviation. Further detail concerning individual country inflation rates both before and after 1971 is presented in Table 1. These facts raise the following questions. Why was the trend in world average inflation downwards during the 1950s and upwards in the 1960s and 1970s? Why are there marked cycles in the inflation rate superimposed on those trends? Why was the spread of inflation rates so much greater in the 1970s than in the '50s and '60s?[7] Why do some countries have persistently higher inflation rates than others? The ability of each of the two main competing groups of hypotheses to answer these questions will now be examined.

---

[5] The most comprehensive survey is Laidler and Parkin (1975). See also, however, Laidler (1976).

[6] The "world" is defined as the Group of Ten, i.e., the U.S., Canada, the U.K., France, Italy, West Germany, the Netherlands, Belgium, Sweden, and Japan; and "inflation" is defined as the annual rate of change of consumer prices.

[7] This question should perhaps be posed more carefully since the dispersion clearly fell during the 1950s and was then rather flat during the late 1950s and 1960s. It grew again after 1970. The former period, not the focus here, was of course dominated by exchange controls and nonconvertibility.

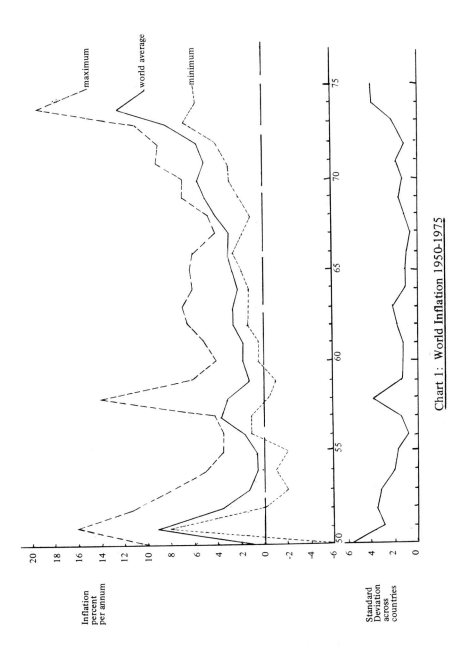

Chart 1: World Inflation 1950-1975

35

Table 1

Inflation in Sixteen Countries

(Average Annual Rates, 1958-1970 and 1971-1975)

Country	1958-1970	1971-1975
Australia	2.4	9.7
Austria	3.1	7.0
Belgium	2.4	8.0
Canada	2.5	7.5
Denmark	4.8	9.1
Ireland	4.1	12.5
France	5.0	8.8
. Italy	3.4	11.5
Japan	4.9	11.3
Netherlands	3.8	8.6
Norway	4.1	8.1
Sweden	3.9	7.8
Switzerland	2.8	7.4
United Kingdom	3.5	12.6
United States	2.6	6.9
West Germany	2.3	6.1
Standard Deviation	0.908	1.966

Source: IMF, International Financial Statistics. The latest data were taken from the May 1976 issue, and earlier data from the July 1968 issue and the supplement to Volume 19, 1966-67, item No. 64: Average of monthly cost of living indices.

The wage-push sociological view takes as its starting point the behavior of money wages which are seen to be entirely (or almost entirely) unresponsive to excess demand variations and dominated by a variety of sociological forces. The following examples by no means exhaust the plethora of specific propositions concerning the sociological determination of money wages which can be found.

> . . .in the planning system (i.e., that part of the economy dominated by large corporations), the normal tendency is to accede to the wage claims of unions. The ceremonial insult that graces the collective bargaining process slightly disguises but does not alter this circumstance. . . . The existence of rival unions of varying power adds to this upward instability. One union seeks naturally to improve on the settlements won by others. The union with the greatest determination and power thus sets the pattern for the others (Galbraith, 1975, pp. 204-5).

> [the amount by which wages rise] depends on what numbers the trade union leaders pick out of the air when they make their wage claims. For the claims are entirely subjective, and though settlements have some relation to objective supply and demand it is an extremely loose one, much influenced by the claims. . . [and]. . .good or bad, . . .rising crime, sex and drug permissiveness, less self-discipline in dress, speech and deportment, less respect for hard work, less religion, loosening of the nuclear family, breakdown of a deferential class structure, etc., etc. . . .raise prices (Wiles, 1973, pp. 392-3).

> But what is the cause of the wage-price explosion? I don't think it is economic. . . .This new wage-price explosion is altogether unprecedented, and my own opinion is that the causes are sociological. The causes of our present

37

difficulties are first cousins to the causes of such things as student unrest. We are dealing with a sort of activism on the part of the people, who want something for themselves– the labour unions if you like but also the corporations saying, 'We'll just make our customers pay'. All of this has been made possible of course by a certain permissiveness. Instead of employers presenting a stern front and saying, 'we can't possibly give you the wage increase you want', they have been permissive. And the consumers have been permissive too; they just take the prices asked for in the shops and don't argue about them as they would have in the old days. So I think the problem is sociological rather than economic (Harrod, 1972, p. 44).

It is no longer the case that the main force that is raising wages is labour scarcity. Wages rise, whether or not there is labour scarcity; so they rise in slumps as much, or nearly as much, as in booms. Everyone, on some comparision or other, feels left behind (Hicks, 1974, p. 71).

And more positively, naming at least three possible ways in which the rise in wages may be transmitted,

One is the pressure for fair wages, . . .second, . . .to make the demand for fair wages effective, profits should also be rising. . . , third, . . .there is a backlash of prices on wages –a Real Wage Resistance, it may be called (Hicks, 1975, pp. 4 - 5).

The last quotation brings in the only systematic economic factor which the wage-push school permits to affect wage change, namely the rate of price change. In Hicks' version, this is Real Wage Resistance. For Galbraith, it is simply allowing for anticipated cost of living changes, i.e.:

> As prices and living costs rise, unions must also seek provision in the settlement for prospective increases in living costs—or negotiate escalation clauses to cover such increases. This means larger increases in prices and leads in the next round to yet greater increases in wages (Galbraith, 1975, p. 205).

Thus, for the wage-push school, wage increases are in part noneconomic and in part a response to price rises. Price rises, in turn, are determined as the difference between wage rises and the rate of productivity growth; the latter is independent of the rate of wage and price increase and is treated as exogenous. This implies that profit margins, like wages, are unresponsive to the state of demand. Taken together these two propositions imply that both the rate of wage change and the rate of price change are determined by sociological factors and are independent of demand and other economic factors.

Most wage-push proponents recognize that if the inflation process which they envisage is to proceed without leading to unemployment and excess capacity, accommodating increases in the money supply will .be necessary. However, they argue that a failure to allow the money supply to expand fast enough to maintain full employment would affect only the level of economic activity and leave the inflation rate largely unchanged. It follows from the primarily sociological view of the wage determination process that changes in the institutional environment, changes in constraints on behavior in the form of wage and price controls, and the setting up of monitoring and policing agencies are seen as the best means for controlling inflation.

The tendency for inflation rates to move together across countries over time is, on the wage-push view, attributed to an international demonstration effect.[8] The systematic tendency for inflation rates to differ across countries at a point in time (and on the average) is attributed to differences in "inflation proneness." This latter factor is seen as the major source of balance of payments

---

[8]This is not to deny or ignore the fact that some "eclectics" admit the possibility of market forces transmitting inflation internationally while arguing that wages are determined nationally by wage push.

disequilibrium and of the need for exchange rate realignments under a fixed exchange rate regime, and as the source of exchange rate movements under floating rates.

On top of the synchronous wage-push source of inflation comes a purely international cost-push factor in the form of oil, other primary product, and food price rises. The strengthening of the OPEC cartel and the two successive years of weak harvests are seen as major contributors to the "two-digit" inflation of 1974-75.

To summarize, the sociological-push view of inflation attributes the explosion of inflation in the 1960s to increasing domestic wage-push forces which were more or less synchronized across the major economies, and attributes the even greater inflation of the 1970s to a continuation of these wage-push forces with the superimposition of international commodity price-push factors.

The alternative monetary explanation of inflation has two components. One develops an analysis of the linkages between monetary and fiscal policy and the behavior of real output and the inflation rate. The other attempts to explain the sources of inflationary monetary and fiscal policy. In this section, only that first set of linkages is investigated.

A monetary explanation of inflation begins with the insistence that a fixed exchange rate world is fundamentally different from a floating rate world. Under fixed exchange rates, there is a well-defined world price level, world inflation rate, and world money supply. Under floating rates, with the price of one national money continuously changing with respect to another national money, these concepts, while definable, serve no useful purpose.

Under a fixed rate regime, the aggregate economy relevant for analyzing inflation becomes the world as a whole (or rather those countries which are linked together by a fixed exchange rate).[9] The basic mechanisms generating world inflation under fixed rates are those postulated to apply to any closed economy.[10] Prices are set by firms or in organized markets to achieve profit maximization and/or market clearing. This implies that individual prices are changed by the amount which prices on the average are expected to change plus an adjustment for the expected state of excess demand in the sector in question.

---

[9] This has been understood (though long neglected) since the time of Hume (1752). The revival of this idea is due to Mundell (1968) and Johnson (1972) and has formed the basis of much empirical work especially in the Manchester Inflation Workshop; see, e.g., Parkin and Zis (1976a, 1976b), and Parkin (1977).

[10] There are two mainstream views on the details of this mechanism, one emerging from the work of Fisher (1911) and one from the Keynesian tradition, supplemented with an expectations augmented excess demand price setting process. It is the latter which is presented here.

Aggregating over the entire economy, this leads to the proposition that the difference between actual and expected inflation is some positive function of excess demand. Expectations of inflation are usually postulated either to follow an adaptive process or to be rational. Most economists would regard rational expectations as the appropriate hypothesis for the long run, but would regard a more mechanical expectations formation scheme as appropriate for periods in which the monetary authorities' response rules had not been stable for long enough to have been learnt. Others would postulate rationality as a universal principle for expectations formation. Thus, the adaptive expectations approach sees current price change as depending on the current state of excess demand and on past price change or, equivalently, on the history of excess demand.[11] The rational expectations approach sees current price change depending on current excess demand and on the history of both excess demand and monetary and fiscal policy.[12]

Although the stories concerning expectations differ, they become hard to distinguish from each other when the forces generating demand are analyzed.[13] Both postulate that the state of aggregate demand depends, in the standard way, on monetary and fiscal policy. However, fiscal policy changes will produce once and for all changes in aggregate demand and, therefore, change the price <u>level</u>; while changes in the rate of growth of the money supply will produce continuing changes in aggregate demand and, hence, affect the ongoing rate of inflation.

Under a regime of fixed exchange rates, world average inflation is thus seen as depending on the rate of growth of the world money supply. Its falling rate during the 1950s is seen as the consequence of tight monetary policies, especially in the second half of the period; its gradual and then more violent acceleration in the 1960s is seen as the consequence of step jumps in the rate of world monetary expansion throughout the 1960s. Its cyclical evolution is seen as a consequence of cycles in the growth rate of the world money supply.

Differences in national inflation rates during an era of fixed exchange rates are explained as a consequence of two interrelated factors. First, equilibrium relative prices are continuously changing because of differences in productivity growth rates. Secondly, the prices of goods which are not easily traded internationally may temporarily change relative to the world price level as a result of temporary domestic demand pressures. Such pressures cannot be

---

[11] Since past price change depends on past excess demand, all past price changes can be equivalently expressed in terms of all past excess demands.

[12] This is so because these are the variables upon which expected future monetary policy and, hence, inflation will be based.

[13] They may, however, be distinguished empirically if there are changes in policy response rules or "policy reaction functions."

permanent, for they will be associated with balance of payments disequilibrium and with equilibrating movements in reserves and, therefore, in national money supplies. Under fixed exchange rates, divergences among national inflation rates will be limited by these two factors.[14]

Under flexible rates, there are no such restrictions on national inflation rates, and the above analysis of the mechanism whereby inflation is generated applies at the national but not at the world level. Thus, national inflation rates will be determined by the behavior of national money supplies. Exchange rate changes will take place to reflect, in the long run, the purchasing power parity relation. In the short run, however, exchange rates will be determined by portfolio equilibrium considerations and may diverge markedly from purchasing power parity.[15] On this view, the wider divergence in inflation rates since 1971 is attributable to the more divergent monetary policies made possible by the adoption by most countries of floating exchange rates.

No attempt has been made in the above to discriminate between the two groups of hypotheses.[16] Attention is now turned to that task.

The point of direct conflict between the two views concerns the determination of prices and wages. The wage-push view sees these as largely independent of demand factors and subject to influence from a variety of ill-defined social factors and from wage and price controls. The monetary view is that wage and price changes are influenced by excess demand and by inflation expectations. The evidence relating to this conflict is voluminous and has already been extensively surveyed for the U.S. and the U.K. in Laidler and Parkin (1975), for six western European countries in Parkin (1976), and for six other (with overlaps) countries in Laidler (1976). Additionally, a recent volume edited by Brunner and Meltzer (1976) and not featured in the surveys cited adds further evidence, especially on the effects of controls. The main conclusions of these surveys are that wages and prices do respond systematically to demand and to inflation expectations, and that wage and price controls and other factors have, at most, small transitory effects.[17]

---

[14] It should be noted that fixed rates with full convertibility only became operational in 1958, prior to which exchange controls and trade restrictions were in force. Hence, the period prior to 1958 is, in some respects, more comparable to the 1970s than to the late 1950s and 1960s.

[15] See Dornbusch (1976), and Mussa (1976).

[16] For an attempt to set out some rigorous discriminating tests, see Gray and Parkin (1974). Also, see Parkin (1975a, 1977), and Brunner and Meltzer (1976).

[17] The dramatic reductions in inflation rates throughout the world during the latest recession are just one example of this mechanism at work and are a confirmation that it is as true now as it ever was that inflation responds strongly to market forces.

42

A further comparative test of the two hypotheses arises from the extensive phenomena which they can explain. The monetary hypothesis explains the falling inflation rate experienced by most countries in the late 1950s, the gentle acceleration of the early 1960s, the strong acceleration of the late 1960s, and the explosion of the 1970s. It also explains the cycles, the synchronous developments, the narrow dispersion across countries in the 1960s, and the widening dispersion of the 1970s, as well as the narrowing dispersion through the 1950s.

The wage-push view is entirely silent on the reasons for a falling inflation rate in the 1950s, on the cycles, and on the change in dispersion, and treats the synchronization of inflation either as coincidence or as the result of an unspecified international demonstration effect.

On these two tests, the monetary view completely dominates the wage-push alternative. It also dominates on a third test, that of "causality" (see Sims, 1972, and Genberg and Swoboda, 1975). However, in posing the two views as alternatives, violence has been done to what is probably the majority "eclectic" position. The most common eclectic position is that, until the second half of the 1960s, the monetary hypothesis is broadly correct, but that, for the period since then, it needs to be augmented by, but not replaced by, a wage-push and international commodity price-push impulse. This "everything is important" view is more difficult to deal with than the two extreme cases. It is all the more difficult to treat since even the pure monetary analysis has to admit that there has been a tendency, during the past decade, for the natural rate of unemployment to rise.[18] This rise in the natural rate could, in principle, be the result of the very wage-push factors to which that school of thought points.[19] However, that has yet to be demonstrated. Further, it has to be shown that a wage-push explanation of the rise in the natural unemployment rate is superior to the alternatives. Those alternatives are that a change in the demographic situation arising from the postwar bulge in the birth rate and improved unemployment compensation provisions have both contributed to a rise in the natural rate of unemployment. How much each has contributed in the various countries has not yet been determined.[20] However, it is clear that,

---

[18]That is, the rate of unemployment at which the rate of inflation is stationary has risen in most countries in the late 1960s and early 1970s.

[19]Indeed, given a monetarist explanation of inflation, the only interpretation which may be placed upon the wage-push view of the world is that push factors might raise the natural unemployment rate.

[20]Clearly what is needed is a combined time-series/cross-section study to control for both demographic factors and the economic incentives to be unemployed contained in the unemployment compensation regulations. There is not enough independent variability in these two factors across countries at a point in time, or over time in a single country.

when allowance is made for these factors, there is no puzzle about the rise in the natural unemployment rate.[21]

Some wage-push proponents argue as if, without wage-price controls, the inflation process has now become unstable. This statment could be given analytic content by interpreting it as implying that the natural unemployment rate no longer exists, i.e., even at 100 percent unemployment, there would be a tendency for inflation to accelerate. Whatever the reason, admittedly still moot, for the rise in the natural unemployment rate, this last proposition is clearly rejected by the available evidence. That evidence suggests that the natural rate has risen (at least in the countries for which there is evidence) from numbers in the range 2-5 percent to numbers in the range 4-7 percent.[22]

II. SOURCES OF INFLATIONARY MONETARY POLICY

The conclusion of the preceding section is that, ". . .inflation is always and everywhere a monetary phenomenon. . .produced by a more rapid increase in the quantity of money than in output" (Friedman, 1970, p. 24). However, the discussion so far has ignored the question: Why has the money supply grown too quickly? It is that question which is now addressed.[23]

The distinction between the fixed exchange rate era, which ended in early 1972 with the collapse of the Smithsonian attempt to patch up the Bretton Woods arrangements with realigned exchange rates, and the subsequent floating rate era remains a crucial distinction for analyzing this question. During the former period, it is the factors determining the world money supply which need to be identified, and for the latter period, separate national developments require attention.

The fixed exchange rate world consisted of one country (the U.S.) representing approximately 50 percent of the "world"; five countries (France, Germany, Italy, Japan, and the U.K.) representing a little less than 10 percent each; and scores of countries, in aggregate, representing the balance.[24] Thus, in terms of size, the fixed exchange rate world was dominated by the U.S. More importantly, the U.S. dollar was, during this period, the major form in

---

[21]See especially Gordon (1972); and Gray, Parkin, and Sumner (1975).

[22]The U.K. natural rate, according to Gray, Parkin, and Sumner (1975), has risen from 1.8 percent in the late 1950s and early 1960s and, by 1974, was 3.2 percent.

[23]There is not a large literature on this subject. See, as representative items, Brunner (1976), Gordon (1975), Meltzer (1975), and Parkin (1975a).

[24]The precise weights, using Group of Ten GNP average weights are: U.S., 55 percent; France, 8 percent; Germany, 10 percent; Italy, 5 percent; Japan, 7 percent; U.K., 7 percent; Canada, 4 percent; and no other country more than 1 1/2 percent.

which international reserves were held by the "small" countries. Further, it was in terms of the U.S. dollar that parities were defined. Each of the small countries pursued monetary policies which, with minor exceptions, were dominated by the aim of preserving the fixed exchange rate structure. This implies that their money supplies were largely endogenous and determined by the demands for the various national monies, and that U.S. monetary policy was the dominant influence on the course of both U.S. and world money supply behavior.[25]

The behavior of U.S. and world monetary aggregates (M2 growth rates) for the period to 1975 is displayed in Chart 2. While it is clear that the detailed year-by-year developments do not align exactly, the broad trends are clearly similar. Money supply growth rates for the Group of Ten aggregate went through one and a half cycles from 1954 to 1960 but, throughout that period, never exceeded 6 percent and averaged less than the world real output growth rate. In 1961, there was a sharp rise to 7.5 percent and, following that, the world money supply growth rate fluctuated between 5 percent and 9 percent, averaging approximately 6 1/2 percent up to 1970. The major explosion came in 1971, the final year of the fixed exchange rate era, when the growth rate jumped to more than 13 percent. The U.S. money supply growth rate has been persistently below the world average, but it has moved in broadly similar ways. Its average in the late 1960s was significantly higher than in the early 1960s, which in turn was higher than in the late 1950s.

What is the explanation for this money supply behavior? Four hypotheses will be examined here (though they are not offered as exhaustive). The first is that inflation is basically a push phenomenon with the money supply passively following. This has already been examined and rejected in the previous section. The second hypothesis is that governments seek to maximize their tax revenue from money creation. This is difficult to reconcile with the data. The principal, though not only, difficulty concerns the 1950s. Why, if governments seek to maximize the yield of the inflation tax, did it take them so long to raise the money supply growth rate? Further, the existing growth rates and, indeed, the peak growth rates hardly seem high enough if that is the objective.[26] A third hypothesis is that there was a major shift of emphasis toward Keynesian policies in the U.S. during 1961, and that the conservative monetary policies specifically aimed at price stability which were pursued in the 1950s were abandoned in favor of fine tuning monetary and fiscal policies aimed at achieving full employment. As a "story" of the late 1950s and early 1960s, that seems

---

[25] For a brief survey of and comprehensive bibliography on the literature on world money supply under the fixed exchange rate arrangements of Bretton Woods, see Parkin (1977).

[26] Sjaastad (1975) has attempted an ingenious explanation of why governments might produce a variable inflation as part of a revenue maximization effort.

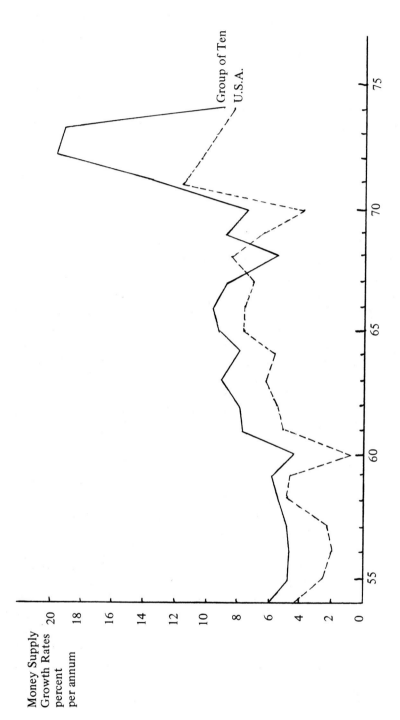

Chart 2: Money Supply Growth Rates (M2)

accurate enough. However, it is a "story," not an explanation. Further, it does not reconcile easily with the events of the past two years during which unemployment rates have been allowed (forced) to rise to unprecedented postwar levels.

A fourth hypothesis looks more promising than any of the above, although it has to be admitted that it is, at this stage, less than fully developed. In its most general, if somewhat empty, form, it is the hypothesis that inflationary monetary policies are the outcome of utility maximizing behavior on the part of politicians and bureaucrats in an indirect democratic political system.[27] The key element in this is the winning of elections.

In a purely empirical study, Fair (1975) has shown that voters are apparently most influenced by the state of the economy in the year of an election. The particular indicator of the state of the economy which most influences voting behavior, at least in U.S. presidential elections, is the rate of growth of real income. In a purely analytical exercise, Nordhaus (1975) has shown that politicians optimizing over a limited time horizon and facing the type of constraint embodied in the Phillips type trade-off between inflation and unemployment will produce a higher and more variable rate of inflation and average level of economic activity than bureaucrats optimizing over an infinite horizon. These two studies point to the notion that it will be optimal for policy to be variable and expansionary in the run-in year to an election. The approximate time lags of real and price level responses reinforce this. Real expansion typically follows reflationary policies within one year, while a change in the rate of inflation typically follows two years after the initial stimulus. Thus, with skill, and provided the policy has not been too widely anticipated, a real growth recovery can be engineered for an election year with the inflationary consequences of that recovery coming through only after the election.

The above factors may go a long way toward explaining the cycles in inflationary policies. They do not, however, explain the trend. A potential explanation for this may be a combination of two related ideas developed by Meltzer (1975) and Parkin (1975a). Meltzer points out that governments can raise their popularity by developing programs which benefit specific groups, while financing them with taxes the effects of which are diffused. This leads to the prediction that government, as measured both by its volume of spending and

---

[27]This is to return to a long-standing tradition in economics started by Adam Smith (1776) of treating politicians like private agents, i.e., as rational maximizers. It stands in contrast to the more fashionable current approach of treating politicians as benevolent maximizers of other peoples' welfare.

the degree of intervention in the private sector, will tend to grow.[28] It also suggests why such growth may well be financed in part by inflation, for rising prices produce an automatic and widely diffused rise in effective marginal tax rates and provide an opportunity for selective "giveaway" higher tax effect allowances. A further reason to suppose that government growth will lead to inflation arises from the fact that growing government expenditure is combined with pegged interest rates. This inevitably leads to accelerating rates of money supply growth. The specific way in which governments can gain electoral advantage by pegging interest rates arises from the debt distribution by age groups. The life cycle of indebtedness has young people as net debtors, middle-aged people breaking even, and old people as net creditors. Low interest rates, therefore, discriminate on the average against the old and in favor of the young. Governments which are more concerned to win the votes of the young will, therefore, pursue low interest rate policies. The demographic features of most western societies make the young the most important voting group and, hence, perhaps explain the low interest rate policies of the past decade. Additionally, it is possible that younger voters are more volatile in their voting habits than older voters[29] providing yet a further reason for pursuing low interest rates. Further, while appearing to address the problems of the old, thereby maintaining some of their support, government pension programs may be introduced, adding yet more to the underlying rise in public spending and inflationary pressures.

The data on public spending growth for the U.S. and the U.K. (taken as representative economies) as well as real after-tax interest rates[30] are set out in Charts 3 and 4. It is clear that whether or not the above "story" is a correct explanation of those phenomena, there has indeed been a rise in public spending, and the public sector deficit in both countries and real interest rates have fallen.

It is also clear from Chart 4 that although both spending on goods and services and transfer payments as fractions of national income have risen, it is the latter which has dominated the growth of total public sector spending. The effects of these inflation inducing policies on allocation and growth will now be analyzed and evaluated.

---

[28] There remains the puzzle as to why governments remained small and almost constant (relative to GNP) throughout the nineteenth century and until World War I. The first wave of expansion of government came in the interwar years and the second wave immediately after World War II. The late 1960s saw the third wave.

[29] This is, of course, a testable proposition and needs to be investigated directly.

[30] A constant tax rate of 30 percent was used for the U.S. This was done to give an indication of the order of magnitude of real after-tax rates in that country.

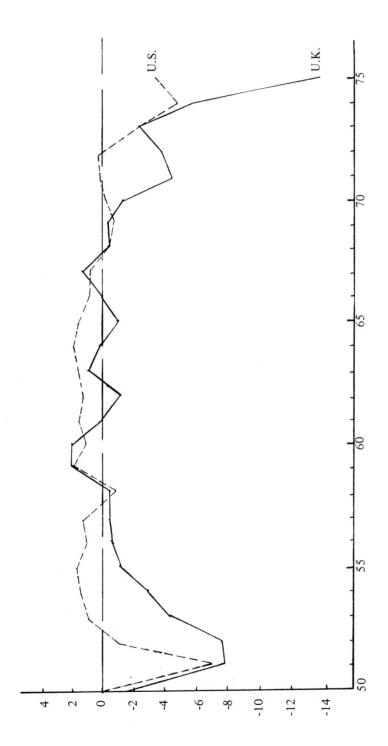

Chart 3: Net-of-Tax Real Rates of Interest

49

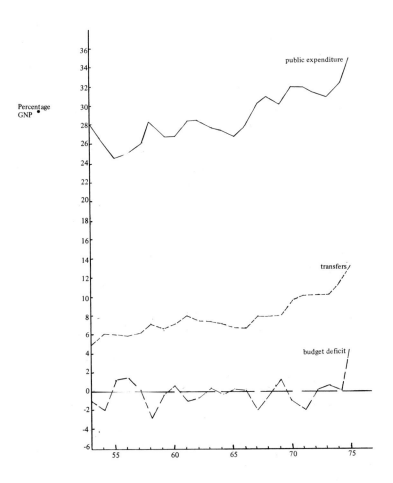

Percentage
GNP

**Chart 4a: Growth of Public Expenditure, Transfers and Budget
Deficit for U.S.**

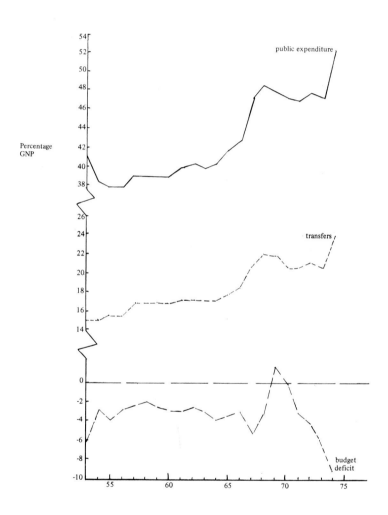

Chart 4b: Growth of Public Expenditure, Transfers and
Budget Deficit for U.K.

51

III. CONSEQUENCES FOR RESOURCE ALLOCATION AND GROWTH

Standard analysis predicts that a fully anticipated inflation, no matter what its rate, has no effect on the steady state growth rate, but may affect such real variables as the capital/labor ratio and output per head, although in an ambiguous direction.[31] In more general models with endogenous and embodied technical change, the growth rate may also be affected. Some recent analyses and speculations have questioned the relevance of these results and have suggested that they probably miss some potentially important effects of even a fully anticipated inflation, especially its effects on the information content of prices and the efficiency of the search process.[32] The usefulness of these results for analyzing the consequences of the current inflation is more seriously undermined by the description of the origins of that inflation contained in the preceding section. From that description, it is clear that the origin of the current inflation is not a neutral and fully anticipated rise in the growth rate of the money supply. Rather, the money supply growth is the consequence of real changes in fiscal policy and in interest rates. In analyzing the effects associated with the current inflation on allocation and growth, it is necessary, therefore, to analyze the effects of these fiscal and interest rate policies.

First, there is a direct "crowding out" effect of fiscal policy.[33] This is the simplest "real crowding out" and in no way depends on a rise in public spending raising interest rates to crowd out private spending. Indeed, by assumption, policy is holding interest rates steady, in nominal terms. The precise consequences of this "real crowding out" will depend in part on what the government expenditure is directed toward. To the extent this expenditure is on items with a low or even negative marginal utility, the effects are of course damaging to growth and welfare.

Whether or not increases in general public expenditure crowd out capital accumulation or consumption will depend on the particular features of the financing of the increase in public expenditure. In current circumstances, there is good reason to suppose that it is primarily the former which is adversely affected. The key elements which lead to this conclusion are the interest rate policies and the tax laws which lead to unambiguous and potentially serious asset reallocations. This needs spelling out more fully.

---

[31] See Laidler and Parkin (1975, section V) for a brief review of the relevant literature.

[32] See, especially, Leijonhufvud (1975), Laidler (1975), Parkin and Swoboda (1976), and Sheshinski and Weiss (1976).

[33] For a useful, if simple-minded, survey of the recently revived "crowding out" literature, see Carlson and Spencer (1975).

It is convenient to distinguish four classes of assets--bonds, equity, durables, and money--and to analyze the consequences of current tax structures in order to define the effects of inflation on the net-of-tax real rates of return on these assets. First, consider bonds. The typical arrangement is for the nominal yield to be subject to income tax at a rate, hardly anywhere, less than 30 percent and rising in extreme cases (e.g., the U.K.) to more than 90 percent at high enough levels of taxable income. Assume for the moment that the nominal yields on a bond always rise to reflect exactly the ongoing rate of inflation. In this case, the net-of-tax real yield r_N will be given by:[34]

$$r_N = (r + p)(1-t) - p = r(1-t) - pt,$$

where r is the real pre-tax yield; p is the rate of inflation; and t is the tax rate. It is clear that, in this case, a rise in the rate of inflation lowers the net real return on bonds by an amount equal to the inflation rate multiplied by the tax rate. With tax rates in the typical 30-50 percent range, quite modest inflation rates will be sufficient to make net-of-tax real returns negative. If, as is common in many countries, monetary policy is conducted by pegging nominal bond yields to prevent them from rising sufficiently to reflect the underlying rate of inflation, then the reduction in real after-tax bond yields becomes even greater. In sum then, the impact effect of a rise in the rate of inflation on real after-tax bond yields is to lower them by an amount not less than the inflation rate times the tax rate, and possibly by as much as the inflation rate itself.

The case of equities is more complicated and in its details more variable across countries. However, the broad principles are similar and clear. The method of computing taxable corporate profits is the central source of distortion here.[35] Fixed capital is, in most cases, depreciated on a "historical cost" valuation basis, and inventories are valued on a "first-in/first-out" basis. These conventions have the effect of overstating true profit by an amount which varies directly with the rate of inflation and, since tax liabilities are computed on the basis of an upward biased measure of profit, of making real after-tax profits an inverse function of the rate of inflation. The tendencies just described will be partly, exactly, or more than offset by the debt/equity position of the

---

[34] This formula first came to my attention in McCulloch (1975, p. 106).

[35] Arnold, Carsberg, and Scapens have conducted extensive investigations of the detailed effects of inflation on U.K. corporate profits as part of the Manchester Inflation Research Programme. For a convenient summary of some of that work, see Scapens, Arnold, and Carsberg (1975).

corporation. A corporation with sufficient debt will obtain an increase in after-tax profits as a function of inflation as a result of the bond yield distortions discussed previously. Thus, in sum, the impact effects of inflation on net-of-tax real corporate profits will depend on the capital structure of the corporation. At one extreme, a corporation with "old" assets and no debt will experience a reduction in real after-tax profits as inflation increases; at the other extreme, a corporation with "new" assets and a high debt/equity ratio may experience a rise in after-tax real profits as inflation increases.

Durables are much simpler. The nonpecuniary yield on such durables as housing, art, and jewelry is not taxed. Nor, in many countries, is the capital gain.[36] In consequence, there is no impact effect of a rise in the rate of inflation on the yields on durables. Finally, money typically has a zero nominal yield so that a rise in the rate of inflation simply lowers its own-real rate of return one for one.

The impact effects described above are not the end of the story. If, prior to a postulated change in the rate of inflation, portfolio equilibrium prevailed, there would be, after the impact effects just described, a portfolio disequilibrium, and asset reallocations would be made. The disequilibrium would relate both to the composition of portfolios and their size. Assuming the usual substitution effects, there should be a movement out of bonds, money, and the losing equities, and into durables and the winning equities. Movements within these groups will be of ambiguous sign. There should also be a reduction in the overall rate of wealth accumulation. It may be presumed that the reallocations of the given stock of wealth will be accomplished quickly by equilibrating asset price changes. However, the change in the actual stock of wealth and in the physical capital stock will take a long period--probably many years or even decades. The physical capital stock adjustment induced by the changes in yields identified above will either slow down the rate of economic growth or, if strong enough, lead to an actual decline in real incomes.

The above discussion has concentrated only on the effects of changes in relative yields, as if these changes were expected to persist. A sharp change in, or a highly variable rate of, inflation will additionally lead to an increase in uncertainty. This can be expected to have two types of effects, neither of which, however, can be unambiguously signed on the usual assumptions. One is that the covariance of returns will, as inflation increases, come more to be dominated by inflation variability rather than by variability in real factors. The second is that uncertainty about the longer term average inflation rate will

---

[36]The capital gain on art and jewelry is taxed on realization in the U.K., but the rate for long-term holdings is low.

become greater, thereby inhibiting long-term loan contracts denominated in money units.

To summarize the above, with taxation of nominal yields, with profits accounting conventions which bias the measurement of taxable profits in inflationary conditions, and with no taxation of the income from durables, a rise in the inflation rate will bias asset allocations away from bonds and some forms of physical capital and into durables.

It is important to emphasize that the quantitative effects of these interest rate and tax policies will depend crucially on the scale of public spending and, the higher the volume, the greater will be the inflation rate and the distortions to the accumulation process. Further, assuming that savings are a direct function of income (or wealth), transfer payments are no different in this respect from purchases of goods and services, for they too will require higher equilibrium interest rates. Indeed, it is precisely the steep growth in transfer payments since the mid-1960s which represents the major change leading to the strong inflation of the past four years. The problem of reducing and containing this expenditure is the topic of the next section.

IV. THE GROWING TRANSFER PAYMENTS PROBLEM

It has been argued above that it is the growth in transfer payments combined with a monetary policy designed to prevent interest rates from rising which has led to the current inflation problem. This section examines some methods for dealing with this problem. One possibility would be to let real interest rates rise to the level necessary for the financing of public expenditure to be achieved without inflationary money creation. Another would be to set taxes sufficiently high to balance the government budget. However, each of these measures would have potentially serious effects on efficiency; they will not be pursued further here. Rather, attention will focus on ways of reducing and containing the volume of redistributive transfer payments.

There is an increasingly vocal minority of economists and political philosophers who are advocating the elimination of compulsory redistribution by the state, and its replacement by voluntary income equilization insurance schemes and voluntary charity. Although the arguments for this solution are powerful, they will neither be presented nor evaluated here, for their lack of popularity makes it unlikely that these or similar schemes would be politically possible. However, the widespread support for the view that some compulsory redistribution is desirable will be taken as a constraint, and alternative methods of achieving an efficient and "just" redistribution will be considered.

55

First, it is well known and widely accepted that redistributions in cash are more efficient than redistributions in kind (see, e.g., Tobin, 1970). It follows that, by eliminating such redistributive subsidies as those on food, housing, and medicine which are common in many countries and sizable in some, and replacing them with cash transfers, the total cash volume of redistribution could be reduced without reducing the welfare of the recipients of the transfers. How much could be saved by replacing all specific subsidies and transfers in kind with transfers in cash is an empirical matter and would vary substantially across countries. However, even in countries such as Sweden and the U.K. where transfer payments are approaching one-third of national income, it is unlikely that savings from this switch would amount to enough to eliminate inflationary pressures at interest rates regarded as politically acceptable.

The real problem then is to reduce the overall scale of redistribution and, at the same time, not violate widely accepted notions of distributive justice.

The problem of distributive justice has, at a high level of abstraction, received a good deal of attention in recent years following the publication of Rawls' (1971) important book on this subject.[37] By way of analysis of an hypothetical individual's maximizing choices in a primeval state in which the individual has no knowledge of his own attributes, Rawls argues that all rational individuals will choose to live in a society in which the welfare of the least well-equipped individual is maximized--a maxi-min criterion. The basic analysis leading to this conclusion can be criticized on the grounds that in the hypothetical choice situation of the primeval state, the individual is simply faced with a choice under uncertainty problem, and maxi-min is not, in general, the expected utility maximizing strategy. Indeed, if individuals were not risk averse, a straightforward utilitarian social welfare function would be chosen. We might, therefore, regard maxi-min and the utilitarian objective of maximizing the sum of utilities as the two limiting cases which span all peoples' views on distributive justice.

These ideas, stemming from Rawls and the subsequent literature, while providing an axiomatic basis for rules for distributive justice are, from an operational point of view, somewhat empty. They have, however, been given greater operational content in recent work by Mirrlees (1971), Atkinson (1973), and others.[38]

---

[37] Also see Rawls (1967) and Phelps (1974).

[38] See, additionally, Sheshinski (1972).

Mirrlees asks the question: Given a state of technology (concave) and a distribution of talents, and assuming each individual has the same preference function defined with respect to effort and consumption, what is the shape of the tax collection function (tax as a function of pre-tax income) which will maximize the sum of individual utilities? On "reasonable" assumptions Mirrlees concludes that a tax function which is <u>linear</u> is approximately optimal. The least talented individuals would receive a lump sum transfer and do no work. Those more talented would receive the lump sum and be taxed at a constant marginal (rising average) rate. In other words, a negative income tax with a constant marginal tax rate is approximately optimal. Atkinson investigates the consequences of using the maxi-min criterion with the restriction that the marginal tax rate be constant. Not surprisingly, maxi-min has a higher lump sum transfer and higher tax rate than the utilitarian solution. On these criteria, there is no case at all for progressive (as distinct from degressive) taxes.

The analyses just considered, although abstract and a long way from the concrete redistribution problem, do seem to provide a powerful and potentially widely acceptable rationale for, and argument in favor of, replacing the complex welfare programs which redistribute toward not only the poor but also the unemployed, the sick, and a variety of other groups, with a single and simple "social dividend" combined with a flat rate tax on all income. The incentives contained in such a structure to greater work effort cannot be numerically evaluated, but may be large. Further, as a result of its effects on effort, if the tax rate is substantially reduced, the total scale of redistribution would surely be much lower than that currently operating in most countries at the present time. Further, the redistribution would unambiguously go to the poor and not, as in all present systems, from one pocket to the other of the same person or group.

The main problem with the proposal that a negative income tax should replace all other forms of state engineered redistribution is, first, settling on the size of the lump sum transfer and on the tax rate and, secondly, of ensuring that those administering the system do not develop modifications, loopholes, and the like to gain political advantage. Both problems could, in principle, be handled by making the entire redistribution scheme a constitutional and referendum matter. That is, the lump sum transfer (preferably indexed to average wages growth) and the tax rate could be voted on directly—where the options are constrained to provide an expected break even—and regard as having the status of a constitutional law, so that there is a presumption in favor of infrequent changes in the rules. Further, a constitutional law is required outlawing all other legislation on redistribution. By implementing such a procedure, the ability of political groups to buy votes by favoring one group or another is eliminated, and legislators can concentrate on their proper tasks.

It has long been advocated that monetary policy should be independent of the political process and that a fixed money supply growth rate be announced and adhered to. This proposal is in the same vein. Indeed, the two are closely related, for without some constitutional limit on the size of total public spending, it is hard to see how, in the long run, money supply growth rates can be held at noninflationary steady levels.

V. CONCLUSIONS

The main conclusions which emerge from the above analysis are clear and simply stated. First, the world inflation take-off in the late 1960s had, as its proximate cause, an expansion in the world money supply growth rate. That money supply growth arose as the effect of a policy of pegging nominal interest rates combined with a sharp rise in public expenditure, especially transfer expenditures, in a variety of countries. In addition to generating inflationary monetary expansion, these policies also disturbed asset market equilibrium and led to portfolio substitutions in favor of the accumulation of durables and against the accumulation of physical capital. Further, the large increases in transfer payments had direct output inhibiting disincentive effects.

The trends in public spending were different in each country, but, while the fixed exchange rate system was held together, these differences did not affect national inflation developments. However, after the collapse of the fixed rate system, inflation rates diverged to reflect the underlying national fiscal and monetary trends.

It is easy to prescribe a solution for the world's economic ills, but, given the constraints imposed by existing political institutions and attitudes, less easy to see how a workable solution can be introduced. The prescription is simply to place the growth rate of the money supply and income redistribution outside the scope of the day-to-day business of politicians and to set rules in both areas with the status of constitutional laws. Further, public spending on goods and services should have a constitutionally imposed upper limit. However, the move from prescription to implementation has to overcome many further problems, for:

> . . .the belief that deliberate regulation of
> all social affairs must necessarily be more
> successful than the apparent haphazard
> interplay of independent individuals has
> continuously gained ground until today
> there is hardly a political group anywhere
> in the world which does not want central
> direction of most human activities in the
> service of one aim or another (Hayek,
> 1935, p. 1).

This attitude is as strong (if not stronger) today than when Hayek wrote and relentessly leads to ever bigger government. In the face of the strong forces in this direction, it is still not clear how institutional changes can be designed to modify the course and make workable solutions acceptable ones as well. Perhaps as a start, nailed to the bedpost of every politician and bureaucrat should be the famous words of Adam Smith:

> I have never known much good done by
> those who affected to trade for the public
> good. . . .
> The statesman who should attempt to
> direct private people in what manner they
> ought to employ their capitals would not
> only load himself with a most unnecessary
> attention, but assume an authority which
> could safely be trusted, not only to no
> single person, but to no council or senate
> whatever, and which would nowhere be
> so dangerous as in the hands of a man who
> had the folly and presumption enough to
> fancy himself fit to exercise it (Smith,
> 1776, 1910 edition, Vol. 1, pp. 400-1).

It is clear that Smith remains as relevant today as he was two hundred years ago. It is also clear, however, that until economists understand why his message has become so unfashionable and why ". . .the belief that deliberate regulation. . .must necessarily be more successful" has become the dominant view, they shall not be able to produce the required changes in government behavior. The research task on this question has hardly begun.

DATA APPENDIX

A1: World Inflation - Sources and Methods

Inflation was calculated as $\ln(P_t/P_{t-1}) \times 100.0$ where P_t is the annual average retail price index for year t from the following sources:

1950-57	International Financial Statistics, IMF, Washington, D.C.;
1957-74	Various national sources–see Inflation Workshop world data base;
1975	OECD Main Economic Indicators.

The aggregate Group of Ten price index was constructed as a weighted average of the national price indices, the weights being as follows:

1950-57	$GNP in 1953 evaluated at par rates (IFS);
1957-75	Series of $GNP evaluated at 1963 par rates and at 1963 prices (Manchester University Inflation Workshop world data base).

A2: Money Supply Growth Rates (M2)

(percent per annum)

Year	Group of Ten	U.S.
1954	6.0	4.2
1955	4.4	2.5
1956	4.3	1.9
1957	4.7	2.3
1958	5.3	4.8
1959	5.7	4.5
1960	4.2	0.9
1961	7.5	5.2
1962	7.8	5.5
1963	8.9	6.4
1964	8.0	5.9
1965	9.1	7.6
1966	9.4	7.8
1967	8.7	7.1
1968	5.3	8.6
1969	8.6	6.4
1970	7.2	3.9
1971	13.3	11.1
1972	19.9	10.0
1973	19.4	9.3
1974	9.0	8.0

Sources and methods:

As for retail prices (see notes to Table A1). The aggregate Group of Ten data were a simple addition of national money stocks evaluated at par rates up to end–1971 and average spot rates 1971-75.

A3: Net-of-Tax Real Rates of Interest

Year	U.K.	U.S.
1950	- 1.868	- 0.162
1951	- 7.485	- 6.746
1952	- 7.473	- 0.707
1953	- 4.323	0.711
1954	- 0.863	1.274
1955	- 1.161	1.750
1956	- 0.559	1.114
1957	- 0.181	1.178
1958	- 0.218	- 0.665
1959	1.969	2.108
1960	2.333	1.294
1961	0.108	1.451
1962	- 0.901	1.338
1963	0.905	1.355
1964	0.164	1.547
1965	- 0.803	1.371
1966	0.142	0.667
1967	1.461	0.803
1968	- 0.131	- 0.187
1969	- 0.128	- 0.503
1970	- 1.537	- 0.560
1971	- 4.933	- 0.119
1972	- 3.715	0.010
1973	- 2.444	- 2.380
1974	- 5.863	- 4.755
1975	-13.940	- 3.701

Sources:
U.K. average redemption yield on short-term (under five years) bonds. Source: Annual Abstract of Statistics and Monthly Digest of Statistics, H.M.S.O., London.

U.S. yield on 3-5 year Government Bonds. Source: Economic Report of the President, 1976, Washington, D.C.

Both adjusted for average tax rate (U.K. standard rate; U.S. 0.3 throughout) and for annual rate of change of consumer prices.

A4: Public Expenditure and Deficits for U.S. and U.K. 1955-1975 as a Percentage of GNP

Year	U.S.				U.K.			
	Goods and Services Expenditure (1)	Transfers (2)	Total (1) plus (2)	Deficit (-) Surplus (+)	Goods and Services Expenditure (1)	Transfers (2)	Total (1) plus (2)	Deficit (-) Surplus (+)
1953	22.54	5.20	27.74	-1.89	25.67	15.14	40.81	-6.04
1954	20.68	5.81	26.49	-1.95	23.45	15.13	38.58	-3.19
1955	18.79	5.74	24.53	+0.79	22.44	15.51	37.95	-4.07
1956	18.87	5.96	24.83	+1.23	22.66	15.46	38.12	-2.95
1957	19.67	6.36	26.03	+0.21	22.23	16.75	38.98	-2.63
1958	21.17	7.26	28.43	-2.81	22.15	16.90	39.05	-2.15
1959	20.06	6.87	26.93	-0.32	22.42	16.89	39.31	-2.62
1960	19.81	7.15	26.96	+0.46	22.27	16.87	39.14	-3.16
1961	20.67	7.82	28.49	-0.81	22.49	17.36	39.85	-3.05
1962	20.93	7.53	28.46	-0.67	23.25	17.41	40.66	-2.44
1963	20.79	7.42	28.21	+0.12	23.07	17.26	40.33	-3.26
1964	20.42	7.31	27.73	-0.36	23.33	17.29	40.62	-3.82
1965	20.18	7.12	27.30	+0.08	23.84	18.39	42.23	-3.51
1966	21.07	7.29	28.36	-0.17	24.69	18.66	43.35	-2.96
1967	22.63	7.81	30.44	-1.79	26.21	21.23	47.44	-5.30
1968	22.88	8.08	30.96	-0.63	26.27	22.38	48.65	-3.09
1969	22.22	8.31	30.53	+1.14	26.01	21.84	47.85	+1.71
1970	22.28	9.47	31.75	-0.95	26.40	21.21	47.61	+0.08
1971	21.98	10.04	32.02	-1.72	26.30	21.08	47.38	-2.49
1972	21.61	10.06	31.67	-1.30	26.57	21.51	48.08	-3.84
1973	20.66	10.35	31.01	+0.46	26.30	21.21	47.40	-6.58
1974	21.40	11.12	32.52	-0.25	28.24	24.25	52.49	-8.98
1975	22.07[P]	12.96[P]	35.03[P]	-4.23[P]	---	---	---	---

P = Provisional estimate

Deficit for U.K. is: Net borrowing, changes in Debtors, Creditors, and Cash Balances (pre-1961), or public sector borrowing requirement plus other net financial transactions (post-1960). These equivalent measures are due to no published measure of PSBR being available prior to 1961.

Sources:

For U.S.: Survey of Current Business, January 1976, Parts I and II.

For U.K.: National Income and Expenditure (Blue Book), various issues, H.M.S.O., London.

REFERENCES

1. Atkinson, A.B., "How Progressive Should Income Tax Be?" in Essays in Modern Economics: A.U.T.E. Conference Proceedings, 1972, (ed. M. Parkin), London: Longmans, 1973.

2. Brunner, K., "The Political Economy of Inflations," University of Rochester paper presented at the Catholic University of Leuven Conference, May 1976.

3. Brunner, K., and Meltzer, A.H. (eds.), "The Economics of Wage and Price Controls," in The Economics of Price and Wage Controls, (eds. K. Brunner and A.H. Meltzer), Carnegie-Rochester Conference Series on Public Policy, Vol. 2, Amsterdam: North-Holland, 1976.

4. _____ , "The Explanation of Inflation: Some International Evidence," forthcoming in American Economic Review, Papers and Proceedings, 1977.

5. Carlson, K.M., and Spencer, R.W., "Crowding Out and Its Critics," Federal Reserve Bank of St. Louis Review, 57, No. 12, (December 1975), 2-17.

6. Dornbusch, R., "The Theory of Flexible Exchange Rate Regimes and Macroeconomic Policy," Scandinavian Journal of Economics, 78, No. 2, 1976, 255-275.

7. Fair, R.C., "On Controlling the Economy to Win Elections," Cowles Foundation, Yale University discussion paper No. 397, August 1975.

8. Fisher, I. The Purchasing Power of Money. New York: Macmillan, 1911.

9. Friedman, M. The Counter-Revolution in Monetary Theory. London: Institute of Economic Affairs (for the Wincott Foundation) occasional paper No. 33, 1970.

10. Galbraith, J.K. Economics and the Public Purpose. Harmondsworth: Penguin Books, 1975.

11. Genberg, H., and Swoboda, A.K., "Causes and Origins of the Current Worldwide Inflation," G.I.I.S.-Ford Foundation International Monetary Research Project discussion paper, Geneva: Graduate Institute of International Studies, November 1975.

12. Gordon, R.J., "Wage-Price Controls and the Shifting Phillips Curve," Brookings Papers on Economic Activity, Washington, D.C.: The Brookings Institution, 3 (1972:2), 385-421.

13. _____ , "The Demand for and Supply of Inflation," Journal of Law and Economics, XVIII (3), (December 1975), 807-836.

14. Gray, M.R., and Parkin, M., "Discriminating Between Alternative Explanations of Inflation," University of Manchester Inflation Workshop paper 7414, mimeo, 1974.

15. Gray, M.R., Parkin, J.M., and Sumner, M.T., "Inflation in the United Kingdom: Causes and Transmission Mechanisms," University of Manchester Inflation Workshop discussion paper 7518, mimeo, paper presented at the Helsinki Conference on the Monetary Mechanism in Open Economies, 1975.

16. Harrod, Sir R. F., "The Issues: Five Views," in Inflation as a Global Problem, (ed. R. Hinshaw), London: Johns Hopkins Press, 1972.

17. Hayek, F. A. (ed.) Collectivist Economic Planning. London: Routledge, 1935.

18. Hicks, Sir J.R. The Crisis in Keynesian Economics. Oxford: Blackwell, 1974.

19. _____ , "The Permissive Economy," in Crisis '75. . ? , London: Institute of Economic Affairs occasional paper special 43, 1975.

20. Hume, D., "Of the Balance of Trade," in Essays, Moral, Political, and Literary, London: Oxford University Press, 1963.

21. Johnson, Harry G., "The Monetary Approach to Balance of Payments Theory," in Further Essays in Monetary Economics, London: G. Allen and Unwin, 1972.

22. Laidler, D., "The Welfare Costs of Inflation in Neo-Classical Theory: Some Unsettled Questions," University of Western Ontario research report No. 7523, forthcoming in Proceedings of the International Economics Association Conference on Inflation, (ed. A. Robinson), Sweden: Saltsjöbaden, 1975.

23. _____, "Inflation–Alternative Explanations and Policies: Tests on Data Drawn from Six Countries," in Institutions, Policies and Economic Performance, (eds. K. Brunner and A.H. Meltzer), Carnegie-Rochester Conference Series on Public Policy, Vol. 4, Amsterdam: North-Holland, 1976.

24. Laidler, D., and Parkin, J.M., "Inflation: A Survey," Economic Journal, 85, No. 340, (December 1975), 741-809.

25. Leijonhufvud, A., "Costs and Consequences of Inflation," mimeo, University of California, Los Angeles, April 1975.

26. McCulloch, J.H. Money and Inflation. New York: Academic Press, 1975.

27. Meltzer, A.H., "Why Governments Grow," Carnegie-Mellon University, mimeo, lecture in "The Economy in Disarray" lecture series, University of Chicago, 1975.

28. Mirrlees, J.A., "An Exploration in the Theory of Optimum Income Taxation," Review of Economic Studies, XXXVIII (2), No. 114, (April 1971), 175-208.

29. Mundell, R.A. International Economics. New York: Macmillan, 1968.

30. Mussa, M., "The Exchange Rate, the Balance of Payments and Monetary and Fiscal Policy under a Regime of Controlled Floating," Scandinavian Journal of Economics, 78, No. 2, (1976), 229-248.

31. Nordhaus, W.D., "Political Business Cycle," Review of Economic Studies, XLII (2), No. 130, (March 1975), 169-190.

32. Parkin, M., "The Politics of Inflation: An Economist's View," Government and Opposition, 10, No. 2, (Spring 1975), 189-202 (a).

33. _____ , "Where is Britain's Inflation Going?" Lloyds Bank Review, 117, (July 1975), 1-13 (b).

34. _____ , "Monetary Union and Stabilization Policy in the European Community," Banca Nazionale de Lavoro Quarterly Review, forthcoming 1976.

35. _____ , "A 'Monetarist' Analysis of the Generation and Transmission of World Inflation: 1958-1971," University of Western Ontario research report No. 7616, forthcoming in American Economic Review, Papers and Proceedings, 1977.

36. Parkin, M., and Swoboda, A.K., "Inflation: The Issues," University of Western Ontario Graduate Institute of International Studies, mimeo, Geneva, 1976, forthcoming in Proceedings of the International Economics Association Conference on Inflation, (ed. A. Robinson), Sweden: Saltsjöbaden, 1976.

37. Parkin, M., and Zis, G. (eds.) Inflation in the World Economy. Manchester and Toronto: Manchester University Press and University of Toronto Press, 1976a.

38. _____ . Inflation in Small Open Economies. Manchester and Toronto: Manchester University Press and University of Toronto Press, 1976b.

39. Phelps, E.S. (ed.) Economic Justice. Harmondsworth: Penguin, 1974.

40. Rawls, J., "Distributive Justice," (1967), in Economic Justice, (ed. E.S. Phelps), 1974.

41. _____ . A Theory of Justice. Cambridge: Harvard University Press, 1971.

42. Scapens, R., Arnold, J., and Carsberg, B., "The Measurement of Business Profits," in Study on the Possible Part Played by Certain Primary Nonemployment Incomes in the Inflationary Process in the United Kingdom, (ed. D.E.W. Laidler), Brussels: Commission of the European Communities, Mediterranean Economic Series, Vol. 6, 1975.

43. Sheshinski, E., "The Optimal Linear Income Tax," Review of Economic Studies, XXXIX (3), No. 119, (July 1972), 297-302.

44. Sheshinski, E., and Weiss, Y., "Inflation and Costs of Price Adjustment," Stanford University Inflation Workshop discussion paper No. 2, January 1976.

45. Sims, C.A., "Money, Income and Causality," American Economic Review, LXII, No. 4, (September 1972), 540-552

46. Sjaastad, L., "Why Stable Inflations Fail," in Inflation in the World Economy, (eds. J.M. Parkin and G. Zis), 1975.

47. Smith, A. The Wealth of Nations, Vols. I and II, (1776), London: Everyman, 1910. Reprinted with introduction by W. Letwin, 1975.

48. Solow, R.M., "Economic Growth and Residential Housing," in Readings in Financial Institutions, (eds. M.D. Ketchum and L.T. Kendall), Boston: Houghton Mifflin, 1965.

49. Tobin, J., "On Limiting the Domain of Inequality," Journal of Law and Economics, XIII (2), (October 1970), 263-278.

50. Wiles, P., "Cost Inflation and the State of Economic Theory," Economic Journal, 83, No. 330, (June 1973), 377-398.

INDEXING THE ECONOMY THROUGH FINANCIAL INTERMEDIATION

Alan S. Blinder*

Princeton University

I. INTRODUCTION AND SUMMARY

This paper attempts to unravel the great mystery in the economic analysis of indexing--why have so few indexed contracts arisen in market economies, except under government instigation?

Part II provides a simple theoretical model of the "market" for indexed contracts, and points out why wage escalators and indexed financial instruments are <u>substitutes</u> in the perceptions of both workers and firms. While the model is very simple, the central point is, I think, very robust. With incomplete indexing in financial markets, real returns on assets decline with unexpected inflation. On general portfolio-diversification grounds, therefore, workers demand wage escalators as hedges against reductions in property income. Firms will be amenable to this idea because inflation reduces their real interest costs; they too find an element of insurance in escalators.[1] Where indexed bonds are more prevalent, workers have less to gain from indexing wages, and firms have more to lose. The suggestion, then, is that a scarcity of indexed bonds will create great incentives to escalate wage contracts.

Part III develops a parallel analysis of the market for indexed bonds, and reaches parallel conclusions. Workers who lack complete cost-of-living protection for their wages will be willing to pay a premium for an indexed bond or, better yet, a security whose real rate of return rises with inflation. Similarly, firms without wage escalators will gain from an inflation which erodes real labor costs, and thus would be eager to hedge these gains by issuing indexed bonds. When wage escalators are widespread, both incentives diminish. Theory thus suggests that a lack of wage escalators will encourage the use of indexed bonds.

Taken together, these models offer a neat explanation of a nonexistent world -- one in which economies have either a great deal of wage indexing or a

*Econometric Research Program. This proposal has gone through several drafts, and many people have contributed helpful criticisms and insights. In addition to those cited directly in the text, I wish to thank William Baumol, William Branson, Lester Chandler, Stephen Goldfeld, Edward Gramlich, Martin Hellwig, Dwight Jaffee, Burton Malkiel, and Stephen Salop. This draft has benefited from seminar presentations at MIT, Rutgers University, University of California at San Diego, University of Florida, and the Federal Reserve Bank of Philadelphia, in addition to the Carnegie-Rochester conference. William Newton provided exceptionally fine research assistance, and financial support was provided by the National Science Foundation.

[1]The argument clearly assumes that firms are risk averse. If they are risk neutral, the relative absence of indexed contracts is truly mysterious. The note by Clifford Smith in this issue uses the possibility of bankruptcy to rationalize risk-averse behavior by firms.

great deal of bond indexing. Unfortunately, the U. S. economy and, indeed, all the advanced market economies have surprisingly little indexing of any kind. Is it because the simple models are misleading? I think not. Their basic point -- that hedging against inflation is a good idea – is too obvious to be wrong.

Part IV, the core of the paper, offers both an hypothesis for why things may have gone awry, and a policy prescription to set things right. I suggest that risk-averse firms would be happy to link factor payments to a price index which follows closely the movements of their own output prices, but shy away from contracts linking wages and interest to some broad price index whose movement might easily outstrip their selling prices. Conversely, workers and bondholders may be unwilling to bear the substantial risks of linking their factor payments to the prices of firms for which they work or to which they lend. Instead, they prefer linkage to a broad price index more or less representative of the things they buy. These asymmetrical perceptions of the risks caused by inflation may have resulted in the absence of both kinds of linked security.

If this is the reason, then a new kind of financial intermediary can solve the problem. Let a mutual fund be established, one holding as its assets bonds linked to the output prices of a broad collection of firms. The total interest received by the fund will then resemble the return on a bond indexed to a broad price index. Such receipts give the fund the wherewithal to issue deposits linked to such an index. Both firms and bondholders, therefore, can have the type of security they want. Of course, things are not quite so simple as this; the fund would have to face several technical problems, and remedies for each are suggested in part IV.

A more fundamental problem is that of verifying that firms and bondholders would want to borrow and lend in these forms. Taking a cue from the theoretical models of parts II and III, I seek such empirical evidence by studying how rates of return on (unindexed) human and financial assets, and corporate profits, behave in inflation. The models of consumer-worker behavior suggest that there will be a substantial demand for indexed deposits if real returns to human and nonhuman capital decline with unanticipated inflation. The models of the firm suggest that businessmen will be eager to enter into contracts linking factor payments to their own industry price if the profit performance of a firm is best when prices in its industry are rising most rapidly. Part V marshals empirical evidence, some of it necessarily impressionistic rather than definitive, in support of these hypotheses.

Despite the apparent contradiction, then, the theory, the empirical evidence, and the policy prescription are all related. The theory views escalator clauses and indexed bonds as ways to hedge inflation losses; the evidence shows that such hedges are in fact needed; and the policy prescription suggests how they may be supplied through financial innovation.

II. THE DEMAND FOR AND SUPPLY OF WAGE ESCALATORS

The major point of this section is that the prevalence of cost-of-living escalators in wage contracts is strongly conditioned by the presence or absence of indexed bonds. Specifically, when bonds are indexed, workers will demand less wage escalation, and firms will supply less, because indexing wages is a substitute for indexing bonds for both workers and firms.

A. The Demand for Escalators

At first, firms are assumed to be risk neutral, and thus indifferent among wage contracts which offer the same expected real wage, $\bar{w}$. Workers, however, are risk averse, and therefore concerned with both the mean real wage and the dispersion around that mean. They must agree on a wage contract, which is a function, $w(\pi)$, stipulating how the real wage, w , depends on the rate of inflation, π . Since firms are indifferent among all functions satisfying

$$(1) \quad E[w(\pi)] = \bar{w}, \text{ a constant,}$$

which contract will workers select?

Suppose the worker lives and works for two periods; enjoys real consumption, c_0 and c_1 , in the two periods; earns w_0 and $w(\pi)$ in the two periods; has real assets, k_0, at the start of first period; and carries over k_1 in real assets to the second period.[2] Then his two budget constraints are

$$(2) \quad c_0 = k_0 + w_0 - k_1 ,$$

$$(3) \quad c_1 = (1+r)k_1 + w(\pi),$$

where r is the real rate of return on wealth. The stochastic properties of r , especially its covariance with π, depend on whether or not financial instruments are indexed.

The worker's problem is to select k_1 and the form of the $w(\cdot)$ function so as to maximize his two-period utility, which is assumed to take the following simple form:

---

[2]The assumption of a two-period life probably is not restrictive if the forms of the wage contracts in different periods are not limited by some institutional constraint, e.g., a three-year contract which must involve the same escalator clause for all three years. In the latter case, since r and π may be serially correlated, the two-period problem misses some intertemporal linkages which might upset the conclusions.

$$J = V(c_0) + E[U(c_1)],$$

subject to (1) – (3).

Since for any choice of a $w(\cdot)$ function, savings will be adjusted optimally to keep $\partial J/\partial k_1 = 0$, I can abstract from savings choices; treat k_1 as fixed; and find the optimal wage contract by maximizing $E[U(c_1)]$, subject to (1) and (3).[3]

Remembering that c_1 is random because both π and r are, the maximand can be expressed as:

$$E[U(c_1)] = \int_a^b \int_a^\beta U(c_1) f(\pi,r) d\pi dr$$

where $f(\pi,r)$ is the joint density function; and where the integrals are taken over the relevant limits. Writing the joint density as $f(\pi,r) = f(\pi)f(r|\pi)$, the integral can be rewritten:

$$\int_a^\beta f(\pi) \int_a^b U(c_1) f(r|\pi)dr \; d\pi \equiv \int_a^\beta f(\pi) g(\pi)d\pi \;;$$

which is to be maximized subject to the integral constraint:

$$\int_a^\beta f(\pi)w(\pi) = \overline{w}.$$

This is a well-known problem in the calculus of variations which is solved by introducing the Lagrange multiplier, λ, a _constant_ whose value depends on $\overline{w}$, and finding an extremum of the integral:

$$\int_a^\beta f(\pi)[g(\pi) + \lambda w(\pi)] \; d\pi.$$

The Euler equation holds that:

$$\frac{\partial}{\partial w} [g(\pi) + \lambda w] = 0$$

for all π; or that $\partial g(\pi)/\partial w = -\lambda$ for all π. Using the definitions of $g(\pi)$ and

---

[3]This is just an application of the "envelope theorem." If γ is any parameter of the wage contract:

$$dJ/d\gamma = \partial J/\partial \gamma \big|_{k_1 = \text{constant}} + dk_1/d\gamma \cdot \partial J/\partial k_1 \big|_{\gamma = \text{constant}}$$

$$= \partial J/\partial \gamma \text{ because } \partial J/\partial k_1 \big|_{\gamma = \text{constant}} = 0.$$

c_1, the Euler equation implies:

$$-\lambda = \int_a^b U'(c_1)f(r|\pi)dr .$$

Since this must hold for all π , we can take the derivative of each side with respect to π , viz.:

$$(4) \qquad 0 = \int_a^b w'(\pi)U''(c_1)\, f(r|\pi)dr + \int_a^b U'(c_1)\, \frac{\partial f(r|\pi)}{\partial \pi}\, dr .$$

In the case of an indexed asset, the second integral in (4) vanishes because real returns are not conditional on the inflation rate.[4] Assuming that $U''(c_1)$ < 0 and $f(r|\pi) > 0$ within the limits of integration, equation (4) then implies that the optimal contract has full cost-of living escalation: $w'(\pi) = 0$ for all π .

Now consider the case of a nonindexed asset, and assume that the distribution of real returns shifts leftward when the inflation rate rises, as depicted in Figure 1. Examination of the figure reveals that $F(r|\pi_2) > F(r|\pi_1)$ everywhere; that is, the relation between the two distribution functions is one of "first degree stochastic dominance."[5] For infinitesimal changes, the dominance relation implies $\partial F(r|\pi)/\partial \pi > 0$. The second term in (4) can be integrated by parts to obtain:

$$w'(\pi)\int_a^b U''(c_1)f(r|\pi)dr = k_1 \int_a^b U''(c_1)\frac{\partial F(r|\pi)}{\partial \pi}\, dr .$$

The optimal wage contract can thus be characterized by the formula:

$$(5) \qquad \frac{w'(\pi)}{w(\pi)} = \frac{k_1}{w(\pi)} \left[\frac{\int_a^b U''(c_1)\frac{\partial F(r|\pi)}{\partial \pi}\, dr}{\int_a^b U''(c_1)f(r|\pi)dr} \right] .$$

---

[4] A riskless indexed bond is a special case where the density function of real returns collapses to a spike. But one can conceive of other indexed securities which retain some risks unassociated with price-level fluctuations.

[5] This is the technical representation of the notion that inflation lowers the real rate of return. Some empirical evidence supporting the proposition is presented later in the paper.

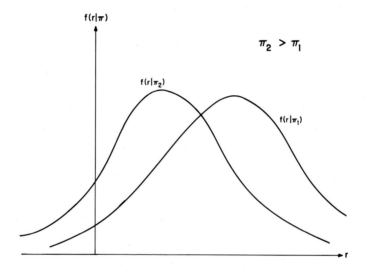

Figure 1
Effect on Distribution of Real Returns
of a Shift in the Inflation Rate

Since the ratio of the two integrals must be positive, $w'(\pi)$ has the same sign as k_1.

In words, workers with positive net worth will demand more-than-100 percent wage escalation; workers with zero net worth will demand precisely 100 percent escalation; and workers with negative net worth will demand less-than-100 percent escalation. The intuition behind this result was provided in part I. Since inflation lowers the real return on net worth (in a stochastic sense), workers with positive net worth will use their wage contract as "insurance" against this contingency -- recouping some of their losses in real property income by gains in real labor income. Workers with negative net worth are in the opposite position; since inflation raises (algebraically) their negative property income, they are willing to incur some losses in labor income to protect themselves against the possibility that inflation will be very low.

The percentage by which wages are escalated is $1 + w'(\pi) / w(\pi)$. By (5) this depends on the ratio of net worth to property income, and on the ratio of the two integrals. Not much can be said in general about the integrals; while the ratio is positive, its magnitude depends on the curvature of the utility function, and on the manner in which inflation alters the probability distribution of real returns. However, there is no reason to think it will be constant, either with respect to π, or with respect to wealth.

Among workers with positive assets, the demand for escalation will be higher the higher the ratio of assets to earnings. Thus, presumably, workers near retirement will want more inflation protection than young workers. More importantly, if most workers have positive net worth, indexed assets reduce the incentive to demand indexed wages.[6]

B. The Supply of Escalators

Thus far I have assumed that workers can have any type of escalator they choose, so long as it is actuarially fair. But, if firms are averse to risk, they will not be so pliable at the bargaining table. In considering this complication, I simplify the problem somewhat by assuming that π, the inflation rate, is the only source of uncertainty; that is, r is stochastic only because of its dependence on π, as would be the case if all assets were risk-free money-fixed bonds. This enables me to adopt the results of a recent paper by Shavell (1976).

Consider a worker and a firm bargaining over the form of the wage contract, $w(\pi)$. Let $R(\pi)$ be the nonwage income of the worker, and assume that $R'(\pi) < 0$. Let $Y(\pi)$ be the net income of the firm exclusive of wage payments; I shall discuss the sign of $Y'(\pi)$ presently. Shavell asks: What sort of

---

[6]The relations between net worth and wage escalators are statements about correlations, not about causation, because both k_1 and $w(\cdot)$ are selected in the same maximization process.

75

wage function would be <u>Pareto optimal</u> for the two parties? For the case in which employer and employee have the same subjective probability distribution for inflation, he shows that the contract satisfies:

$$(6) \quad w'(\pi) = \frac{Y'(\pi)\rho_F - R'(\pi)\rho_w}{\rho_F + \rho_w} \quad \text{for all } \pi \, ,$$

where ρ_F and ρ_w are the (positive) degrees of absolute risk aversion of the firm and worker, respectively.[7]

If firms are risk neutral $(\rho_F = 0)$, (6) implies that the wage contract completely insures the worker against income fluctuations: $w'(\pi) + R'(\pi) = 0$. This result would have emerged from the previous analysis if inflation were the only source of uncertainty.

If firms are risk averse $(\rho_F > 0)$, but their other income is unaffected by inflation $[Y'(\pi) = 0]$, they will sell insurance to workers, but only on actuarially unfair terms. As a result, workers will find it optimal to buy less than complete insurance, i.e., $w'(\pi) > 0$, but $w'(\pi) + R'(\pi) < 0$.

If the firm is both risk averse and affected by inflation in ways other than through its wage payments, real wages will rise unambiguously in inflation only if $Y'(\pi) > 0$. This is the first instance of "supply side" responses in the "escalator market." Firms which tend to do well in inflation $[Y'(\pi) > 0]$ will be eager to give generous escalators as a form of insurance to workers– in return for lower mean wages. Conversely, and for the same reasons, firms which tend to fair poorly in inflation $[Y'(\pi) < 0]$ will be reluctant to escalate wages very much, even though that implies lower mean wage costs.

What is the likely sign of $Y'(\pi)$? In part V, some indirect empirical evidence on this question is presented. It is indirect enough, however, that the issue merits some qualitative discussion. As is true of almost every question in the theory of indexing, the outcome is very different in the cases of demand-induced versus supply-induced inflations. An approximate accounting identity for $Y(\pi)$ is

$Y(\pi)$ = real sales revenue - real materials costs - real interest payments + real inventory profits - real profits taxes.

---

[7]In general, ρ_F and ρ_w are not constants, but depend upon the income levels of firm and worker, respectively, and thus upon π. I note in passing that (6) can be modified to account for differences in subjective probability distributions. A similar problem is considered by Azariadis (1976).

Consider first a demand-pull inflation. Presumably, in such a situation, real sales revenues rise much faster than real materials costs. Real interest payments, at least on long-term debt, fall in any kind of inflation so long as bonds are not indexed. Inflation also leads to inventory revaluations, which represent genuine profits in the short run. The only negative argument is that real corporate taxes increase because inflation erodes the real value of depreciation allowances. On balance, then, it seems safe to assume that $Y'(\pi) > 0$ in demand-pull inflation; this means that firms will be eager to index wage payments. Note the role of indexed bonds in this analysis--indexing interest payments reduces $Y'(\pi)$, and thus reduces firms' willingness to index wages. To firms, as to workers, indexed bonds and indexed wages are substitutes.

Now turn to cost-push inflations, where things are quite different. Since the quantity of goods sold presumably falls in a supply-side inflation, real sales receipts drop (nominal sales rise less rapidly than prices). At the same time, materials costs may rise faster than product prices. Interest payments, inventory profits, and corporate taxes behave in much the same way as under demand-pull inflation. On balance, then, it would not be surprising if $Y'(\pi) < 0$. If so, firms will be reluctant to exacerbate the burden of inflation by indexing wages; and if bonds are indexed, their resistance to wage escalation will stiffen.[8]

III. THE DEMAND FOR AND SUPPLY OF INDEXED BONDS

The question I address in this section is the mirror image of the question considered in part II: How does the degree of wage escalation influence the demand for and the supply of indexed bonds? The demand for indexed bonds has been treated very elegantly by Fischer (1975).[9] What follows is a highly simplified variant of Fischer's analysis which, I hope, preserves the intuitions while stripping away almost all of the mathematical complexities. I use this watered-down model to focus on the interaction of human and non-human capital, a point not stressed by Fischer although it is implicit in his analysis.

A. A Simple Model of Portfolio Choice

I adopt unabashedly both mean-variance analysis and a one-period horizon in order to simplify the mathematics. Consider a worker-investor deciding how to allocate his total wealth among three assets in such a way as to maximize the expected value of his von Neumann-Morgenstern utility indicator:

---

[8]$Y'(\pi) < 0$ does not mean, however, that no escalation will be offered, nor even that $w'(\pi) < 0$. See equation (6).

[9]Siegel (1974) presents a similar argument in less mathematical form, using the capital assets pricing model.

$U = (\bar{z},\sigma)$, where $\bar{z}$ is the mean rate of return and σ is its standard deviation. The assets are the following.

(a) Human Wealth. The unique feature of human wealth is that it cannot be sold. The total amount of human wealth and, therefore, the fraction of start-of-period wealth held in human form is <u>given</u> and not subject to choice. I call this fraction <u>a</u> . The stochastic nature of the returns from human wealth can be parameterized in a convenient manner developed in Body (1975). Let H be the nominal rate of return on human wealth, and $h = H - \pi$ be the real rate of return. Express the deviation of H from its mean, $\bar{H}$, as consisting of two stochastic components, one of which is proportional to <u>unanticipated</u> inflation, $u \equiv \pi - \bar{\pi}$; the other is uncorrelated with unanticipated inflation.[10] In symbols:

$$(7) \quad H = \bar{H} + au + \epsilon .$$

Treating these rates of return as continuously compounded rates,[11] the interpretation of the parameter, a, is the <u>degree of wage escalation</u> --what I denoted by $1 + w'(\pi) /w(\pi)$ in part II. Subtracting π from both sides of (7) gives an expression for the ex post real rate of return on human wealth:

$$h = H - \pi = \bar{H} - \bar{\pi} + (a - 1) u + \epsilon ; \text{ or}$$

$$(8) \quad h = \bar{h} + \beta u + \epsilon , \beta \equiv a - 1 .$$

(b) Indexed Bonds. This is the simplest possible type of asset with a fixed, riskless, real return denoted by r . Let <u>b</u> denote the fraction of total wealth held in indexed bonds.

(c) Nominal Bonds. I assume that nominal bonds are riskless except for inflation risk. Thus, if the nominal return is $i = R + \bar{\pi}$, the real rate of return is[12]

$$i - \pi = R + \bar{\pi} - \pi = R - u .$$

The fraction of wealth held in this form is $1 - a - b$.

---

[10]The mean return, $\bar{H}$, may well depend on the expected rate of inflation, $\bar{\pi}$, but that is not of direct concern here.

[11]This validates writing $h = H - \pi$.

[12]This is not meant to imply that R is a constant unaffected by $\bar{\pi}$. That question is irrelevant for present purposes.

Since the real rate of return on the entire portfolio is

$$z = ah + br + (1\text{-}a\text{-}b)(R\text{-}u)$$

$$= \{a\bar{h} + br + (1\text{-}a\text{-}b)\,R\} + \{a\beta - (1\text{-}a\text{-}b)\}u + a\epsilon \quad \text{by (8)},$$

it follows that the mean and variance of z are

(9) $\bar{z} = a\bar{h} + br + (1\text{-}a\text{-}b)R$,

and

(10) $\sigma^2 = a^2 V(\epsilon) + (1\text{-}b\text{-}aa)^2 V(u)$.

Remember that a is given, so the only choice variable is b, the fraction held in indexed bonds. The first-order condition for utility maximization is

$$0 = \frac{dU}{db} = U_1\,\frac{d\bar{z}}{db} + U_2\,\frac{d\sigma}{db} \;,\; \text{or}$$

(11) $U_1 \cdot (r\text{-}R) = U_2\,\dfrac{V(u)}{\sigma}\,(1\text{-}b\text{-}aa)$.

A major point of Fischer's (1975) paper is that r-R may actually be positive, though, for reasons explained below, my guess is that it would be negative. It is simplest to start with the case, R=r .

The case where R=r .

R=r means that the guaranteed real rate of return on indexed bonds is equal to the ex ante expected real rate of nominal bonds. If this is so, (11) simply implies:

(12) $b = 1 - aa$.

Complete wage indexing would make a=1, so that (12) would imply that the demand for nominal bonds is exactly zero; all financial wealth would be held in indexed bonds. This is because full wage indexing eliminates all covariances among the real returns. Since nominal bonds carry some risk, and bear no premium over indexed bonds, they are a dominated asset.

If there is literally no indexing of wages, not even tacit indexing, so that a=0 , (12) states that holdings of indexed bonds equal total wealth. Since the fixed stock of human wealth is presumably very large, this implies tremendous short sales of nominal bonds. The reason is again obvious. Human capital fares badly in inflation, as do nominal bonds, while indexed bonds are "inflation neutral." Selling short a volume of nominal bonds equal to one's human capital stock creates a perfect hedge, in the sense that the only remaining risk in the portfolio is the undiversifiable component of risk in human returns.

The case where there is partial indexing is intermediate between these two extremes. The central point is clear enough–the demand for indexed bonds falls as the degree of wage indexing increases.

The case where $R > r$.

This tendency is muddied by introducing an expected premium for holding nominal bonds, a premium which the previous case strongly suggests would exist. If $R > r$, equation (11) implies that $1-b-aa$ is positive.

Under full wage indexing $(a=1)$, then, there will be a positive demand for nominal bonds if they pay a premium. Will there be a demand for indexed bonds? One cannot say, in general, that b must be positive. For a large enough premium, the demand for indexed bonds would vanish. But this only means that the market premium would not have to be this large to induce consumers to hold nominal bonds.

For other cases, although at least one of the bonds must be held in positive amounts, we cannot establish which that will be, nor whether both are held. Of course, in the limit as the premium gets small, we can apply the results of the previous case.

The case where $R < r$.

If indexed bonds pay a premium – a possibility raised by Fischer (1975) – the analysis is once again simple. Equation (11) states that $1-b-aa < 0$, which, so long as $0 \leq aa \leq a$, also implies that $1-b-a < 0$. That is, everyone will sell nominal bonds short because short sales of nominal bonds provide a hedge against inflation-induced losses on human capital. Only more-than-100 percent indexing of wages $(a>1)$ could possibly induce worker-investors to hold nominal bonds in positive amounts. This suggests that $R < r$ is very unlikely to obtain.

Which case is realistic?

If indexed bonds existed, one could read the answer to this question from published tables of bond yields. The OECD (1973) reports, in fact, that indexed bonds paid consistently lower interest rates during the nine years in which they coexisted with nominal bonds in France. Given the absence of indexed bonds in the U.S., however, one is free to speculate.

Fischer's analysis guides the speculation. His investigation of the demand for indexed bonds concluded that the real return on indexed bonds would probably be below that on nominal bonds (R>r) if: (a) real returns on common stocks are negatively correlated with inflation; and, (b) real wage income is negatively correlated with inflation. Some documentation that both of these conditions have held in the postwar United States is provided in part V. I conclude that, if both types of bonds coexisted, R would exceed r .

B. The Supply of Indexed Bonds

Will firms want to borrow on an indexed basis, given that they can probably sell such securities at real interest rates below those which they now pay on nominal bonds? If they are risk neutral, they will, for risk-neutral firms simply want to float debt at the lowest expected real interest cost.

But, if firms are risk averse, certain complexities arise. I can turn Shavell's analysis on its head to analyze this problem in the same way I analyzed wage contracts. If $R(\pi)$ now denotes the noninterest income of the bondholder, and $Y(\pi)$ denotes the net income of the firm exclusive of interest payments, equation (6) will again hold, with $w(\pi)$ now interpreted as the real value of debt service.

If most "other income" of bondholders is wage income, then $R'(\pi)$ will presumably be negative, and less so the greater the prevalence of wage indexing. The previous analysis of costs and benefits to the firm can be repeated, with real wage payments replacing real interest payments. Given only partial wage escalation, this item of costs also declines in inflation. Again the situation may be that $Y'(\pi) > 0$ for demand-pull inflations, and $Y'(\pi) < 0$ for cost-push inflations.

In a word, risk-averse firms will be eager to sell indexed bonds if: (a) they are not indexing wages heavily; and, (b) they tend to do well in inflation. Risk-averse firms will be reluctant to issue indexed debt if: (a) they have large wage escalators; and, (b) they tend to suffer heavy cost increases in inflation.

IV. THE NATIONAL INFLATION MUTUAL FUND

A. Recapitulation

The models of the previous two sections hold three main messages.

(a) There are good reasons to believe that workers will demand substantial escalation in wage contracts, perhaps even more-than-100 percent escalation, and that bondholders would welcome indexed bonds even if they paid lower real interest rates than nominal bonds.

(b) The case for indexing is much less clear-cut for firms. But given the diversity of firms in the U.S. economy, there must be many which could profit by indexing their debt instruments and/or escalating their wage payments.

(c) Indexed bonds and escalated wages are substitutes, from the points of view of both workers and firms. Having more of one dulls the incentive to seek more of the other. s

As noted in part I, the theory explains a phenomenon that, unfortunately, does not exist in the world. The models suggest that economies with substantial wage escalation should have very few indexed loan agreements, while economies with many indexed bonds should have few escalated wage contracts. In most economies, however, there is rather little indexing of any kind.

There are no indexed bonds in the United States. In addition, the notion that cost-of-living escalators are extremely widespread is a myth. The latest Bureau of Labor Statistics data show that, even after nine years of the worst inflation in modern U.S. history, a little over half the workers covered by major collective bargaining agreements (1,000 or more employees) have any sort of cost-of-living escalator. Almost none of these contracts offer complete protection of real wages, not to mention the fanciful more-than-100 percent escalation discussed in part II. Furthermore, major collective bargaining agreements cover only about 10 percent of the U.S. labor force, and wage escalators in smaller establishments are almost nonexistent. [13]

The models do, however, suggest one possible explanation for the dearth of indexing. The really virulent inflation of the past few years has certainly come from the supply side, and has been accompanied by falling profits. For the years 1972-75, indexed bonds and highly escalated wages would not have been in the best interests of stockholders. If firms foresaw these events (or had an irrational fear of cost-push inflation which proved true!), then this could explain the absence of indexing.

But this is stretching a point. Until recently, demand-pull inflation has been the rule, not the exception. The 1966-1971 inflationary period fits this pattern. The absence of indexed bonds must have another explanation. Let me suggest one. [14]

B. Asymmetries in Risk and the Need for an Intermediary

Workers and bondholders reduce risk by linking their nominal incomes to a broad price index, more or less representative of the things they buy. But the same may not be true of firms. In a world where relative prices change rapidly, no firm is sure that the prices of the product mix it sells will move in the same way as, say, the private GNP deflator. A firm considering an indexed bond will worry -- and not without reason -- that its product prices

[13] See Kuhmerker (1976) and David (1974) for documentation of these points.

[14] A variety of other explanations is considered by Fischer (1976).

will lag behind the deflator, leaving it with a burdensome level of interest payments.

The remedy for the firm is obvious. Suppose it could tie its interest payments to the prices of its own products, or at least to an index more closely tailored to its own sales. This type of indexed bond would offer a very safe way to borrow. But it would not be a safe way to lend. As viewed by consumers, such an instrument would be almost as risky as common stock, since it's returns would depend on relative price fluctuations.

The outcome, then, of the operation of free markets may be that the latent demand for bonds indexed to a broad price index, and the latent supply of bonds indexed to firm-specific prices both go unsatisfied. The fact that these very real private risks are not social risks -- because, on average, the selling prices of firms and the buying prices of consumers must move together[15] -- motivates my proposal for a new type of financial intermediary.

Suppose a "National Inflation Mutual Fund" (henceforth NIMF) were created and instructed to: (a) purchase bonds from firms, with the interest and principal linked to the specific price index applicable to each firm's industry; (b) issue deposits to consumers, paying a guaranteed real interest rate in terms of some broad price index. Both firms and bondholders would find the instruments far safer than the present nominal bonds. NIMF itself would be simply an intermediary. Given the right set of weights for each industry in NIMF, the fund would be literally self-insured.

C. A Mutual Fund of Indexed Bonds

While many different variants of NIMF might be designed, depending on the maturity structure of its assets and liabilities, I will concentrate -- solely for concreteness -- on a version in which NIMF purchases one-year bonds from firms, and simultaneously issues one-year certificates of deposit to consumers.

Let $i = 1,...,n$ denote the n industries. Let the price index of each industry at the end of the year, with all prices normalized to unity at the beginning of the year, be P_i. Let $I \equiv \sum_i \lambda_i P_i$ be the aggregate price index at the end of the year, so that λ_i represents the weight of industry i in the index. Let r_i be the real rate of interest which industry i pays into NIMF.[16]

---

[15]This proposition is stated rather too baldly; most of what follows is concerned with qualifications.

[16]The following analysis abstracts from any risk that the firm will default. Thus, firms are distinguished only by the industry to which they belong. In practice, firms would have to be cross-classified by both industry and risk class (e.g., by their Moody's rating), and interest rates assigned accordingly. It is perhaps most useful to think of the r_i analyzed in the text as the prime rate charged to each industry.

Then if B_i is the face value of the bonds which industry i sells to NIMF at the beginning of the year, its nominal payments at the end of the year will be $(1+r_i)B_i P_i$. Deflating by the general price index, the real payment is $(1+r_i)B_i p_i$, where the $p_i \equiv P_i/I$ are henceforth called the "real prices" or "relative prices" of each industry, and are assumed to have well-behaved probability distributions.

The face value of the fund is $B = \sum_i B_i$. If $w_i \equiv B_i/B$ is the weight of industry i in NIMF, then total deflated receipts are

$$\sum_i (1+r_i)B_i p_i = [\sum_i (1+r_i)w_i p_i] B.$$

In general, this will be a random variable since all the p_i are random. Payments from NIMF to bondholders at the end of the year would be simply $(1+r_0)BI$ in nominal terms, or $(1+r_0)B$ in real terms, where r_0 is the guaranteed real rate paid on NIMF deposits. Thus, the real profit rate of NIMF is $\sum_i (1+r_i)w_i p_i -$ $(1+r_0)$. Now, by the definition of the price index, the weighted sum of random variables, $\sum_i \lambda_i p_i$, is equal to unity <u>with certainty</u>. So NIMF will be perfectly self-insured if, and only if, $(1+r_i)w_i = k\lambda_i$, for all i, for some constant k .

Can a fund be designed which meets this requirement? I shall argue that it can.[17] However, if equal real interest rates (r_i) are charged to all firms, there is no reason to expect open participation in NIMF to result in $w_i = \lambda_i$. Indeed, there is every reason to expect w_i to differ from λ_i in a systematic way that would threaten the solvency of NIMF.

The reason is <u>adverse selection,</u> a phenomenon which is common to all insurance schemes. To cite one prominent example, it is well known that purchasers of health insurance are sicker on average than the population as a whole. The corresponding danger for NIMF is that firms which borrow from NIMF might have lower average rates of price increase than the economy as a whole, so that the fund's income would grow more slowly than its outlays. If NIMF posted equal real borrowing rates (r_i) for each industry, this would probably happen; for if every industry could borrow at a uniform real rate, r, linked to its own price index, industry i would view the real interest factor as $(1+r)p_i$. Industries expecting small price increases $[E(p_i) < 1]$ would view this as "cheap," while industries expecting rapid inflation $[E(p_i) > 1]$ would

---

[17]The reader may have noticed that the question of self-insurance has no inherent connection with the aggregate inflation rate. Relative prices change with or without inflation, so the viability of NIMF is subject to the same questions in either regime. The difference is that the existence of money -- or any other asset with a sure nominal return -- makes NIMF superfluous if there is no inflation. NIMF deposits will be a "riskless" asset for consumers in an inflationary environment only in the same limited sense that money is riskless in a world of zero inflation. Neither asset will move precisely in accord with the particular bundle of commodities any individual consumer might purchase, that is, neither asset offers insurance against relative price fluctuations.

find NIMF an expensive source of funds.

One way to cope with such adverse selection is to post a set of industry-specific interest factors satisfying $(1+r_i)E(p_i) = 1 + \bar{r}$ for all industries. If the price projections of firms correspond to, or deviate randomly from, the price projections made by NIMF, adverse selection would be eliminated. If the two sets of price expectations differed systematically, _firms_ which expected _industry_ price performance superior to NIMF projections would prefer to borrow elsewhere, while firms anticipating less inflation in their industry than NIMF projections would participate actively in the fund. If businesses are better forecasters of relative prices than NIMF, this would present another – though less serious – adverse selection problem; but it is not obvious to me that they need be better.

However, even if some degree of adverse selection occurs, it need not be fatal to NIMF. Private insurance is a thriving industry in the United States today despite actual or potential adverse selection in virtually every line of insurance. Further, in coping with adverse selection, NIMF would have an important advantage over most commercial insurers because it would not continually be presented with applications from _new industries_, with which it had no past experience. NIMF could, therefore, more readily identify industries whose real price is likely to fall than, for example, could a commercial insurance company identify which of a set of new drivers is more likely to have an accident.[18] _New firms_ may, of course, seek to borrow from NIMF; but they will usually be from familiar industries. New industries are simply not born as frequently as new people.

Thus far I have enumerated two constraints on NIMF. If it is to be self-insured, it must satisfy

$$(1+r_i)w_i = k\lambda_i \; ;$$

and, if it is to obviate adverse selection, it must set interest rates such that

$$(1+r_i)E(p_i) = 1 + \bar{r}.$$

---

[18]This assumes that the recent past gives some ability to predict the near-term future, i.e., that relative prices are not a random walk. It should be noted, however, that while a mis-classification of a new driver is an inconsequential error to an insurance company, many industries will be of nonnegligible importance to NIMF.

These two jointly determine the required NIMF-weights since

$$w_i = \frac{k\lambda_i}{1+r_i} = \frac{k\lambda_i}{1+\bar{r}} \ E(p_i) = \lambda_i E(p_i) \,,$$

because k must equal $(1+\bar{r})$ if the w_i's are to sum to unity. There is no particular reason to expect the ratio of an industry's NIMF-weight to its weight in the price index to be equal to its expected relative price. Therefore, if NIMF simply posts <u>any</u> vector of interest rates and accepts all comers, it probably will not acquire the risk-free weights.

But there is a simple alternative. Suppose it has been decided that an NIMF of face value B should be established as a risk-free fund. This means that NIMF must buy bonds worth $B_i = \lambda_i E(p_i)B$ from industry, i. It can achieve this by a "Dutch auction," whereby the rate, r_i, that NIMF charges to industry i is set by the requirement that the firms in the industry wish to borrow precisely this amount from NIMF. Call these the "market clearing" rates.

The perceptive reader will have noticed that I have now imposed two restrictions on the r_i: first, that they clear markets; and second, that they eliminate adverse selection. However, these requirements come to roughly the same thing because markets can only clear at rates that satisfy $(1+r_i)E(p_i) = 1 + \bar{r}$ approximately. If NIMF's lending rates were such that $(1+r_1)E(p_1)$ was very much less than $(1+r_2)E(p_2)$, it would be profitable for firms in industry 1 to borrow from NIMF at interest factor $(1+r_1)p_1$, and lend to firms in industry 2 at interest factor $(1+r^*)p_2$, where $r_1 < r^* < r_2$. Perhaps only a small spread between $(1+r_1)E(p_1)$ and $(1+r_2)E(p_2)$ would induce the two firms to enter into such a contract if their price expectations were basically alike. But such operations would raise industry 1's supply of bonds to NIMF, thus increasing r_1. And, as industry 2 borrows from industry 1, instead of from NIMF, r_2 would decline. The process would continue until the gap between $(1+r_1)E(p_1)$ and $(1+r_2)E(p_2)$ shrunk to the point where the incentive to "arbitrage" disappeared.[19] Thus competition automatically establishes relative interest rates which minimize adverse selection.

A similar "no arbitrage" argument establishes that $\bar{r}$ must be at least as large as r_0; that is, the NIMF cannot – even by accident – have a structure of borrowing and lending rates that would lose money! To see why not, suppose that $r_0 > \bar{r}$. Then firms could borrow from NIMF at expected interest factors

---

[19] Literally, these are not arbitrage operations, for there is some risk.

$(1+r_i)E(p_i)$, use the funds to purchase an NIMF deposit with a guaranteed re-turn of $1+r_0$, and earn an expected profit. As firms sought to exploit these possibilities, $\bar{r}$ would be driven up.

How big would NIMF be? The general equilibrium of the financial markets would provide the answer. There would be a supply function of bonds to NIMF, $B^S = B^S(\bar{r}, R^f)$, where R^f is a vector of alternative rates at which firms can borrow, and where $\partial B^S / \partial \bar{r}$ is presumptively negative. And there will be a demand function for NIMF deposits, $B^d = B^d(r_0, R^c)$, where R^c is a vector of alternative rates at which consumers can lend, and where $\partial B^d / \partial r_0$ is presumptively positive. Figure 2 shows how the profitability of NIMF -- the margin between its borrowing and lending rates -- depends on its size. A very small fund, like b, will have a large profit rate, while a much larger fund, like B, will be less profitable. In the long run, competition will insure that the margin between $\bar{r}$ and r_0 is just sufficient to cover the costs of oper-ating NIMF. However, during the transitional period, there may be monopoly profits to be reaped by some enterprising financial institution.

The real empirical question is whether or not demand and supply would be strong enough (i.e., the intersection point shown in Figure 2 would be far enough to the right) to support a fund of at least the minimum viable size.

D. <u>An NIMF Miscellany</u>

Now that general equilibrium issues have been raised, it is worth noting that NIMF would probably have side effects on both the financial and real sectors of the economy. First, the establishment of NIMF would obviously affect other financial institutions, and this would affect both vectors of "alternative rates" mentioned above. Second, by changing the terms on which firms can borrow, NIMF would affect relative prices and resource allocation. Both of these are familiar, though complex, phenomena in general equilibrium analysis which require no further comment here.

There are many variants on the NIMF theme. In order to secure wider participation, NIMF might forswear the requirement that it be risk free, and let the weights, w_i, be determined through open participation by firms. In this case, either the return to NIMF deposits would have to be risky (a proportionate share in NIMF receipts), or some other institution (the govern-ment?) would have to underwrite the risk. As a large mutual fund investing in a diversified portfolio of securities linked to specific commodity prices, it is reasonable to suppose that most (though not all) of the risk could be eliminated by pooling. The law of large numbers should rescue this variant of NIMF just as it rescues commercial insurers.

Another variant would be to establish an NIMF which paid interest linked

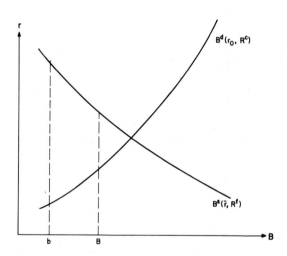

Figure 2
The Demand for NIMF Deposits and Supply
of NIMF Loans

to the CPI, or other index of consumer prices, rather than to the private GNP deflator used as an illustration here. I have not concentrated on such a fund here – though consumers might prefer it -- as it is desirable to open participation to all firms. An NIMF with deposits linked to the CPI, for example, could not lend to industries with no weight in that index. However, there is no real reason why NIMF need be monolithic. Different NIMFs could be established, each linked to a distinct price index. Indeed, this arrangement would be preferable to a single NIMF, since different households purchase different market baskets of goods and services.

With what sort of index would NIMF work best? I have used the private GNP deflator as an illustration, but the deflator for nonfarm business product might be a more likely candidate, unless farmers also borrowed from NIMF. It is arguable whether exports and imports should also be excluded on the grounds that domestic wage earners and bondholders ought not to be insulated from changes in the terms of trade.[20] In some cases (e.g., the 1973-74 oil debacle) such protection would have been most welcome.

Some readers may wonder why I propose to index loans to the industry's price rather than to the firm's price. The reason is that the latter alternative invites abuses – a kind of "window dressing" in reverse, whereby firms, by manipulating specific commodity prices and/or sales weights, attempt to make their average price performance look worse than it really is. Industry price indices are far less subject to manipulation by firms, although some care would have to be taken in highly concentrated industries. This suggests that NIMF should use a fairly coarse level of industrial classification. Monopoly typically disappears as industries are aggregated.

Just as industries dominated by few firms pose problems for NIMF, so do firms participating in many industries. NIMF could create for such firms a weighted average of the industry-specific price indices for those industries in which the firm does business. This assumes, however, that multi-industry firms are willing to reveal their sales weights to NIMF; it could be that some of them wish to keep this information from public view.[21] In that case, I suppose, NIMF could offer to let the firm borrow with payments linked to any of the P_i for industries in which it participates, relying on the firm to apportion its borrowing weights to its sales weights. However, even this procedure involves a (tacit) revelation by the firm of some aspects of its business and, rather than do this, some firms might simply shun participation in NIMF. I do not know how big a problem this might be in practice.

[20] The "insulation" would only hold for the short run; nothing can insulate them in the long run.

[21] I owe this point to Philip Friedman.

Finally, there is the question of matching the maturities of NIMF assets and liabilities. In the illustration, I assumed perfect matching, in that NIMF only borrowed and lent for precisely one year. In reality, firms might want to borrow for various durations – as they now do from banks and in the bond market. And the popularity of NIMF deposits would be enhanced greatly if the deposits were of no fixed maturity, like passbook savings accounts. It is true that, if NIMF deviates from perfect matching of maturities of assets and liabilities, it can no longer hope to be literally riskless. Like banks and all other financial intermediaries, it would be subject to random deposit outflows. Banks and other intermediaries – even thrift institutions – manage to cope with this problem quite well. I imagine that NIMF could, too.

E. Wage Escalation through NIMF

The theoretical discussion stressed the similarities between indexed bonds and wage contracts with cost-of-living escalators. Yet wages have not been mentioned in my discussion of NIMF.

If NIMF deposits were available with any starting date, or with any desired maturity, then firms could use NIMF to enter into escalated wage contracts linked to a broad price index with no risk to themselves. For example, $I in wages (an uncertain nominal sum) could be paid at the end of a period by depositing $I(1+r_0)$ in an NIMF account at the beginning of a period.

One objection frequently raised against any scheme for comprehensive wage indexation is that linking many, or all, money-wage rates to the same index effectively freezes the relative wage structure, thus preventing relative wage movements from accommodating shifts in demand. However, this is true of any long-term labor contract, whether or not tied to a price index. With or without indexing, relative wages are free to adjust each time a contract expires. A difference would arise only if the average duration of labor contracts were lengthened by the advent of comprehensive indexing. It is not obvious that this need occur, though it might.

Indexing wages through NIMF, rather than through conventional escalator clauses, is especially beneficial to firms when prices rise due to an external supply shock, as in 1974. In this case, workers' purchasing power is maintained, but most firms do not pay the costs of higher wages. NIMF does this instead, essentially by transferring income from firms with high P_i to firms with low P_i.[22]

---

[22]I owe this point to Edmund Phelps.

F. NIMF and Wage-Price Controls

NIMF, or indexing in general, cleárly affects the trade-off between real output growth and inflation, not because it "shifts the Phillips curve," but because it significantly lowers the welfare costs of inflation. As such, it can be looked on as an alternative to wage-price controls.

Wage-price controls may, nevertheless, recur. It is worth asking, therefore, how the chance that controls might be reimposed affects the viability of NIMF. On the surface, the effect would seem to be devastating, since the price index, I, and some, but not all, of the P_i would be artifically held down by controls. But who would gain and who would lose?

Until controls reached the point where the prices recorded in the index seriously understated true transactions prices, consumers would be neither helped nor harmed. While their interest receipts from NIMF would be lower under controls, so would commodity prices. Real interest received from NIMF would be unaffected.

Redistributions among firms, however, would be substantial. But they might be in a desirable direction. The firms which suffer most from controls are, presumably, those on whom the controls are most binding, that is, those whose controlled p_i fall most short of the p_i expected before controls. But, since firms borrowing from NIMF pay an ex post real interest factor

$$(1+\bar{r}) \ \frac{p_i}{E(p_i)} \ ,$$

NIMF loans would ease their burdens. Conversely, firms not subject to controls would have high $p_i/E(p_i)$, since P_i would be allowed to rise while I was held down. These firms -- the "winners" from controls -- would have to make larger payments into NIMF. Thus, NIMF offers a unique form of (partial) insurance against the institution of price controls.

Wage-price controls could work against NIMF -- or against any indexed contract -- if they include provisions for vacating contract clauses calling for index linking, as was done, for example, to some wage contracts during the 1971 wage-price freeze.[23] Investor fears that government might make it il-legal for NIMF to pay depositors $(1+r_0)I$ at the end of the period, even at the artifically depressed level of I, could seriously damage the attractiveness of NIMF deposits. On the other hand, if firms think that the government may mandate payments into NIMF less than the $(1+r_i)P_i$ specified in the contract,

---

[23]See Poole (1976).

borrowing from NIMF would be made more attractive. Whether these two forces, on balance, enhance or undermine the viability of NIMF is unclear on a priori grounds. However, my guess is that they would be very harmful.

G. The Gulf between Theory and Practice

Given enough supply and demand, then, NIMF can obviate the problem of asymmetrical risks which, as I suggested, may explain the dearth of indexed contracts. But would firms and workers want to participate?

To me, it is obvious that worker-savers would be eager to subscribe, at least if the reduction in mean wage and interest payments were not too large.[24] Part V attempts to provide some reasons why NIMF would be well received by consumer-workers. The idea behind the "evidence" is simple. Workers and savers have an incentive to participate in NIMF to the extent that (a) the real returns to human capital suffer from unanticipated inflation, and (b) the existing menu of financial instruments offers an inadequate hedge against inflation. In parts V. A and V. B, I argue that, in the postwar United States, these have both been true.

It is a more difficult story for firms. They will be eager to link factor payments to their own prices if profits and prices tend to move together (as in demand-pull inflations), but not if profits and prices tend to move in opposite directions (as in cost-push inflations). Part V.C presents an initial attempt to shed some light on this question for U.S. manufacturing corporations.

V. EMPIRICAL EVIDENCE ON THE NEED FOR NIMF

A. Inflation and the Returns on Human Capital

How does unanticipated inflation affect the returns to human capital? Given the paucity of complete escalator clauses in our economy, it would be very surprising if the answer were anything but that it falls.

Before examining the data, I want to clarify one point that may be confusing. Asserting that wages fare badly in unanticipated inflation does not imply that inflation hurts labor in the long run. The indexing issue is only a live one in the short run; in the long run, everything is effectively indexed de facto, if not de jure. For the period I consider, the U.S. in 1948-1975,[25] compensation per manhour in the private nonfarm economy rose at a compound annual rate of 5.6 percent, while productivity (output per manhour) rose at 2.3 percent per year. The excess of wage growth over productivity growth was thus 3.3 percent per year, which slightly exceeds the average compound growth rate of the CPI (3.0 percent per year). In a word, wages kept

---

[24] The size of these "insurance premia" depends on the willingness of firms to participate.

[25] Data cited here and elsewhere in this section are from various tables in Economic Report of the President, 1976.

pace with inflation in the long run.

There is no such close correspondence over shorter periods. From 1973: IV to 1974: IV, for example, compensation per manhour grew 9.7 percent, while consumer prices rose 12.1 percent. As measured by the CPI, the five years of greatest inflation in the 1948-1975 period were (in order of inflation rates) 1974, 1975, 1951, 1948, and 1973. Over these five years, inflation averaged 8.4 percent, while compensation per manhour grew at an average rate of 8.6 percent. The margin is clearly well below trend productivity growth. Conversely, the five years of lowest inflation were (in inverse order of inflation rates) 1949, 1955, 1954, 1953, and 1959, during which time inflation averaged a scant 0.1 percent per year. Over the same five years, compensation per manhour averaged 3.9 percent growth per year; the difference is well above trend productivity.

These gross statistics may or may not be compelling. A more serious job of answering the question requires some measure of the "return on human capital" for the overall economy. It is not hard to see that compensation per manhour will not do. Its drawbacks are many. No allowance is made for the cyclical variation of hours of work per week, nor for weeks of work per year. Neither is allowance made for changes in tax burdens on labor income (payroll taxes and income taxes).

But what is a satisfactory empirical proxy? Problems abound in applying the rate-of-return notion to human capital. How does one value the stock at the beginning and end of the period? Even if this is answered, should capital gains be included? On the one hand, such gains cannot be cashed in. But, on the other hand, any revaluation of the human capital stock presumably means higher earnings at some future date; thus, by omitting the capital gains, we attribute these returns to subsequent years. Worse yet, human investment-- not capital gains-- accounts for some of the year-to-year increase in the market value of the human capital stock. Because I could neither isolate the capital gains, nor know what to do with them had I succeeded in measuring them, I concentrated instead on getting a more refined series on wage changes. As a representation of human capital returns, the series is probably too smooth.

Existing BLS data do most of the work for me. Their series on Average Spendable Weekly Earnings in the Total Private Nonagricultural Sector adjusts average gross hourly earnings for both variations in the work week and changes in payroll and income taxes (based on a worker with three dependents). Furthermore, it does not make any correction for inter-industrial movements of labor, which are, after all, elements of the return on human capital. I made only one adjustment to this series. Because it represents the return on human capital only to _employed_ workers, I multiplied each yearly figure by one minus the unemployment rate.[26]   The <u>rate of change</u> of the average earnings series so derived, henceforth denoted by h, is my rough empirical proxy for the returns to human capital.[27]

A simple regression of h on the rate of inflation[28] yields:

$$h_t = 2.84 - 0.61\pi_t \ ,$$
$$ (.64) \quad (.15)$$

where π is the inflation rate and standard errors are in parentheses. The simple correlation between h and π is - 0.62, which connotes a substantial negative covariance. The suggestion is clearly that real human-capital returns decline in inflation--and by quite a considerable amount.

It might be objected that the correlation between real returns on human capital and <u>unanticipated</u> inflation would be a more revealing statistic. Though possibly more revealing, it is difficult to obtain because the desired correlation is between two variables which are very hard to measure. I made an attempt to compute this correlation from data on expected inflation recently constructed by de Menil (1974). An annual series on <u>unanticipated</u> inflation, from 1955 to 1972, was constructed by the identity:

$$u_t = \pi_t - \bar{\pi}_t \ ,$$

where $\bar{\pi}_t$ is de Menil's series for expected inflation.[29]   A simple regression of h_t on u_t yields:

$$h_t = 1.51 - 1.10u_t \ .$$
$$ (.58) \quad (.64)$$

---

[26]The labor force data and the wage data are not strictly comparable. See the footnote to Table B-7 in <u>Economic Report of the President, 1976.</u>

[27]The rationale for using the rate of change is that the "stock" of human capital should be roughly proportional to w_{t-1}, while w_t represents the "yield" on the investment if capital gains are ignored. Thus, the rate of return should be proportional to w_t/w_{t-1}. Note that this can only be an approximation, since the factor of proportionality depends on the real rate of interest, and thus on the inflation rate.

[28]The CPI is used both to deflate the nominal return on human capital and to measure inflation. The period of the regression is 1949-1975.

[29]de Menil's series is quarterly, 1953:IV-1972:III. An annual series was constructed as follows. Each quarterly expectation reported by de Menil pertains to the <u>average</u> inflation rate for the <u>following</u> four quarters. Since I seek expectations of the <u>year-over-year</u> inflation rate, it seems most appropriate to take an <u>average</u> of the expectations in the four quarters of year t as indicating the expected inflation rate from year t to year t+1 . I wish to thank George de Menil for furnishing me with his data.

The correlation in this case is -0.40. Given the wide margins of error in measuring each variable, the point estimate accords remarkably well with the notion that the expected rate of inflation is incorporated exactly into nominal human capital returns, so that real human capital returns decline point-for-point with unanticipated inflation.

Poole (1976), however, recently suggested an alternative hypothesis, "that U. S. experience has been for inflation surprises to be associated with lower real yields on human and physical capital independently of whether the inflation is higher or lower than anticipated" (p. 201). This can be tested, in a very rough way, by replacing u_t in the preceding regression by its absolute value. The result is:

$$h_t = 3.75 - 2.90 \, |u_t| \, ,$$
$$\quad\;\; (1.17) \;\; (1.28)$$

and the simple correlation between h_t and $|u_t|$ is -0.49. While the standard error on the slope coefficient is regrettably large, the correlation slightly exceeds that between h_t and u_t, thus lending some credence to Poole's conjecture. However, the issue clearly cannot be decided on the basis of a difference of 0.09 between two correlation coefficients.

B. Inflation and the Returns on Financial Instruments

To what extent are the financial instruments held by the typical household hedges against inflation? For some assets the answer is painfully obvious. Because of interest rate ceilings, deposits in thrift institutions, for example, often do not even compensate the holder fully for anticipated inflation. Short-term money market instruments such as Treasury bills and commercial paper probably offer adequate compensation for expected inflation, but none for unanticipated inflation; these instruments would have to be sold short in great volume to hedge against inflation. The practical difficulties of carrying this out need no elaboration, for there is a more fundamental point. Households with positive financial net worth must take a long position in some asset; they cannot sell everything short. Thus, inflation hedging requires the existence of some asset which actually gains from unanticipated inflation. Is there any?

Jaffe and Mandelker (1975) report strong negative correlations between monthly inflation rates and holding period returns on short-duration Treasury bills in the 1953-1971 period, but very little correlation between inflation and holding period yields on long-term obligations. The more important question, however, concerns the correlation between real bond returns and unanticipated inflation, u_t. Both Body (1975) and Jaffe and Mandelker (1975) find almost no correlation between u_t and the nominal returns on bonds of various maturities, which must imply a negative correlation between real returns and u_t.[30]

Common stocks are the financial asset traditionally touted as a hedge against inflation. Yet Cagan's (1974) comparison of 24 countries over the 1939-1969 period turned up a negative association between real stock market values and inflation rates.[31] Three recent studies, varying somewhat in statistical techniques and in period of coverage, all conclude that even nominal returns on common stocks in the U.S. are negatively correlated with unanticipated changes in the CPI. Real stock returns, therefore, must be affected extremely adversely by unanticipated inflation. Studying the U.S. from 1953 until the early 1970s, Body (1975), Jaffe and Mandelker (1975), and Nelson (1976) all found either a zero or negative correlation between nominal stock market returns and unanticipated inflation. The latter two studies even reported that anticipated inflation hurt common stock returns.[32]

The case for assuming that returns on households' financial portfolios decline with unanticipated inflation, then, seems quite strong. However, I have ignored owner-occupied homes, an important asset in the portfolio of many consumers.[33] Since prices of houses generally rise with the rate of inflation, while nominal payments on nonindexed mortgages do not, unanticipated inflation provides a windfall gain to homeowners. Essentially, homeowners enjoy a capital gain as the market value of their mortgage indebtedness falls.

C. Inflation and Corporate Profits

The last two sections suggest that the typical household – one which has positive net worth and receives most of its income from wages and salaries – stands to lose from unanticipated inflation. This, in turn, suggests that there would be substantial demand for NIMF deposits, and also ample supply

---

[30]One caveat must be entered here, although I do not know how important it is. Both Jaffe and Mandelker (1975) and Body (1975) make substantial use of Fama's (1975) analysis which suggests that the Treasury bill rate is the sum of a constant real interest rate plus the unbiased estimator of future inflation. However, there are well-known theoretical reasons–first spelled out by Mundell (1963)–for expecting anticipated inflation to lower real interest rates; this suggests that changes in the nominal bill rate should understate changes in inflationary expectations.

[31]Using Cagan's (1974) data, I computed a rank correlation of - 0.64 between real stock market appreciation and inflation.

[32]Nelson (1976) proxied anticipated inflation by various leads and lags on actual inflation. Jaffe and Mandelker (1975) used the Treasury bill rate (see footnote 30 above). Body (1975) used both the bill rate and a variant of adaptive expectations.

[33]I am grateful to Robert Barro for pointing out this oversight.

of labor to firms which promised perfectly indexed wages (accomplished through NIMF, as explained earlier).

But will firms wish to participate? If they are risk neutral, they undoubtedly will, because workers and bondholders will be willing to pay for inflation protection by accepting lower expected real wages and expected real interest rates. However, the theoretical analysis reveals that risk-averse firms may or may not wish to participate, depending on their degree of risk aversion and on how their "other income" fares in inflation.

The latter can be assessed empirically, at least in principle. Ideally, one would like several time series of complete income statements, aggregated to the industry level, in order to see how a concept like "net income before wage and interest payments" behaves in inflation. Unfortunately, such ideal data are not available.

An indirect test can be designed as follows. The theory points out that firms whose positions improve when their industry's prices rise will be eager to hedge their positions by borrowing from NIMF, while firms who suffer when industry prices rise will want to avoid NIMF. The correlation between profits and prices, then, is an important datum in guessing whether or not NIMF would be well received by firms.

Matched profit and price data by industry are not readily available, but a close approximation can be created by linking the Federal Trade Commission's (FTC) quarterly data on profits of manufacturing corporations with the Bureau of Labor Statistics' (BLS) detailed breakdown of the Wholesale Price Index (WPI). These data are particularly suitable for this problem because the industrial classification is roughly at the level of disaggregation that I imagine NIMF would want to use (approximately two-digit industries in the Standard Industrial Classification). However, there are shortcomings. First, multi-industry firms are assigned to a single industry; this is not how I imagine NIMF would handle them. Second, precise matching of FTC and BLS classifications was not always possible. Judgment was exercised in deciding where a tolerably close match-up could be created; the Appendix explains the details. Third, profits as defined for corporate income tax purposes may be far from the ideal definition. Finally, the manufacturing sector may not be representative of the entire private business sector.

While theoretical interest attaches to the sign of $Y'(\pi)$, the usefulness of simple correlations between industry-specific <u>inflation rates</u> and <u>levels of profit</u> is vitiated by common time trends. To circumvent this problem, several alternatives were tried. The first two columns of Table 1 report correlations between industry-specific <u>inflation rates</u> and the two measures of <u>profit rates</u>

Table 1

Correlations Between Profits and Price Increases for U.S. Manufacturing Corporations, 1947-1975

Industry groups[b]	Period	Correlations Between Inflation Rate and: Profits/Sales Ratio	Correlations Between Inflation Rate and: Profits/Equity Ratio	Correlation Between Deviations from Logarithmic Time Trends
(1) Food and kindred products (.145)	Quarterly: 1947:I-1975:I[a] Annual: 1948-1974	+.30 +.12	+.42 +.52	+.42 +.63
(a) Dairy products (.017)	Quarterly: 1963:I-1973:IV Annual: 1963-1973	+.05 +.05	+.29 +.59	-.19 -.26
(b) Bakery products (.010)	Quarterly: 1962:I-1973:IV Annual: 1962-1973	-.48 -.81	-.34 -.63	-.33 -.63
(c) Alcoholic beverages (.012)	Quarterly: 1956:II-1973:IV Annual: 1957-1973	+.16 +.31	+.21 +.38	+.01 +.04
(2) Tobacco manufactures (.012)	Quarterly: 1951:II-1975:I Annual: 1948-1974	+.37 +.10	+.23 +.21	+.28 -.09
(3) Apparel and other finished textile products (.030)	Quarterly: 1947:I-1973:IV[a] Annual: 1948-1973	+.62 +.26	+.58 +.35	-.03 +.30
(4) Paper and allied products (.025)	Quarterly: 1947:I-1975:I[a] Annual: 1948-1974	+.55 +.35	+.73 +.64	+.46 +.49
(5) Chemicals and allied products (.080)	Quarterly: 1947:I-1975:I[a] Annual: 1947-1974	+.32 +.27	+.56 +.53	+.31 +.38
(a) Industrial chemicals and synthetics (.038)	Quarterly: 1956:II-1975:I Annual: 1957-1974	+.12 +.10	+.55 +.63	+.22 +.48
(b) Drugs (.015)	Quarterly: 1956:II-1975:I Annual: 1957-1974	+.36 +.57	+.05 +.26	-.32 -.37
(6) Petroleum and coal products (.107)	Quarterly: 1957:I-1975:I Annual: 1948-50, 1957-74	+.26 +.30	+.65 +.80	+.51 +.71
(a) Petroleum refining (.105)	Quarterly: 1954:II-1973:IV Annual: 1951-1973	-.15 -.22	+.24 +.28	+.10 +.05

	Period			
(7) Rubber and miscellaneous plastic products (0.026)	Quarterly: 1951:II-1975:I Annual: 1947-1974	+.35 +.66	+.33 +.73	+.03 +.32
(8) Leather and leather products (.006)	Quarterly: 1947:I-1973:IV[a] Annual: 1947-1973	+.48 +.53	+.48 +.48	-.06 +.18
(9) Stone, clay, and glass products (.025)	Quarterly: 1951:II-1975:I Annual: 1947-1974	-.28 -.06	-.11 +.20	-.21 +.48
(10) Primary metal industries (.064)	NA	NA	NA	NA
(a) Iron and steel (.039)	Quarterly: 1947:I-1975:I[a] Annual: 1947-1974	+.22 +.36	+.41 +.68	+.18 +.46
(b) Nonferrous metals (.025)	Quarterly: 1947:I-1975:I[a] Annual: 1947-1974	+.46 +.47	+.56 +.62	+.51 +.60
(11) Electrical and electronic equipment (.092)	Quarterly: 1951:II-1975:I Annual: 1947-1974	-.20 +.40	-.01 +.47	-.41 -.41
(12) Machinery, except electrical (.086)	NA	NA	NA	NA
(a) Metalworking machinery and equipment (.007)	Quarterly: 1956:II-1973:IV Annual: 1957-1973	+.33 +.32	+.37 +.44	-.43 -.60
(13) Transportation equipment (.119)	Quarterly: 1969:II-1975:I Annual: 1969-1974	-.34 -.61	-.32 -.57	-.41 -.43
(a) Motor vehicles and equipment (.083)	Quarterly: 1947:I-1975:I[a] Annual: 1947-1974	-.16 -.15	-.09 -.04	-.38 -.25
(14) Furniture and fixtures (.011)	Quarterly: 1947:I-1973:IV[a] Annual: 1947-1973	+.58 +.71	+.55 +.60	-.06 -.39
(15) Lumber and wood products except furniture (.026)	Quarterly: 1947:I-1973:IV[a] Annual: 1947-1973	+.53 +.79	+.55 +.86	+.53 +.66

[a] Omitting 1951:II
[b] Numbers below each title are the 1973:IV sales weights.
NA = not available

available in the FTC data. The rate of return on equity is generally regarded as superior to profits per dollar of sales for most purposes. However, for getting an indication of the sign of $Y'(\pi)$, the profits/sales ratio may be more appropriate, especially since the FTC's "stockholders' equity" is based on book value rather than true market value.

An alternative approach is to compute the deviations of each industry's price and profit levels from their respective logarithmic time trends, and to calculate the correlation between these two deviations. This method of detrending is reported in the third column of Table 1.

For each of the three alternative measures of the price-profit correlation, the table reports results based on both quarterly and annual data.[34] Thus, for each industry, there are six measures in all.

In view of the many conflicting signs, what useful generalizations can be made from these correlations? Using the correlations between profits/sales ratios and inflation as the measure, price change and profitability are positively correlated in 17 of 23 cases in the quarterly data, and in 18 of 23 cases in the annual data. This looks highly favorable to NIMF. It is an unfair way to keep score, however, first, because it double-counts, and second, because the very large motor vehicle industry is among the industries showing the "wrong" sign. A more relevant way to summarize the results is to compare the fractions of total sales accounted for by industries showing positive versus negative correlations.[35] Based on 1973:IV sales weights,[36] the set of industries with positive correlations is about 2.8 times as large as the set of industries with negative correlations.[37]

---

[34]WPI data are reported monthly. Quarterly and annual inflation rates are computed from appropriately averaged quarterly and annual price levels. Similarly, FTC quarterly profit rates were aggregated to years by separately averaging numerators and denominators.

[35]These two classes do not exhaust the manufacturing sector because some of the FTC industries could not be matched up with WPI price components, and because the electrical equipment and petroleum industries fall in neither category. The petroleum and coal products industry, 99 percent of which is petroleum refining, is not put in either category because of its puzzling behavior. Over some time periods, the correlation is positive; over others, it is negative.

[36]This is the last quarter before several of the subdivisions listed in Table 1 were dropped from the FTC reports. It also avoids the distortions caused by the 1974-75 recession.

[37]This ratio rises to 3.5 if petroleum is assigned a positive correlation, and falls to 1.6 if petroleum is assigned a negative correlation.

Using the correlation between profits/equity ratios and inflation rates instead, price change and profitability are positively correlated in 18 of 23 cases in the quarterly data, and in 20 of 23 cases in the annual data. The 18 industries with unambiguously positive correlation now account for 3.3 times as much sales volume as the three industries with unambiguously negative correlation.[38]

While these two measures agree quite well, a somewhat weaker picture emerges when we look at correlations between deviations of prices and profits from their logarithmic trends. In this case, a positive correlation emerges in only 12 of 23 cases with quarterly observations, and in 14 of 23 cases with annual data. The 11 industries with unambiguously positive correlation account for about 1.6 times as much sales volume as do the eight industries with unambiguously negative correlation.

In brief, then, a substantial majority of manufacturing industries, but certainly not all, seem to be characterized by the positive correlation between prices and profits which is necessary if NIMF is to work. While the theoretical discussion of parts II and III suggests that we might learn more by looking separately at periods of "supply side" versus "demand side" inflation, a preliminary investigation of this was inconclusive.

One final shred of evidence pointing to a willingness of firms to borrow from NIMF is the apparent popularity of some recent financial innovations which can be viewed as halfway houses between conventional and index-linked borrowing. The best known of these are probably the floating-prime-rate loans now being made by Citibank in New York.[39] If instruments like these are attractive to businessman, then perhaps NIMF loans would be too.

D. Conclusion: Would NIMF Work?

In part IV, I argued that NIMF can be made to work if there is sufficient demand for NIMF deposits and a sufficient supply of bonds to NIMF. It seems to me that the evidence cited above on the effects of unanticipated inflation on the returns to human and financial assets and on corporate profits provides at least mild support for the notion that consumers and firms would welcome NIMF. However, the case remains weak enough so that the skeptic will rightfully remain unconvinced. The proof of this particular theoretical pudding will most assuredly come in the empirical tasting.

---

[38]In this case, electrical equipment and stone, clay, and glass products fall in neither group, but petroleum and coal products clearly gets a positive correlation. If electrical equipment is grouped in the positive category, the 3.3 ratio cited in the text rises to 4.

[39]Thomas Huertas of Citibank pointed out to me the similarity between floating-rate loans and index-linked loans. However, I stress that it is only a loose kinship; floating-rate loans certainly are not indexed.

APPENDIX

This section explains the procedures used to match FTC data on profits by industry to components of the WPI. For convenience, the information is given in tabular form. The first column lists all industrial categories used by the FTC since 1947 to which a price series could be matched. Some of them do not go back to 1947; others were eliminated before 1975. The second column gives the component of the WPI which was used as a proxy for each industry's price. The final column ("Comments") explains imperfections in the matching, gaps in the data, and so on.

Table A-1

Matching of Profits and Price Data

FTC Industrial Classification	Component of WPI	Comments
(1) Food and kindred products (a) Dairy products	Processed Foods and Feeds Dairy Products	FTC carried this classification only from 1963 to 1973.
(b) Bakery products	Cereal and Bakery Products	FTC carried this classification only from 1962 to 1973.
(c) Alcoholic beverages	Alcoholic Beverages	FTC carried this classification only from 1956: II to 1973: IV.
(2) Tobacco manufactures	Tobacco Products	Prior to 1951, insufficient data were available to construct quarterly price series.
(3) Apparel and other finished textile products	Apparel	This FTC industry includes nonapparel textile products made outside of textile mills. Products manufactured in textile mills constitute a separate industry in FTC's classification, to which no price series could be matched.
(4) Paper and allied products	Pulp, Paper, and Allied Products	
(5) Chemicals and allied products (a) Industrial chemicals and synthetics	Chemicals and Allied Products Industrial Chemicals	
(b) Drugs	Drugs and Pharmaceuticals	

102

FTC Industrial Classification	Component of WPI	Comments
(6) Petroleum and coal products	"Petroleum Products, refined" and "Coal"	A price series was created by averaging (with BLS weights) the WPI components, "Petroleum products, refined" and "coal." Monthly data on the former began only in 1954. 1951-56 are omitted because FTC did not use this industrial classification for those years.
(a) Petroleum refining	Petroleum Products, refined	Monthly price data began only in 1954.
(7) Rubber and miscellaneous plastic products	Rubber and Plastic Products	Monthly price data began only in 1951.
(8) Leather and leather products	Hides, Skins, Leather, and Related Products	
(9) Stone, clay, and glass products	Nonmetallic Mineral Products	Monthly price data began only in 1951.
(10) Primary metal industries (a) Iron and steel	NA Iron and Steel	No suitable price index.
(b) Nonferrous metals	Nonferrous Metals	
(11) Electrical and electronic equipment	Electrical Machinery and Equipment	Monthly price data began only in 1951.
(12) Machinery, except electrical (a) Metalworking machinery and equipment	NA Metalworking Machinery and Equipment	No suitable price index.
(13) Transportation equipment	Transportation Equipment	Monthly price data began only in 1951.
(a) Motor vehicles and equipment	Motor Vehicles and Equipment	
(14) Furniture and fixtures	Furniture and Household Durables	
(15) Lumber and wood products, except furniture	Lumber and Wood Products	

103

REFERENCES

1. Azariadis, C., "Escalator Clauses and the Allocation of Cyclical Risks," unpublished, Brown University, 1976.

2. Body, Z., "Hedging Against Inflation," unpublished Ph. D. dissertation, MIT, 1975.

3. Cagan, P., "Common Stock Values and Inflation – The Historical Record of Many Countries," Supplement to National Bureau of Economic Research Report, 1974.

4. Council of Economic Advisers, <u>Annual Report</u>, in the <u>Economic Report of the President, 1976</u>, Washington, D.C.: U. S. Government Printing Office, 1976.

5. David, L. M., "Cost of Living Escalation in Collective Bargaining, Price and Wage Control: An Evaluation of Current Policies," Hearings before the Joint Economic Committee, 92nd Congress, 1974.

6. Fama, E., "Short-term Interest Rates as Predictors of Inflation," <u>American Economic Review</u>, LXV, No. 3, (June 1975), 269-282.

7. Fischer, S., "The Demand for Index Bonds," <u>Journal of Political Economy</u>, 83, No. 3, (June 1975), 509-534.

8. _____, "Corporate Supply of Index Bonds," unpublished paper, M.I.T, 1976.

9. Jaffe, J. F., and Mandelker, G., "The 'Fisher Effect' for Risky Assets: An Empirical Investigation," <u>Journal of Finance</u>, XXXI, No. 2, (May 1976), 447-458.

10. Kuhmerker, P., "Scheduled Wage Increases and Escalator Provisions in 1976," <u>Monthly Labor Review</u>, 99, (January 1976), 42-48.

11. de Menil, G., "The Rationality of Popular Price Expectations," unpublished paper, Princeton Univeristy, 1974.

12. Mundell, R. A., "Inflation and Real Interest," Journal of Political Economy, LXXI, No. 1, (February 1963), 280-283.

13. Nelson, C. R., "Inflation and Rates of Return on Common Stocks," Journal of Finance, forthcoming, 1976.

14. Organization for Economic Cooperation and Development. Indexation of Fixed-Interest Securities. Paris: OECD, 1973.

15. Poole, W., "Indexing and the Capital Markets," American Economic Review, LXVI, No. 2, (May 1976), 200-204.

16. Shavell, S., "Sharing Risks of Deferred Payment," Journal of Political Economy, 84, No. 1, (February 1976), 161-168.

17. Siegel, J.J., "Indexed versus Nominal Contracting: A Theoretical Examination," unpublished paper, University of Chicago, 1974.

18. U. S. Bureau of Labor Statistics. Handbook of Labor Statistics. Washington, D. C.: U. S. Government Printing Office, 1974.

19. _____. Wholesale Prices and Price Indices, various monthly issues. Washington, D. C.: U. S. Government Printing Office.

20. U. S. Federal Trade Commission. Quarterly Financial Report for Manufacturing, Mining and Trade Corporations (formerly Quarterly Financial Report for Manufacturing Corporations), various quarterly issues. Washington, D. C.: U.S. Government Printing Office.

WAGE INDEXATION AND MACROECONOMIC STABILITY*

Stanley Fischer**
Institute for Advanced Studies
Hebrew University of Jerusalem

Wages with escalator clauses are flexible nominal wages; wages without escalator clauses are flexible real wages.[1] Accordingly, the relevant consideration in analyzing the effects of wage indexation on macroeconomic stability is whether sticky real wages or sticky nominal wages are more conducive to stability.

There are at least two prevalent views on the effects of wage indexation on economic stability, by which is meant the variability of output and prices. One, associated with Friedman (1974) and Giersch (1974), is that wage indexation stabilizes real output. In making this argument, Friedman points to the 1967-1970 period in the U. S. during which, he claims, sticky nominal wages in conjunction with rising prices led to an excessive expansion of output. Both Giersch and Friedman suggest that in 1974 a contractionary monetary policy would have had smaller output effects with indexed than with non-indexed wages. The second argument is that wage indexation exacerbates real economic instability by reducing the responsiveness of the economy to disturbances that require real wage changes. Bernstein (1974) points to the oil and food shocks of 1973-74 in arguing for the potentially destabilizing effects of wage indexation. The end of Finnish indexing in 1968 and the Israeli government's successful attempt to abrogate or at least delay wage indexing in 1974, each following a devaluation, can also be cited in support of the latter view, as can the Belgian government's proposal at the end of 1975 to suspend indexing.

The analysis of this paper shows that each view is correct under appropriate circumstances. Real output tends to be more stable in an indexed than in a non-indexed system when disturbances to the system are primarily nominal

---

*This is a revised version of a paper presented at the Helsinki Conference on the Monetary Mechanism in Open Economies, August 1975. I am indebted to Milton Assis, Adolfo Diz, Rudiger Dornbusch, Michael Parkin, and Edmund Phelps for useful comments. Research support from the National Science Foundation is gratefully acknowledged.

**On leave from the Massachusetts Institute of Technology.

[1]With apologies to Giersch (1974, p. 6), who notes, "Wages with escalator provisions are flexible wages."

and persistent; output tends to be more stable in a non-indexed than in an indexed system when disturbances are primarily real.[2]

Recent discussion of wage indexation has taken place in a short-run context in which it is desired to reduce the rate of inflation over the next few years. Accordingly, I shall discuss the short-run impacts on output and the price level of a change in the money stock in indexed and non-indexed systems, respectively. But indexation is a relatively complicated instrument to introduce into the economy, and it is unlikely that it can be turned on and off at will by the monetary authority or other economic policymakers. Therefore, I also examine the steady state behavior of non-indexed and indexed economies that are subjected to random real and nominal disturbances each period.

Two important features of wage indexation should be noted before proceeding to the analysis. First, wage indexing exists in most economies.[3] In the absence of legal impediments, the extent of indexation of contracts is endogenous, and apparently related to the rate of inflation, though theoretical considerations would suggest that the variance of the inflation rate is the major determinant.[4] That endogeneity suggests that the extent of indexing not only affects, but also is affected by, macroeconomic stability, and further raises the question of whether the private economy produces the optimal amount of indexing. In this paper, I do not treat indexation as endogenous but instead compare two economies in which wages are and are not indexed, respectively. However, I recognize that a complete theory of the effects of indexation on macroeconomic stability will have to begin from the work contract by analyzing the circumstances under which wage contracts are indexed,[5] embodying such contracts in a complete macro model, and then examining the consequences of the prohibition of indexing on stability.

Second, the form wage indexing takes in practice is not the same as the method of indexing for debt instruments in which the payment for a given

---

[2]This result is also obtained by Gray (1976). I am informed by Harry Johnson that Keynes reached such a conclusion in discussing Australian indexation. A similar point was made by an Israeli Committee of Experts in 1964, whose membership included Ephraim Kleiman and David Levhari; see Brenner and Patinkin (1975). Recent analyses of the effects of wage indexation are those by Arak (1975), Cukierman and Razin (1974), and Parkin (1975). Related papers are by Barro (1975), Brenner and Patinkin (1975), and Grady and Stephenson (1975).

[3]See the appendix to Giersch (1974) for a summary of international experience, and Perna (1973) and January issues of the Monthly Labor Review for the U. S. experience.

[4]However, on an international basis, the mean rate of inflation and the variance of inflation are positively correlated. See Jaffee and Kleiman (1975).

[5]The one attempt I am aware of to do this is by Gray (1975).

period is adjusted ex post on the basis of the realized price change for the period. Instead, wage indexing typically applies to long-term contracts and adjusts the wage for later periods of a contract in accordance with the realized behavior of the price level over the preceding periods. In a typical indexed wage contract, the nominal wage for a given period is known at the beginning of the period; further, the period is likely to be three months or longer,[6] though it doubtless shortens with increases in the variance of the inflation rate. The analysis in sections IV-VI below is designed to reflect this feature of wage indexation–labor contracts are assumed to last two periods and to differ between indexed and non-indexed economies according to whether the nominal wage for the second period of each contract is allowed to adjust to price changes realized since the beginning of the contract. In each period, though, the nominal wage is predetermined in that it is known at the beginning of the period.

This paper contains three models of wage indexing, each of which suggests that whether wage indexing is stabilizing or not depends on the nature of the disturbances affecting the economy; taken together, they suggest that the basic results of the paper are robust. Each model has three elements: wage setting behavior; an output supply equation (or a markup equation); and an aggregate demand equation. The first model–Case Zero[7]– focuses as directly as possible on the question posed at the start by examining the consequences for output variation of fixed nominal and real wages in an extremely simple model economy disturbed by real and nominal shocks. The second model, presented in section II, contains a simple Phillips curve for wage determination and is included because the model, indexing aside, is a standard textbook macro model.

The third model provides the major theoretical innovation. It uses the basic result of research on the labor contract and stylized facts about wage indexing to build a model with overlapping two-period labor contracts to study the effects of indexing on stability. Recent research on the wage contract is reviewed in section III and is used in the subsequent specification of wage adjustment equations. The model of a non-indexed economy is examined in section IV, and that of an indexed economy in section V. The behavior of the two economies is compared in section VI. The source of the basic conclusions is discussed in section VII, together with the results of an extension of the model to include an interest elastic demand for money which are presented in an

---

[6]In Israel, the indexation adjustment usually occurs one year after the start of the initial contract, but the period has been as short as three months; in the U. S. in 1972, 2 million of the 4.3 million workers covered by escalation clauses received adjustments after a year, and 1.7 million every three months. See Sparrough and Bolton (1972) p. 7.

[7]Edmund Phelps suggested the inclusion of Case Zero, and Michael Parkin recommended the use of Figure 1 below.

Appendix. Concluding comments are contained in section VIII. Since it is clear that wage indexing makes no difference when inflation is correctly anticipated, the assumption throughout is that prices fluctuate around a stationary price level; fluctuations could as well be thought of as occurring around a rising price trend.

I. CASE ZERO

The three elements of each of the models discussed are wage setting behavior, an output supply equation, and an aggregate demand equation. In all the models, output is assumed to be a decreasing function of the real wage:

$$(1) \quad Y_t = P_t - W_t + u_t$$

where Y_t is the level of real output,[8] P_t the logarithm of the price level, W_t the logarithm of the wage rate, and u_t is (until section IV) a serially uncorrelated real or aggregate supply disturbance term with expectation zero and variance σ_u^2. The disturbance u should be thought of as representing the effects of weather, etc., on real output. An alternative interpretation of (1) is that it is a markup equation with the markup depending on the level of output.

Aggregate demand is given by a simple velocity equation:

$$(2) \quad M_t - P_t = Y_t + v_t$$

where M_t is the logarithm of the nominal money stock; and v_t is a serially uncorrelated nominal or aggregate demand disturbance with expectation zero, and variance σ_v^2, and is uncorrelated with u_t.[9] The strong simplifying assumption implicit in (2) is that velocity is independent of the nominal interest rate. This assumption is relaxed in the Appendix which discusses a Keynesian interpretation of (2) as the reduced form of a two-equation system embodying goods and money market clearing conditions.

Since we are chiefly interested in the effects of indexing per se and not in the interactions of indexing and policy,[10] we shall assume throughout that monetary policy is passive in that M_t is constant at the level M.

---

[8] Although (1) appears to make negative output levels possible, the reader can prevent that possibility by adding a sufficiently large constant to the right-hand side, or else may view (1) as a relationship that applies to deviations of output from a specified level.

[9] Although we shall generally refer to the disturbances as real or nominal, the reader should feel free to substitute "supply" for "real" and "demand" for "nominal."

[10] The latter topic is analyzed in Fischer (1976).

The third element of the model is wage setting behavior. In the non-indexed case, the nominal wage is assumed to be predetermined at a level $\overline{W}$, which is expected to produce a specified real wage and level of employment. In the indexed case, the real wage is assumed to be set at the same expected level $\overline{w} = (\overline{W} - P)$, which is also expected to produce the same level of employment as $\overline{W}$. The indexed wage, in other words, responds to the current price level, while the nominal wage does not.[11]

Using the prescripts NI for non-indexed and PI for price-indexed, the resultant behavior of output is

(3) $\quad {}_{NI}Y_t = \frac{1}{2}(M - \overline{W} + u_t - v_t)$;

(4) $\quad {}_{PI}Y_t = -\overline{w} + u_t$.

Now suppose there is a nominal or demand disturbance v_t that tends to reduce the price level. In the non-indexed system, we see from (3) that an increase in v_t increases the real wage (since $\overline{W}$ is fixed) and tends to reduce output. In the price indexed system, by contrast, the nominal wage adjusts with the price level; the real wage is unaffected; and as (4) shows, output is unaffected. Hence, wage indexing is stabilizing for the behavior of output if disturbances are nominal.

Next, suppose there is a positive real or supply disturbance, u_t. In (4), u_t has its full effect on output since whatever effects the real disturbance has on the price level have no effect on the real wage. But, if wages are not indexed, we see from (3) that the effects of the real disturbance on output are mitigated. How? The increase in output tends to reduce the price level and that, given the nominal wage, tends to increase the real wage; hence, the effects of the initial real disturbance on output are reduced. Thus, wage indexing is destabilizing for the behavior of output if disturbances are real.

Figure 1 illustrates these results. It represents the aggregate demand (DD) and supply (SS) functions in the (Y,P) plane. The aggregate demand curve, equation (2), is the same in both cases. Figure 1a shows the non-indexed case for which the aggregate supply function, from (1) with $W_t = \overline{W}$, is

(1a) $\quad Y_t = P_t - \overline{W} + u_t$.

---

[11]This is precisely the analysis of Gray (1976).

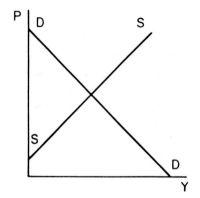

Figure Ia : Non-indexed

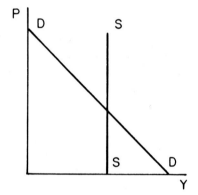

Figure Ib : Indexed

FIGURE I

112

Figure lb is the indexed case in which the aggregate supply function, from (1) with $(W_t - P_t) = \bar{w}$, is

(lb) $Y_t = -\bar{w} + u_t$.

Aggregate supply in the indexed case does not respond to the absolute price level. The curves in Figure 1 are drawn for $u_t = 0 = v_t$. The reader may gain understanding of the basic results by shifting the supply and demand curves by letting u_t and v_t, respectively, take on nonzero values.

Note that indexing totally removes the effects of nominal disturbances on output while non-indexing only partially offsets the effects of real disturbances on output. In general, where both types of disturbances are possible, the question of whether the system is more stable with or without indexing turns on the size of the variances of the disturbances. It is possible to develop an analysis of the optimal extent of indexing from the viewpoint of stability, as Gray (1976) does.

In summary, indexing shields real output from nominal disturbances by permitting constancy of the real wage in the face of such disturbances; indexing does not permit the stabilizing effect on real wages that would otherwise result from price level movements when disturbances are real. This simple analysis provides the essence of the results presented below.

II. A SIMPLE PHILLIPS CURVE MODEL

We now replace the wage setting behavior of the above model with a postulated Phillips curve, the fundamental notion of which is that wages respond to aggregate demand. The stabilizing effects of indexing on the response of output to nominal disturbances emerge clearly from the analysis. The output supply equation (1) and the aggregate demand equation (2) are retained.

A. Indexed Wages

The Phillips curve for an indexed economy can be written as:

(5) $W_t = W_{t-1} + a(Y_{t-1} - Y^*) + \beta(P_t - P_{t-1}) \quad a > 0, 1 \geqslant \beta > 0$

where Y^* is the full employment level of output; and β is a coefficient representing the degree of indexing, which will later generally be assumed equal to unity. Equation (5) asserts that the nominal wage responds to lagged aggregate demand, Y_{t-1}, and also to the realized one-period rate of inflation. For $\beta = 1$, the real wage changes in response to lagged aggregate demand. Notice that we

113

are not treating the nominal wage here as predetermined, but are allowing it to respond to the current price level. This does not accord with the stylized facts outlined above, but is a simple way of allowing the nominal wage to adjust more rapidly to prices in the indexed system than in the non-indexed system discussed in section II.B below.

We will want later to compare the dynamic responses of the indexed and non-indexed systems to disturbances. Accordingly, we use (1), (2), and (5) to solve for the levels of output and prices as functions of their own lagged values and current and lagged values of the disturbances. We obtain:

(6) $\quad Y_t (2-\beta) = a Y^* + Y_{t-1}[(1-\beta) + (1-a)] + u_t - u_{t-1} - v_t(1-\beta) + v_{t-1}(1-\beta).$

(7) $\quad Y_t = aY^* + (1-a) Y_{t-1} + u_t - u_{t-1} \qquad$ for $\beta=1$.

(8) $\quad P_t (2-\beta) = a(M-Y^*) + P_{t-1}[(1-\beta) + (1-a)] - u_t + u_{t-1} - v_t + v_{t-1} (1-a).$

(9) $\quad P_t = a(M-Y^*) + (1-a) P_{t-1} - u_t + u_{t-1} - v_t + v_{t-1}(1-a) \qquad$ for $\beta= 1$.

It is apparent from (7) that full indexation shields output from the effects of nominal disturbances, as is the case in the model examined in section I, and for the same reason. We defer further discussion of (6) - (9) to section II. C below.

We want to use (6) and (8) also to calculate the steady state variances of output and prices in the system given by (1), (2), and (5). That is, we are asking what the variances of output and prices are once the economy has been operating sufficiently long for the effects of any particular initial conditions to have worn off. The steady state variances of output, σ_Y^2, and the price level, σ_P^2, are given by (10) and (11) respectively.

(10) $\quad \sigma_Y^2 = 2(\zeta_1\zeta_2)^{-1} [\sigma_u^2 + (1 - \beta)^2 \sigma_v^2]$

$\qquad = a_{11}\sigma_u^2 + a_{12}\sigma_v^2 \; ;$

(11) $\sigma_p^2 = (\zeta_1\zeta_2)^{-1}\{2\sigma_u^2 + \sigma_v^2[a(1-\beta) + (2-a)]\}$

$$= a_{21}\sigma_u^2 + a_{22}\sigma_v^2$$

where $\zeta_1 = 2 - \beta$.

$\zeta_2 = (2-a) + 2(1-\beta)$.

It is necessary for stability of the system that ζ_2 be positive; this can also be seen by examining (6) and (7), and we shall henceforth assume $2 > a$. This stability condition restricts the effects of lagged output on the current real wage and thus on current output. It is immediate from (10) that nominal disturbances have no effect on the variance of output if wages are fully indexed ($\beta = 1$) and also clear from (11) that, for $\beta = 1$, nominal disturbances are consequently fully reflected in the price level. Further comments appear in section II.D.

B. Non-Indexed Wages

The only change made from the Phillips curve model of the indexed economy in studying the non-indexed economy is to replace the wage equation by an expectational Phillips curve, in which the wage rate responds not to the actual price level but rather to the expected price level.

(12) $W_t = W_{t-1} + a(Y_{t-1} - Y^*) + b(_{t-1}P_t - P_{t-1})$ $\qquad 1 \geqslant b > 0$

where $_{t-1}P_t$ is the price level expected at the end of period t-1 to prevail in period t.

We shall assume that expectations are formed rationally, so that

(13) $_{t-1}P_t = (2-b)^{-1}(a + W_{t-1} + a Y_{t-1} - bP_{t-1})$

where $a = M - aY^*$. The major reason for using rational expectations[12] in the present context is that such expectations are unbiased; accordingly, we are certain that none of the results obtained turn on expectational errors that

---

[12]For discussion of the hypothesis, see Barro and Fischer (1976).

differ in any but an unavoidable way between indexed and non-indexed systems.

Once more, we shall want to study the dynamic impacts of real and nominal disturbances on output and prices and accordingly solve (1), (2), (12), and (13) to obtain expressions for Y_t and P_t, respectively, in terms of their own lagged values and the values of the disturbances.

$$(14) \quad 2Y_t = \frac{2aY^*}{2-b} + 2Y_{t-1}(2-b)^{-1}[(1-a)+(1-b)]$$

$$+ u_t - \frac{2}{2-b} u_{t-1} - v_t + \frac{2(1-b)}{2-b} v_{t-1}.$$

$$(15) \quad Y_t = aY^* + (1-a)Y_{t-1} + \frac{u_t}{2} - u_{t-1} - \frac{v_t}{2} \quad \text{for } b = 1.$$

$$(16) \quad 2P_t = \frac{2a}{2-b}(M-Y^*) + 2P_{t-1}(2-b)^{-1}[(1-a)+(1-b)]$$

$$-u_t + \frac{2}{2-b} u_{t-1} - v_t + \frac{2(1-a)}{2-b} v_{t-1}.$$

$$(17) \quad P_t = a(M-Y^*) + (1-a)P_{t-1} - \frac{u_t}{2} + u_{t-1} - \frac{v_t}{2} + (1-a)v_{t-1} \quad \text{for } b = 1.$$

We now use (14) and (16) to solve for the asymptotic variances of output, S_Y^2, and the price level, S_P^2, in the non-indexed economy. The variances are:

$$(18) \quad S_Y^2 = (\xi_3)^{-1} \{ \sigma_u^2 [b^2 + 4a] + \sigma_v^2 [b^2 + 4a(1-b)] \}$$

$$= a_{11} \sigma_u^2 + a_{12} \sigma_v^2 ;$$

116

(19) $S_P^2 = (\xi_3)^{-1} \{\sigma_u^2 [b^2 + 4a] + \sigma_v^2 [(2a-b)^2 + 4a(1-a)]\}$

$= a_{21} \sigma_u^2 + a_{22} \sigma_v^2$

where $\xi_3 = 4a [2(1-b) + (2-a)]$.

It is necessary for stability that ξ_3 be positive which, given our earlier assumption that $2 > a$, requires $a > 0$.

C. The Short-Run Responses of Output and Prices to Disturbances

In order to examine the dynamic responses of output and prices to disturbances, Y_t and P_t are written as functions of current and lagged values of the disturbances.[13] We shall examine only the cases $\beta = 1 = b$, i.e., we use (7), (9), (15), and (17), leaving the general case for the reader. Using once again the PI and NI prescripts for "price-indexed" and "non-indexed," respectively, we obtain:

(20) $\displaystyle {}_{PI}Y_t = u_t - a \sum_{i=0}^{\infty} (1-a)^i u_{t-1-i}$;

(21) $\displaystyle {}_{NI}Y_t = \frac{u_t}{2} - \frac{1+a}{2} \sum_{i=0}^{\infty} (1-a)^i u_{t-1-i} - \frac{1}{2} \sum_{i=0}^{\infty} (1-a)^i v_{t-i}$;

(22) $\displaystyle {}_{PI}P_t = -u_t + a \sum_{i=0}^{\infty} (1-a)^i u_{t-1-i} - v_t$;

(23) $\displaystyle {}_{NI}P_t = \frac{-u_t}{2} + \frac{(1+a)}{2} \sum_{i=0}^{\infty} (1-a)^i u_{t-1-i} \frac{-v_t}{2} + \frac{1}{2} \sum_{i=1}^{\infty} (1-a)^i v_{t-i}$.

---

[13] Since lag coefficients are notoriously sensitive to specification, the short-run responses discussed below should be viewed as broadly representative of the dynamic impacts of disturbances rather than as the precise patterns that would emerge in indexed and non-indexed economies.

We discuss first the impacts of nominal shocks, the v_t. From (20), we observe again that indexing protects real output from nominal shocks, and from (22) that, with indexing, the full impact on prices of a nominal shock occurs in the period of the shock. In the rational expectations context, it is probably most reasonable to think of a monetary stabilization policy as a nominal shock; accordingly, we see the basis for the view that a deceleration of the inflation rate is more easily achieved (comparing (22) with (23) and with less real consequences comparing (20) with (21)) with indexing than without. Equation (21) shows that without indexing nominal shocks have an effect on output that is distributed over time, and (23) makes it clear that the effects of a nominal shock on prices are distributed over time in the non-indexed system. However, the initial impact on the price level of a nominal shock is smaller in the non-indexed than in the indexed system, precisely because in such a case the nominal shock also affects output. Notice also from (23) that in the non-indexed system a nominal shock that increases the price level on impact will tend to produce a lower price level in subsequent periods.

Second, consider the dynamic impacts of real shocks. In this case, the impacts of real shocks on output in each system are the mirror image of the effects of prices, so we discuss only the impact of a real shock on output. Figure 2 shows the dynamic multipliers for a real shock in the two systems for the case $a = \frac{1}{2}$. In each system, the impact effect of a real shock on output is positive but the lagged effects are negative. In the indexed case, the lagged effects are negative because the initial increase in output increases the real wage in subsequent periods. In the non-indexed case, the lagged effects are negative for the reason just outlined, and also because the real wage rises initially as the result of a price level fall that occurs in the first period.

While the impact effect of a real shock on output is larger in the non-indexed system, lagged effects on output are (absolutely) smaller (for $a < 1$). Thus for $a > 1$, it is clear that output is more stable without than with indexation in the face of real shocks, but for $a < 1$, a clearly specified stability criterion is needed to compare stability of the two systems. Such a criterion is provided in section II.D.

Accordingly, this section confirms the basic results of the initial simple model with respect to the role of indexing in dealing with nominal or demand shocks. However, the comparison between the full dynamic impacts of real shocks on output and prices is ambiguous for $a < 1$. It is clear that monetary stabilization affects the price level more rapidly and with less real consequences in an indexed than in a non-indexed system; it is probably this argument that is behind the recent support for indexation.

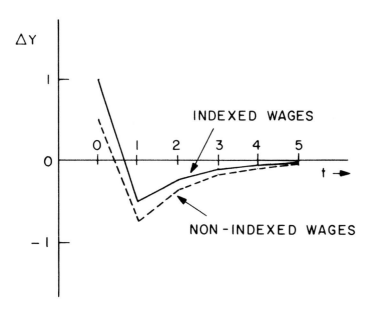

FIGURE 2: Dynamic Multipliers for Effects
of a Unit Real Shock on Output
($a = 1/2$)

D. Asymptotic Stability Comparisons

We use (10), (11), (18), and (19) to compare the steady state variances of the levels of output and prices in the two systems. The asymptotic variance is a convenient measure of how far away from steady state values Y and P are likely to be when the two systems are subjected to repeated shocks. Using the relevant equations and again setting $\beta=1=b$:

$$(24) \quad {}_{PI}\sigma_Y^2 - {}_{NI}\sigma_Y^2 = (a_{11} - a_{11}) \sigma_u^2 + (a_{12} - a_{12}) \sigma_v^2$$

$$= \left[\frac{2}{2-a} - \frac{1+4a}{4a(2-a)} \right] \sigma_u^2 - \frac{1}{4a(2-a)} \sigma_v^2$$

$$= \frac{4a-1}{4a(2-a)} \sigma_u^2 - \frac{1}{4a(2-a)} \sigma_v^2 \; ;$$

$$(25) \quad {}_{PI}\sigma_P^2 - {}_{NI}\sigma_P^2 = (a_{21} - a_{21}) \sigma_u^2 - (a_{22} - a_{22}) \sigma_v^2$$

$$= \left[\frac{2}{2-a} - \frac{1+4a}{4a(2-a)} \right] \sigma_u^2 + \left[1 - \frac{1}{4a(2-a)} \right] \sigma_v^2$$

$$= \frac{4a-1}{4a(2-a)} \sigma_u^2 - \left[\frac{(2a-1)^2 - 4a}{4a(2-a)} \right] \sigma_v^2 \; .$$

Consider first $(a_{11} - a_{11})$ which gives the relevant comparison for the effect of real shocks on output. For large a ($>.25$), real shocks have a greater impact on output in the indexed system, and for $a < .25$, real shocks have a smaller impact on output in the indexed system. The reason can be seen in Figure 1 and from (21) and (23); although the initial impact of a real shock on output is always larger in the indexed system, the lagged impacts will be smaller in the indexed than in the non-indexed system for small a. The variance measure of fluctuations weights deviations in either direction equally so that

120

all that is relevant is the sum of squares of the two curves in Figure 1 from the zero axis. At the limit, as a goes to zero, the indexed system is stable and the non-indexed system unstable, as there are no forces in the non-indexed system driving the real wage back to the appropriate value. The same analysis is relevant for the effects of real disturbances on prices.

The comparative effect of nominal disturbances on output is clear-- nominal disturbances have a greater impact on output in the non-indexed system. The relative effects of nominal disturbances on prices depends on the value of a. For $.13 < a < 1.85$, nominal disturbances have a greater impact on prices in the indexed system; outside those limits, the non-indexed system has less stable prices.

E. Summary

From the viewpoint of the stability of output, indexing is fully appro- priate in an economy subject predominantly to nominal disturbances, but may not be appropriate in an economy subject to real disturbances. However, the ambiguity of some of the results, the essentially ad hoc nature of the wage equations, and particularly the absence of one feature of actual wage indexing noted in the introduction-- that indexed wages provide automatic adjustments in wages in the later periods of a contract but do not actually adjust to the current price level--make it desirable to study the wage equation and con- tracting more carefully.

III. THE LABOR CONTRACT

Recent research on the optimal labor contract has emphasized differences in risk aversion between workers and employers. Facing a worker with a choice between a stream of income from a spot labor market and income derived from a contract with a risk-neutral employer, Baily (1974) shows that a risk-averse worker would, in effect, be willing to buy insurance from the employer by agreeing to a fixed wage contract, even with some probability of his being laid off. The employer could thus obtain a given amount of labor at lower expected cost by offering a fixed wage contract than by varying the wage in accord with labor market conditions. Grossman (1975) points out that the fixed wage contract with variable employment is dominated for the worker by one with constant income. He notes also that, in the absence of default costs, the type of contract analyzed by Baily and also by Azariadis (1975) is not viable in that one side or the other would always find it profitable to repudiate the contract: if the spot market wage was below the contract wage, the employer would repudiate; if the contract wage were below the spot wage, the worker would repudiate. By incorporating the possibility of default, Grossman shows that workers may prefer the fixed wage contract to the fixed income contract.

Although the above-mentioned studies do not explicitly discuss indexing, they imply that wage contracts would be indexed, since workers are concerned with real and not nominal income. Such a conclusion is also implied for workers whose entire income is from labor by a result due to Shavell (1976) who shows that in contracting between a risk-averse individual and one who is risk neutral, the payments function would leave the former with constant income. Partial indexing could obtain if both parties were risk averse.[14] Using a model in which firms minimize the expected costs of deviations of labor input from desired levels, plus an assumed fixed per contract cost of contracting, Gray (1975) produces labor contracts in which the degree of indexing is dependent upon the source (real or nominal) of macroeconomic disturbances.

The fundamental result of the work on the labor contract, then, is that contracts attempt to maintain constancy of the real wage (in a stationary economy subject to random disturbances). We shall also incorporate in our models the existence of long-term labor contracts of finite duration, although we do not provide the analysis which explains the existence of such contracts.[15] In any period, some workers will be in the first year of contracts drawn up at the end of the previous period; some workers will be in the second year of contracts, etc.[16] Typically, wages in the pre-existing contracts will be changing in accordance with a formula fixed at the previous contract date. We now investigate the implications of alternative indexed and non-indexed contracts with their respective wage formulae for macroeconomic stability.

IV. NON-INDEXED LABOR CONTRACTS

We have now set the stage for the introduction of the third model used to study indexing. As before, the model consists of an output supply equation, an aggregate demand equation, and wage setting behavior. The innovation of the model is in wage setting and the consequent output supply equation. All labor contracts run for two periods. In the non-indexed case, the contract specifies a nominal wage for each period. The model differs from those in

---

[14] See Stiglitz (1975) for a discussion of firms behaving as risk averters.

[15] See Williamson, Wachter and Harris (1975) for an interesting examination of labor contracts.

[16] Not all labor works on long-term contracts; for the purposes of this paper, it is necessary only that some labor does so.

sections I and II in another respect--the real and nominal disturbances are no longer treated as serially independent.

In period t, half the firms are operating in the first year of a labor contract drawn up at the end of (t-1) and the other half in the second year of a contract drawn up at the end of (t-2). Given that the wage is predetermined for each firm, and assuming employment is determined by the demand for labor, the aggregate supply of output is:

$$(26) \quad Y_t^s = \frac{1}{2} \sum_{i=1}^{2} (P_t - {}_{t-i}W_t) + u_t$$

where ${}_{t-i}W_t$ is the wage to be paid in period t, as specified in contracts drawn up at the end of period (t-i). The properties of the real disturbance term will be specified below.

The aggregate demand equation (2) is repeated here for convenience:

$$(27) \quad Y_t = M_t - P_t - v_t$$

where the properties of the nominal disturbance v_t remain to be specified. The inclusion of an interest elastic velocity function is discussed in the Appendix.

Next we consider wage setting. The labor contract drawn up at time t specifies nominal wages for times (t+1) and (t+2). Assuming, in accordance with the discussion in section III, that contracts are drawn up to maintain constancy of the expected real wage, we specify[17]

$$(28) \quad {}_{t-i}W_t = {}_{t-i}P_t \qquad i = 1,2$$

where ${}_{t-i}P_t$ is the price level expected at the end of period (t-i) to prevail in period t. To prevent misunderstanding, it should be noted that the use of a one-period contract, and not a two-period contract, is optimal from the viewpoint of minimizing the variance of the real wage; there must be reasons other

---

[17]No substantive results would be changed by the inclusion of a constant in (28) to reflect an equilibrium real wage other than e.

than stability of the real wage, such as the costs of frequent contract negotiations and/or wage setting, for the use of long-term contracts. It should be noted too that, in this model, the goal of maintaining constancy of the real wage and that of maintaining constancy of labor income both imply (28); (28) could also be thought of as the result of a process of wage setting in which each worker tries to set a wage equal to that of others at full employment, as in the Phelpsian process modelled by Parkin (1975).

It is now assumed that each of the disturbances follows a first-order autoregressive scheme:

(29) $u_t = \rho_1 u_{t-1} + \epsilon_t$ $\qquad$ $\left| \rho_1 \right| < 1$;

(30) $v_t = \rho_2 v_{t-1} + \eta_t$ $\qquad$ $\left| \rho_2 \right| < 1$

where ϵ_t and η_t are serially and mutually uncorrelated stochastic terms with means zero, and variances, σ_ϵ^2 and σ_η^2, respectively. It should be clear that if the disturbances are not serially correlated, and given that the nominal wage is predetermined in both the indexed and non-indexed systems, then there will be no difference in the behavior of the two systems. To attempt to maintain constancy of the real wage, the nominal wage would be set at the same level each period in both systems. It is only when current price and output movements convey information about future movements-- when disturbances are serially correlated--that any differences between the behavior of the systems can arise.[18] It should be appreciated that the assumption of serial correlation of disturbances is central to the analysis of the differences between the systems presented below.

Finally, we shall again assume that expectations are determined rationally. Using (28), and eliminating Y_t between (26) and (27), which is equivalent to assuming the price level adjusts to equate aggregate supply to demand:

---

[18]This was not true of the previous models in which the nominal wage could react to the current price level in the indexed system while it could not do so in the non-indexed system.

(31) $\quad 2P_t = M + 1/2 \sum\limits_{i=1}^{2} {}_{t-i}P_t - (u_t + v_t)$.

Using rational expectations, and noting that $E_{t-2}\left({}_{t-1}P_t\right) = {}_{t-2}P_t$,

We obtain:

(32) $\quad {}_{t-2}P_t = -{}_{t-2}(u_t + v_t) = {}_{t-2}W_t$;

(33) $\quad {}_{t-1}P_t = -1/3\,{}_{t-2}(u_t + v_t) -2/3\,{}_{t-1}(u_t + v_t) = {}_{t-1}W_t$

where ${}_{t-j}X_t$ denotes the expectation of variable, X_t, taken at time $(t-j)$, except for W; and where M, the logarithm of the money supply, has for convenience been set at zero.

Substituting (32) and (33) into (31), we obtain:

(34) $\quad 2P_t = -(u_t + v_t) - 1/3\,(\rho_1 u_{t-1} + \rho_2 v_{t-1}) - 2/3(\rho_1^2 u_{t-2} + \rho_2^2 v_{t-2})$;

(34') $\quad 2P_t = -(\epsilon_t + \eta_t) - \dfrac{4}{3}(\rho_1 \epsilon_{t-1} + \rho_2 \eta_{t-1}) -2\left(\sum\limits_2^{\infty} \rho_1^i \epsilon_{t-i} + \sum\limits_2^{\infty} \rho_2^i \eta_{t-i}\right)$.

Then, using (34) in (26):

(35) $\quad 2Y_t = u_t - v_t + \dfrac{1}{3}(\rho_1 u_{t-1} + \rho_2 v_{t-1}) + \dfrac{2}{3}(\rho_1^2 u_{t-2} + \rho_2^2 v_{t-2})$;

(35') $\quad 2Y_t = \epsilon_t - \eta_t + \dfrac{4}{3}\rho_1 \epsilon_{t-1} - \dfrac{2}{3}\rho_2 \eta_{t-1} + 2\sum\limits_2^{\infty}\rho_1^i \epsilon_{t-i}$.

Examination of (34') indicates that all current and lagged disturbances affect the price level. (35'), however, shows only the current nominal disturbance, and that disturbance lagged once, affecting output. All earlier nominal disturbances were known at the time the oldest existing labor contract was drawn up, and the nominal wage has accordingly adjusted to remove any real effect of such disturbances. The term η_{t-1} affects current output because the real wage in the second year of the oldest existing contract is affected by that nominal disturbance. All current and lagged real disturbances, by contrast, affect output.

Equations (34') and (35') will be used in section VI to examine the dynamic responses of prices and output in the non-indexed system to disturbances. They are also used to calculate the asymptotic variances of the price level and output:

$$(36) \quad \sigma_P^2 = \sigma_\epsilon^2 \left(1/4 + 4/9\rho_1^2 + \frac{\rho_1^4}{1-\rho_1^2} \right) + \sigma_\eta^2 \left(1/4 + 4/9\rho_2^2 + \frac{\rho_2^4}{1-\rho_2^2} \right) ;$$

$$(37) \quad \sigma_Y^2 = \sigma_\epsilon^2 \left(1/4 + 4/9\rho_1^2 + \frac{\rho_1^4}{1-\rho_1^2} \right) + \sigma_\eta^2 \left(1/4 + 1/9\rho_2^2 \right) .$$

V. INDEXED WAGES

The formula by which wages are indexed is one of the major determinants of the effects of indexing on stability. In this section we use an indexing formula, "general indexing," which minimizes the variance of the real wage, subject to the nominal wage being predetermined. However, because the implied indexing formula is unlike most seen in practice, we discuss in section VII the implications of an alternative "price indexing" formula in which wages adjust solely on the basis of realized inflation.

An essential difference between indexed and non-indexed contracts is that wages for a subsequent period in indexed contracts can be adjusted in accord with events which occur after the signing of the contract. Given that the wage to prevail in period t can be adjusted on the basis of events occurring up to and during period (t-1), it is clear that the nominal wage which minimizes the variance of the real wage is

$$(38) \qquad {}_{t-i}W_t = {}_{t-1}P_t .$$

Any contract, of any length, could specify (38) as the wage adjustment formula. The contract can be taken to be of length m, where m is determined by considerations not involving the variance of the real wage.

126

Now, replace (26), the supply equation, by

$$(39) \quad Y_t = \frac{1}{m} \sum_{i=1}^{m} (P_t - {}_{t-i}W_t) + u_t$$

$$= P_t - {}_{t-1}P_t + u_t \,,$$

and retain

$$(27) \quad Y_t = M_t - P_t - v_t \,.$$

Using (27) and (39), rational expectations, and assuming $M_t = 0$, we obtain

$$(40) \quad {}_{t-1}P_t = W_t = bP_{t-1} + cY_{t-1} - \rho_1 W_{t-1}$$

where $\quad b = (\rho_1 + \rho_2) \quad c = (\rho_2 - \rho_1) \,.$

Alternatively,

$$(41) \quad {}_{t-1}P_t = W_t = b \sum_{i=0}^{\infty} (-\rho_1)^i (P_{t-1-i})$$

$$+ c \sum_{i=0}^{\infty} (-\rho_1)^i (Y_{t-1-i}) \,.$$

For $.5 = \rho_2 = \rho_1$, we obtain

$$(42) \quad W_t = \sum_{i=0}^{\infty} (.5)^i (P_{t-1-i} - P_{t-2-i}) \,,$$

which approximates a contract indexed to the rate of inflation.

In general, however, it is clear that (40) and (41) are not similar to contracts indexed to the price level, nor for that matter, do they produce wage setting equations which look much like those used in typical Phillips curves, except for $\rho_1 < 0$. For $\rho_1 < 0$, (40) perhaps resembles some form of profit-sharing contract.

Using (40), (39), and (27), we solve for the price level in terms of current and lagged disturbances:

$$(43) \quad P_t = -\frac{1}{2}(\epsilon_t + \eta_t) - \sum_1^\infty \rho_1^i \epsilon_{t-i} - \sum_1^\infty \rho_2^i \eta_{t-i} \; .$$

The price level is accordingly affected by all current and lagged disturbances. Using the same equations to solve for the level of output;

$$(44) \quad Y_t = \frac{1}{2}(\epsilon_t - \eta_t) + \sum_1^\infty \rho_1^i \epsilon_{t-i} \; .$$

The level of output is unaffected by lagged nominal disturbances since these are embodied in the setting of the nominal wage.

The asymptotic variances of the price level and output are obtained by using (43) and (44):

$$(45) \quad \sigma_P^2 = \sigma_\epsilon^2 \left[1/4 + \frac{\rho_1^2}{1-\rho_1^2} \right] + \sigma_\eta^2 \left[1/4 + \frac{\rho_2^2}{1-\rho_2^2} \right] \; ;$$

$$(46) \quad \sigma_Y^2 = \sigma_\epsilon^2 \left[1/4 + \frac{\rho_1^2}{1-\rho_1^2} \right] + \frac{\sigma_\eta^2}{4} \; .$$

VI. SHORT-RUN RESPONSES TO DISTURBANCES AND STEADY STATE VARIANCES IN THE MULTI-PERIOD LABOR CONTRACT MODEL

I want now to draw together the analyses of the last two sections. To compare short-run responses to disturbances, I use (34') and (35') and (43) and (44). Table 1 summarizes the relevant information concerning the dynamic multipliers.

The results are clear. The only period in which there is any difference in response pattern is the first lagged period. The reason should also be clear. There cannot be any differential response to a current disturbance because the nominal wage is predetermined in both cases. Nor can there be any differential response to disturbances two periods or more old, since all contracts are renegotiated over that time span in both systems. The only difference arises from the assumed inability to renegotiate the nominal wage for the second year of the two-period non-indexed contract. That short-run stickiness of the nominal wage tends to reduce the effects on output of real disturbances by creating changes in the real wage. By the same token, that stickiness of the nominal wage transmits nominal disturbances to real income in the non-indexed system in period one which are not transmitted in the indexed system.

Thus, viewing a monetary stabilization policy as a nominal disturbance, it follows that policy has more rapid effects on prices and smaller effects on output in the indexed than in the non-indexed system. The dynamic multipliers of Table 1 should be regarded as illustrative of a general point. If non-indexed labor contracts are for longer than two periods, then there will be differences in the dynamic responses over periods as long as the contract period. In general, the difference is that output responses to nominal disturbances will be smaller in the indexed system, and output responses to real disturbances will be larger in the indexed system.

The comparisons among asymptotic variances are in accord with the short-run results. Using (36), (37), (45), and (46):

$$(47) \quad {}_{NI}\sigma_Y^2 - {}_{GI}\sigma_Y^2 = \sigma_\epsilon^2 \left(-\frac{5}{9} \rho_1^2 \right) + \sigma_\eta^2 \left(\frac{\rho_2^2}{9} \right) ;$$

$$(48) \quad {}_{NI}\sigma_P^2 - {}_{GI}\sigma_P^2 = \sigma_\epsilon^2 \left(-\frac{5}{9} \rho_1^2 \right) + \sigma_\eta^2 \left(-\frac{5}{9} \rho_2^2 \right) .$$

Table 1

Dynamic Multipliers for Real and Nominal Disturbances

in Multi-Period Contract Model

Variable	Disturbance	Period			
		0	1	2	i
NI^Y	Real	1/2	$2/3\rho_1$	ρ_1^2	ρ_1^i
GI^Y	Real	1/2	ρ_1	ρ_1^2	ρ_1^i
NY^Y	Nominal	-1/2	$-1/3\rho_1$	0	0
GI^Y	Nominal	-1/2	0	0	0
NI^P	Real	-1/2	$-2/3\rho_1$	$-\rho_1^2$	$-\rho_1^i$
GI^P	Real	-1/2	$-\rho_1$	$-\rho_1^2$	$-\rho_1^i$
NI^P	Nominal	-1/2	$-2/3\rho_2$	$-\rho_2^2$	$-\rho_2^i$
GI^P	Nominal	-1/2	$-\rho_2$	$-\rho_2^2$	$-\rho_2^i$

Thus, the non-indexed system has a more stable price level than the indexed system; the non-indexed system has more stable output in the face of real disturbances and less stable output in the face of nominal disturbances. These results confirm the result of section I--that indexing stabilizes output in the face of nominal disturbances.

VII. FURTHER CONSIDERATIONS

In this section we shall first provide a further explanation for the strong results of sections IV - VI, and then proceed to discuss elements omitted from the analysis that might affect those results.

The models of this paper indicate that wage indexing destabilizes output in the face of real disturbances while stabilizing output in the face of nominal disturbances. The source of these results is simple: the models of sections IV and V assume that the nominal wage is set in such a way as to try to maintain constancy of the real wage and/or labor income: our criterion of stability has been the variance of output. That wage rate, set at the end of period (t-1), which minimizes the variance of the real wage (the indexed wage of section V) is not the wage which minimizes the variance of output.[19] Thus, the same conflict that has been invoked to explain the existence of unemployment explains the results of this paper. Nonetheless, we should recognize that the professional presumption is that private contracts, freely entered into, lead to desirable outcomes in the absence of externalities. Accordingly, the welfare question of the desirability of the stability of real output requires further analysis, which is beyond the scope of this paper.

There are five major considerations that could alter the above conclusions: interest elasticity of velocity; the use of alternative indexing formulae; expectational errors; the consideration of relative wage and price changes; and inflexibility of the absolute price level.

In the Appendix, I present a Keynesian-type model in which the demand for goods is a function of the real interest rate, the demand for money a function of the nominal rate, and expectations are formed rationally. The aggregate demand or velocity equation (2), then, becomes a function of the expected rate of inflation. Depending on whether contracts are indexed or not, current price and output are differentially affected by current disturbances— in contrast to the results depicted in Table 1. In particular, in an indexed system in which nominal wages are relatively flexible, a current nominal disturbance creates the expectation of a higher price level next period if nominal disturbances are positively correlated than would be expected if wages were

---

[19] I leave it as an exercise to find the indexing formula for wages which minimizes output variance.

sticky. Such a disturbance accordingly has a greater effect on the current price level in the indexed than in the non-indexed system and thus a greater current effect on output in the indexed system. It therefore appears possible that real output could fluctuate more in the indexed system than in the non-indexed system in response to nominal disturbances, although it is shown in the Appendix that that does not happen in the model studied therein.

Second, I noted in section V that the general indexing formula is unlike most seen in practice. A more usual type of indexing formula is of the nature:

$$(49) \quad W_{t-i\ t} = W_{t-i\ t-i+1} + P_{t-1} - P_{t-i} \ ,$$

in which the wage paid in period t on a contract made at the end of (t-i) is the wage specified for the first year of the contract adjusted for inflation over the intervening period. Such contracts stabilize output in the face of nominal disturbances only if the nominal disturbances tend to persist— in other words for large positive values of ρ_2 in (30). They will destabilize output if nominal disturbances are transitory or if disturbances are predominantly real. Thus, the indexing formulae used in practice may be a far cry from the idealized general indexing formula given in section V and are certain to be less stabilizing in the face of nominal disturbances than that formula. They may by good fortune provide a stabilizing influence against real shocks, but there is no guarantee of that.

Third, I consider expectational errors. One of the benefits of indexing is that it allows nominal wages to react to actual rather than expected events. To the extent that the resultant behavior of the real wage is appropriate for stability of output, indexing will accordingly produce more stable real output. For a contract of given length and with an appropriate indexing formula, an indexed contract produces real wages closer on average to those anticipated than does a nominal contract. It is always possible, as in the models discussed, that the expectational errors of non-indexed contracts are actually stabilizing -- as they will be for unanticipated real disturbances. However, without a good theory of expectational errors, it is not in general possible to conclude how the smaller errors that generally occur with indexing affect the stability of output, unless indexed contracts are drawn up with the aim of maintaining stability of output.

Fourth, consider relative wage and price changes. Suppose that some wages are indexed and some not. Then, in response to disturbances, relative wages change, at least on contracts of a given vintage. Such changes can themselves exacerbate unemployment by making it more profitable to search longer for the higher wages.[20] Indexing of wages in one sector--such as government employment-- and not in others might accordingly have output effects in a manner not considered here. Similarly, this one-good model does not analyze the effects of indexation on relative price variability[21] and the consequences, if any, of such variability for macroeconomic stability. A priori, it is not clear how such considerations would affect our results.

Finally, the aggregate price level has been assumed to adjust instantly to equate the supply of and demand for output; the effects of price inflexibility have not been considered. It would seem that price indexing cannot be of consequence if the absolute price level is fixed so that it is unlikely the results would be revised by limiting the flexibility of prices.

VIII. CONCLUDING COMMENTS

This final section comments on a number of issues connected with wage indexing, some of which can be analyzed using the models of the preceding section, before summarizing the basic results.

A. Stabilizing Monetary Policy

In the non-indexed economy of section IV, monetary policy, even when fully anticipated, can play a role in stabilizing output. In that economy, output stabilization requires money stock increases in response to real disturbances that tend to increase the price level and money stock decreases in response to nominal disturbances tending to increase the price level.[22] In the generally indexed system, pre-announced monetary policy has no effect on output which fluctuates more than in the non-indexed system. If wages are indexed by any other formula, there is room for an active stabilizing monetary policy.

Since monetary authorities sometimes want to use monetary policy to affect real output – at which times they would prefer non-indexed wages – and at other times want to reduce the inflation rate without affecting output– at which times they would prefer indexed wages --there is no presumption that either system would always be preferable to the monetary authority. There is probably a temptation to believe that indexing can be encouraged and discouraged at the appropriate times, but that temptation should be avoided. Those factors that make wages and prices sticky and give monetary policy real effects also mean that indexation is slow to be introduced and probably slow to be abandoned. Wage indexation is not a short-run stabilization device even though

---

[20]This point is inspired by a recent paper by Hall (1975).

[21]Relative price variability is the focus of Barro's (1975) indexing paper.

[22]This point is analyzed in Fischer (1976).

its presence or absence affects the success of short-run stabilization policy.

B. Indexing the Money Stock

Increasing the money stock in response to the lagged inflation rate is usually, but not always, destabilizing in the models under discussion; the serial correlation properties of the disturbances may be such as to prevent instability if the money stock is indexed. However, in a more general context, indexing the money stock by means of interest payments on money does not rule out potentially stabilizing open market operations.[23]

C. The Use of Special Indexes and Partial Indexing

The question of the price index to be used for wage indexing has already received attention.[24] Following the general principle of not allowing nominal wages to adjust for real disturbances, an index excluding import prices and indirect taxes, such as a price index of domestic value added, might be appropriate. The models I examine here do not bear directly on the issue, though it is clear that a general indexing formula, in the sense described in section V, could be constructed which would adjust nominal wages only in response to nominal disturbances. Such a formula would imply tying wages to the lagged value of velocity; partial indexation in which wages adjust less than proportionately to prices is not equivalent to this formula.

D. Identification of Disturbances

This is not the first paper in which results have depended on the source of economic disturbances.[25] At this stage, we do not have a good notion of the relative variances of real and nominal disturbances. Since the identification of disturbances also requires the classification of policy actions as offsetting disturbances or creating them, the problem is not simple.

E. Conclusion

Wage indexation stabilizes real output if the disturbances impinging on the economic system are nominal and destabilizes output if the disturbances are real. Further, the short-run response of the economy to monetary shocks and monetary stabilization provides greater and more rapid price level effects

---

[23] This point is due to Franco Modigliani.

[24] For instance, the Israeli Committee of Experts (see footnote 2) discussed this issue. I have also benefited from the views of Franco Modigliani on this question.

[25] See Fischer (1974) and Poole (1970) for previous examples.

and smaller real effects in an indexed than in a non-indexed system. Thus, monetary policies designed to reduce the inflation rate will operate more rapidly and with less impact on output in an economy with indexed wages than in a non-indexed economy. By the same token, expansionary monetary policies will have a smaller real effect and a more rapid effect on prices in an indexed than in a non-indexed economy.

Indexing and the Interest Elasticity of the Demand for Money

In this appendix we examine the consequences for the basic results of the paper of having an interest elastic demand for money. The reason for undertaking the enquiry is the suspicion that current nominal disturbances will have differential impacts on prices in indexed and non-indexed systems and may thus have differential impacts on output if the demand for money is interest elastic.

To keep the Appendix to a reasonable length, the exposition is terse. Familiarity with the non-indexed and indexed systems discussed in sections IV and V is assumed. Variables retain the same definitions. The aggregate supply equations of the text are retained, as is the assumption that the nominal wage is set to maintain constancy of the real wage.

1. The Model

The aggregate demand or velocity equation (2) of the text is replaced by IS and LM curves:

$$(1) \quad Y_t = a_1 Y_t + b_1 r_t + c_1 (M_t - P_t) + \epsilon_{1t} \qquad 1 > a_1 > 0, \, b_1 < 0, \, c_1 > 0$$

where r_t is the logarithm of the real interest rate; and

$$(2) \quad M_t - P_t = a_2 Y_t + b_2 (r_t + {}_tP_{t+1} - P_t) + \epsilon_{2t} \qquad a_2 > 0, \, b_2 < 0$$

where ${}_tP_{t+1} - P_t$ is the expected one-period inflation rate, and ϵ_{1t} and ϵ_{2t} are mutually uncorrelated random disturbances. Substituting (2) into (1) and eliminating r_t, we obtain

$$(3) \quad (M_t - P_t) \left(1 + \frac{b_2 c_1}{b_1}\right) + b_2 P_t = Y_t \left[a_2 + (1-a_1) \frac{b_2}{b_1} \right] + b_2 P_{t+1}$$
$$+ \epsilon_{2t} - \frac{b_2}{b_1} \epsilon_{1t}.$$

Setting $M_t = 0$, we write

(3') $\quad a\, P_t \quad = \quad -\beta Y_t - b\, P_t\, _{t+1} - v_t$

where $\quad a = 1 + \dfrac{b_2 c_1}{b_1} - b_2 > 0$,

$$\beta = a_2 + (1-a_1)\, \frac{b_2}{b_1} > 0 ,$$

$$b = b_2 < 0 ,$$

$$v_t = \epsilon_{2t} - \frac{b_2}{b_1} \cdot \epsilon_{1t} .$$

Henceforth, we assume v_t has the same properties as v_t in equation (30) above, i.e.,

(4) $\quad v_t = \rho_2 v_{t-1} + \eta_t .$ $\qquad\qquad \left| \, \rho_2 \, \right| < 1$

It is assumed that both ϵ_{1t} and ϵ_{2t} have the same coefficient of serial correlation.

2. General Indexing

Consider first the general indexing case of section V in which output is determined by

(5) $\quad Y_t = P_t - _{t-1}P_t + u_t$

137

with the properties of u_t described by (29) above.

Substituting (5) into (3'):

(6) $\quad (a + \beta) P_t = \beta_{t-1} P_t - b P_t {}_{t+1} - v_t - \beta u_t .$

Using a trial solution of the form (7) to obtain the rational expectation

(7) $\quad P_t = \sum_0^\infty \Pi_i u_{t-i} + \sum_0^\infty \omega_i v_{t-i} ,$

and selecting out the stable solution for P_t (an assumption that sometimes masquerades under the guise of "ruling out speculative bubbles"), we find

(8) $\quad \Pi_o = -[(a+\beta)(a+b\rho_1)]^{-1} a\beta, \qquad \Pi_1 = -[(a+\beta)(a+b\rho_1)]^{-1} \beta^2 \rho_1 ,$

$\qquad \Pi_i = 0, i = 2, 3, \ldots ;$

(9) $\quad \omega_o = -a[(a+\beta)(a+b\rho_2)]^{-1}, \qquad \omega_1 = -[(a+\beta)(a+b\rho_2)]^{-1} \beta \rho_2 ,$

$\qquad \omega_i = 0, i = 2, 3, \ldots .$

Accordingly,

(10) $\quad {}_{GI} P_t = \Pi_o \epsilon_t - (a+b\rho_1)^{-1} \beta \sum_1^\infty \rho_1^i \epsilon_{t-i} + \omega_o \eta_t - (a+b\rho_2)^{-1} \sum_1^\infty \rho_2^i \eta_{t-i}$

and

$$(11) \quad _{GI}Y_t = (1+\Pi_o)\,\epsilon_t + \sum_1^\infty \rho_1^i\,\epsilon_{t-i} + \omega_o\eta_t\,.$$

Equations (10) and (11) provide the dynamic responses of prices and output to disturbances. Asymptotic variances are:

$$(12) \quad _{GI}\sigma_P^2 = \sigma_\epsilon^2\,(a+b\rho_1)^{-2}\beta^2\,[(a+\beta)^{-2}a^2 + (1-\rho_1^2)^{-1}\rho_1^2]$$

$$+ \sigma_\eta^2\,(a+b\rho_2)^{-2}\,[(a+\beta)^{-2}a^2 + (1-\rho_2^2)^{-1}\rho_2^2]\,;$$

and

$$(13) \quad _{GI}\sigma_Y^2 = \sigma_\epsilon^2\,\{\,[(a+\beta)(a+b\rho_1)]^{-2}\,[a^2 + (a+\beta)b\rho_1]^2$$

$$+ (1-\rho_1^2)^{-1}\rho_1^2\,\} + \sigma_\eta^2\,a^2\,[(a+\beta)(a+b\rho_2)]^{-2}.$$

We return to (10) - (13) below.

3. Two-Period Nominal Contracts

Next we proceed to two-period nominal wage contracting—the model discussed in section IV above. The output equation becomes

$$(14) \quad Y_t = P_t - \frac{1}{2}(\,_{t-1}P_t + \,_{t-2}P_t) + u_t\,,$$

resulting in

$$(15) \quad (a+\beta)P_t = \frac{\beta}{2}\,_{t-1}P_t + \frac{\beta}{2}\,_{t-2}P_t - b\,_t P_{t+1} - \beta u_t - v_t\,.$$

139

We now use a trial solution for the rational expectations equations for P_t:

(16) $\quad P_t = \sum_{i=0}^{\infty} \theta_i u_{t-i} + \sum_{i=0}^{\infty} \xi_i v_{t-i}$.

Again selecting out the stable solution for P_t, we obtain:

(17) $\quad \theta_o = -\beta[(a+\beta)(2a+\beta)(a+b\rho_1)]^{-1} [a(2a+\beta) + b\beta\rho_1]$,

$\theta_1 = -\beta^2\rho_1 [(a+\beta)(2a+\beta)(a+b\rho_1)]^{-1} (a-b\rho_1)$,

$\theta_2 = -\beta^2\rho_1^2 [(2a+\beta)(a+b\rho_1)]^{-1}$,

$\theta_i = 0 \quad i = 3,4,\ldots$;

(18) $\quad \xi_o = -[(a+\beta)(2a+\beta)(a+b\rho_2)]^{-1} [a(2a+\beta) + b\beta\rho_2]$,

$\xi_1 = -\beta\rho_2 [(a+\beta)(2a+\beta)(a+b\rho_2)]^{-1} (a-b\rho_2)$,

$\xi_2 = -\beta\rho_2^2 [(2a+\beta)(a+b\rho_2)]^{-1}$,

$\xi_i = 0 \quad i = 3,4,\ldots$.

Hence,

$$(19) \quad _{NI}P_t = \theta_o \epsilon_t - 2a\beta\rho_1 \left[(2a+\beta)(a+b\rho_1)\right]^{-1} \epsilon_{t-1} - (a+b\rho_1)^{-1}\beta \sum_2^\infty \rho_1^i \epsilon_{t-i}$$

$$+ \xi_o \eta_t - 2a\rho_2 \left[(2a+\beta)(a+b\rho_2)\right]^{-1} \eta_{t-1} - (a+b\rho_2)^{-1} \sum_2^\infty \rho_2^i \eta_{t-i},$$

and

$$(20) \quad _{NI}Y_t = (\theta_{o+1})\epsilon_t - \left\{ a\beta\rho_1 \left[(2a+\beta)(a+b\rho_1)\right]^{-1} - \rho_1 \right\}\epsilon_{t-1} + \sum_2^\infty \rho_1^i \epsilon_{t-i}$$

$$+ \xi_o \eta_t - a\rho_2 \left[(2a+\beta)(a+b\rho_2)\right]^{-1} \eta_{t-1}.$$

The asymptotic variances are:

$$(21) \quad _{NI}\sigma_P^2 = \sigma_\epsilon^2 \left\{ \theta_o^2 + 4a^2\beta^2\rho_1^2\left[(2a+\beta)(a+b\rho_1)\right]^{-2} + (a+b\rho_1)^{-2}\beta^2\rho_1^4 \right.$$

$$\left. \cdot (1-\rho_1^2)^{-1} \right\} + \sigma_\eta^2 \left\{ \xi_o^2 + 4a^2\rho_2^2\left[(2a+\beta)(a+b\rho_2)\right]^{-2} \right.$$

$$\left. + (a+b\rho_2)^{-2}\rho_2^4(1-\rho_2^2)^{-1} \right\};$$

$$(22) \quad _{NI}\sigma_Y^2 = \sigma_\epsilon^2 \left[(1+\theta_o)^2 + \left\{ a\beta\rho_1\left[(2a+\beta)(a+b\rho_1)\right]^{-1} - \rho_1 \right\}^2 \right.$$

$$\left. + \rho_1^4(1-\rho_1^2)^{-1} \right] + \sigma_\eta^2 \left\{ \xi_o^2 + a^2\rho_2^2\left[(2a+\beta)(2+b\rho_2)\right]^{-2} \right\}.$$

4. Short-Run Responses to Disturbances

(i)   Effects of current nominal disturbances on output and price. From (11) and (20), we note that a unit current nominal disturbance ($\eta_t=1$) affects current output by the amounts w_o and ξ_o in the indexed and non-indexed systems, respectively. It can be shown that both w_o and ξ_o are negative. Further,

$$(23) \quad \omega_o - \xi_o = [(2a+\beta)(a+\beta)(a+b\rho_2)]^{-1} b\beta\rho_2.$$

Since b is negative, we know, if $\rho_2 > 0$, that a current nominal disturbance has a smaller effect on output in a non-indexed than in an indexed system. The reason has already been given. A current nominal disturbance that increases the price level can also be expected to increase next period's price level if $\rho_2 > 0$. The implied expected inflation will increase velocity and thus affect the current price level. In the non-indexed system, wages are relatively sticky and next period's price should be expected to move less than in the indexed system. Accordingly, the current price level also moves less in the non-indexed system, and there is a smaller impact on output of a nominal disturbance than in the indexed system.

It is clear from (10) and (19) that the comparative effects of a current nominal disturbance on prices is also given by (23) and the above verbal discussion applies exactly.

(ii)   Effects of lagged nominal disturbances on output and prices. In the generally indexed systems lagged nominal disturbances have no effects on output whereas the first lagged nominal disturbance does have an impact on output in the non-indexed system. The reason is clearly that the lagged disturbance affects the real wage of those currently in the second year of their contracts. Interestingly, the cumulative impact of a nominal disturbance is greater for $\rho_2 > 0$ with non-indexed than with indexed wages, i.e.,

$$(24) \quad \omega_o - \xi_o + a\rho_2 [(2a+\beta)(a+b\rho_2)]^{-1} > 0;$$

and since each effect is negative, the cumulative impact of a given nominal disturbance on output is clearly larger in the non-indexed than in the indexed system.

Examination of (10) and (18) also shows that the η_{t-1} disturbance has the greater impact on the current price level in the indexed system, and that disturbances lagged two or more periods have precisely the same effect on price in both systems.

(iii) Effects of current real disturbances on output and price. From (11), (20), and (23), making the appropriate substitutions and since $(\theta_0 + 1)$ and $(\Pi_0 + 1)$ are both positive, we know that a current real disturbance has a greater effect on current output in the non-indexed than in the indexed system if $\rho_1 > 0$. The reasoning is the same as that employed in 4.(i) above. In this instance, the fact that prices do not move as much in the non-indexed system offsets the effect of the output disturbance by less than in the indexed system. By allowing the current position of the economy to be affected by future prices, we obtain an interesting reversal of roles of indexing and non-indexing with regard to the current impacts of disturbances. Note from (10) and (19) that a current real disturbance moves price more in the indexed than in the non-indexed system.

(iv) Effects of lagged real disturbances on output and price. Lagged real disturbances have a differential impact on output and price in the two systems only in period (t-1). The disturbance ϵ_{t-1} has a larger (positive) impact on output in the indexed than in the non-indexed system (for $\rho_1 > 0$), but the relative magnitude of the price effect is indeterminate. The comparative cumulative effect of a given real disturbance on output is of indeterminate sign, but for plausible parameter values it appears that a given real disturbance produces smaller cumulative output effects (for $\rho_1 > 0$) in the non-indexed than in the indexed economy. We obtain

$$(25) \quad \theta_o + 1 + \rho_1 - a\beta\rho_1 [(2a+\beta)(a+b\rho_1)]^{-1} - (1 + \Pi_o + \rho_1)$$

$$= -\beta\rho_1 [a(a+\beta) - b\beta] [(a+\beta)(2a+\beta)(a+b\rho_1)]^{-1}.$$

For small or any plausible values of b this expression is negative given $\rho_1 > 0$. Thus, while the initial impact of a real disturbance is larger in the non-indexed than in the indexed system, its cumulative effect is smaller in the non-indexed system.

143

5. Asymptotic Variances

In terms of the asymptotic variance, output is, for small (and plausible) values of b, more stable in the face of real disturbances in a non-indexed system and is definitely more stable subject to nominal disturbances in the indexed system. Prices are more stable in the non-indexed system in the face of both types of shocks for positive serial correlation of the errors.

6. Conclusion

This analysis shows that the dynamic pattern of the response of the systems to given shocks changes when the demand for money is interest elastic-- in particular, a current nominal shock may have a greater current output effect in the indexed than in the non-indexed system--but that the asymptotic properties of the model are largely unaffected by the change.

REFERENCES

1. Arak, M., "The Effect of Wage Indexation on the Behavior of Output, Un-
    employment and Prices," unpublished, Federal Reserve Bank of New
    York, (March 1975).

2. Azariadis, C., "Implicit Contracts and Underemployment Equilibria,"
    Journal of Political Economy, 83, No. 6, (December 1975), 1183-1202.

3. Baily, M.N., "Wages and Employment Under Uncertain Demand," Review
    of Economic Studies, XLI, No. 125, (January 1974), 37-50.

4. Barro, R.J., "Indexation in a Rational Expectations Model," unpublished,
    University of Chicago, (May 1975).

5. Barro, R.J., and Fischer, S., "Recent Developments in Monetary Theory,"
    Journal of Monetary Economics, 2, No. 2, (April 1976), 133-167.

6. Bernstein, E.M., "Indexing Money Payments in a Large and Prolonged
    Inflation," in Giersch et al., Essays on Inflation and Indexation, 1974.

7. Brenner, R., and Patinkin, D., "Indexation in Israel," unpublished, Hebrew
    University of Jerusalem, (October 1975).

8. Cukierman, A., and Razin, A., "The Short-Run Effects of Indexation of
    Wage Contracts on Macro-Economic Fluctuations," unpublished, Tel
    Aviv University, (October 1974).

9. Fischer, S., "Stability and Exchange Rate Systems in a Monetarist Model
    of the Balance of Payments," unpublished, M.I.T., (August 1974).

10. _____ , "Long-Term Contracts, Rational Expectations and the Optimal
    Money Supply Rule," forthcoming, Journal of Political Economy,
    1976.

11. Friedman, M., "Monetary Correction," in Giersch et al., Essays on Inflation
    and Indexation, 1974.

12. Giersch, H., "Index Clauses and the Fight Against Inflation," in Giersch, et al., Essays on Inflation and Indexation, Washington, D.C.: American Enterprise Institute, 1974.

13. Grady, P., and Stephenson, D.R., "Some Macroeconomic Effects of Tax Reform and Indexing," unpublished, Bank of Canada, (June 1975).

14. Gray, J.A., "Some Economic Aspects of Contracting and Indexation," unpublished, University of Chicago, (June 1975).

15. _____ , "Wage Indexation: A Macroeconomic Approach," Journal of Monetary Economics, 2, No. 2, (April 1976), 221-235.

16. Grossman, H.I., "The Nature of Optimal Labor Contracts: Towards a Theory of Wage and Employment Adjustment," unpublished, Brown University, (March 1975).

17. Hall, R.E., "The Rigidity of Wages and the Persistence of Unemployment," Brookings Papers on Economic Activity, Washington, D.C.: The Brookings Institution, 5 (1975:2), 301-350.

18. Jaffee, D., and Kleiman, E., "The Welfare Implications of Uneven Inflation," unpublished, Princeton University, (June 1975).

19. Parkin, M., "Inflation and Unemployment in an Indexed Economy: Some Analytical Issues," unpublished, University of Manchester, (June 1975).

20. Perna, N., "Cost of Living Escalator Clauses in Collective Bargaining Contracts," unpublished, Federal Reserve Bank of New York, (1973).

21. Poole, W., "Optimal Choice of Monetary Policy Instruments in a Simple Stochastic Macro Model," Quarterly Journal of Economics, LXXXIV, No. 2, (May 1970), 197-216.

22. Shavell, S., "Sharing Risks of Deferred Payment," Journal of Political Economy, 84, No. 1, (February 1976), 161-168.

23. Sparrough, M.E., and Bolton, L.W., "Calendar of Wage Increases and Negotiations for 1972," <u>Monthly Labor Review</u>, 95, No. 1, (January 1972), 3-14. (Articles with similar information for other calendar years can be found in January issues of the <u>Monthly Labor Review</u>.)

24. Stiglitz, J.E., "Monopolistic Competition and the Capital Market," unpublished, Stanford University, (February 1975).

25. Williamson, O.E., Wachter, M.L., and Harris, J.E., "Understanding the Employment Relation: The Analysis of Idiosyncratic Exchange," <u>Bell Journal of Economics</u>, 6, No. 1, (Spring 1975), 250-278.

INDEXATION ISSUES:
A COMMENT ON THE BLINDER AND FISCHER PAPERS

Edmund S. Phelps*
Columbia University

Indexing, I take it, means tying some or all elements of a transaction to one or more contingencies--to events or reports not counted as certain at the initial decision. Bonds that promise to pay future in proportion to the future price level are said to be indexed. Some retirement benefits are indexed to money wage levels. Banks and insurance companies have begun to index their loan rates and premium rates by market interest rates. Some public spending programs are automatically started and shut off by the rise and fall of the unemployment rate. Insurance is the best example of indexation because the "indicator" is typically capable of manipulation or misrepresentation.

I focus here upon recent issues in the positive and normative theory of wage indexation--the voluntary indexing of the money wage rate commitments, or implicit contracts, offered by some or all firms.[1] As the first paragraph tediously suggests, a firm now deciding its money wage commitment over some future period could choose to index that wage to a nearly infinite variety of events between now and then. Hence, those wage commitments which are indexed only to the so-called escalator clause represent just one type of indexation.[2] In respect both to its viability and desirability, that type needs to be compared to more general types of indexation, not merely to no indexation at all.

The agenda of issues to be discussed is prompted by the creeping index-ationism of the past few years. In that vision, indexed contracts will soon be sweeping the economy. These contracts will ultimately offer full escalation of

---

*My fixed opinions on this subject were prepared for the January 1975 Sao Paulo Conference on Indexation where I took the solitary position that parties to indexed labor contracts would not freely choose full escalation of wages to the price level and that compulsory full escalation would serve them ill. A grant from the National Bureau of Economic Research is gratefully acknowledged.
The present paper ventures to give reasons for these opinions. The Appendix is largely the work of Guillermo Calvo, and both he and John Taylor contributed to the argument at several points.

[1] I shall not have in mind the Brazilian variant in which there is, by fiat, a retroactive "monetary adjustment" of wages for work previously performed. It will be supposed that the contingencies upon which the current money wage depends are known by the firm and its employees by the time the current work performed at that wage takes place; and that such contingent wage commitments are neither mandated nor enforced by the government.

[2] Under the escalator clause the money wage is an increasing function of the price level.

money wages to the general price level (making the real wage independent of the price level). A dual consequence is the abolition--or, more realistically in view of price data lags, the rapid attenuation–of the employment effects of demand shocks and, as a corollary, the abolition (or rapid attenuation) of the central bank's power to moderate the employment effects of supply shocks (which effects will be magnified by escalation). But, the latter consequence is not a real cost because unemployment brought about by unanticipated supply shocks is "contractual" and the contracts are Pareto-optimal with regard to an individual's ex ante expected utilities.[3]

I think it should be conceded that there are some grains of truth in the models that have generated these conclusions. There is no doubt that the fascinating developments in "contract theory" have opened up a new line of research of great promise. Nevertheless, in perhaps an allergic reaction to those grains of truth, I shall argue that realistic contract theory will not support the conclusions overreached by the indexationists.

1. Where in the economy are there tendencies toward indexation of some kind?

Many firms are so situated that they find it (ultimately) profitable regularly to make and to keep advance commitments regarding the terms on which they will employ certain kinds of workers (if hired). One of the reasons recently glimpsed is that the firm will find a recruiting advantage in having a pre-announced wage scale that reduces the time and trouble of information gathering for the potential employee.[4] If he has to negotiate his wage at one firm but not at others, and then only when he can show the firm he is in earnest, the recruit is apt not to bother with that firm. Another reason for pre-arrangement is that, without it, the prospective employee may worry that the firm will exploit his having distanced himself from alternative employment prospects.[5] The presence of mobility costs tempts every firm to pay its current employees something less than their "going wage."[6]

These remarks, obvious or problematic, leave open the form that wage and employment commitments may take. If a degree of uncertainty about economic conditions during the period of the commitment is added to the above considerations, then it is plausible to expect that such commitments will take

---

[3]As Fischer puts it, " . . . it should be recognized that the professional presumption. . .that private contracts, freely entered into, lead to desirable outcomes in the absence of externalities.

[4]See Okun (1975).

[5]Calvo (conversation).

[6]William Vickrey, in conversation, has noted a similar problem for the existence of equilibrium in the taxi industry.

the form of contingency agreements. If, as I shall suppose, all (or at any rate most) workers are averse to risk, they may be willing to pay for some "insurance" against certain contingencies; and the firm, even the risk-neutral firm, may be willing to pay for contingency clauses allowing it to make employment or wage adjustments.

The tendency toward contingent or indexed commitments appears to be limited to the situations just described. Where the prospective employment is nearly immediate and short-term, it would seem that the firm might as well offer certain employment at a certain money wage. Unless the prospective duration of the job is long, or the job is far in the future, so that substantial uncertainties loom over the horizon, it will not be worth the administrative and evaluational costs to deal in indexed commitments. Where conditions of costless information and costless mobility prevail, the potential worker who can always supply other services at the average wage might welcome fluctuations rather than stability in the wage periodically paid for that service. There may normally exist a dominant arrangement by which the supplier of the service effectively indentures himself to some firm in return for some retainer fee; but, for such an arrangement to exist, the firm must trust the supplier's availability when it is needed and the supplier must trust that the firm will not demand his service when it is not warranted by the firm's true needs.

The nature of the indexation provided by bilaterally optimal contingent commitments, where they exist, is the next question. The implicit contract theories of Azariadis (1975), Baily (1974), and Gordon (1976) appear to imply that optimal commitments will stabilize the real wage--full escalation of the money wage to the price level--and leave workers with some risk of undesired layoffs. Whether or not these conclusions are intended and valid deductions, they are crucially dependent upon the model adopted.

2. Do optimal indexed contracts protect the real wage rate from all shocks?

Azariadis (1975) has constructed a theory of state contingent contracts from a model in which, knowing only the probabilities of each possible "state of the world" before it occurs, risk-neutral firms choose contingent contracts that maximize their expected profits and (homogeneous) risk-averse workers choose the firms at which to locate so as to maximize their expected utilities. This model is subject to the conditions that workers are then immobilized at the firms of their choice for the life of the contracts, so that the firm cannot hire more persons than have come to it and, if it hires fewer, the firm's workers will have an equal probability of not being hired.[7]

The first result pertains to the employment terms of the contract. Given the optimal wage rate to be paid in each state, the firm commits itself to hire generously--beyond the point where marginal value product equals the real wage--when the state is "poor" in order to attract a desirably large pool of workers to be available when the state turns out "good."[8]

A more striking result pertains to the wage terms of the contract. The optimal contract of a firm specifies a wage that is independent of the state (and therefore independent of the employment level corresponding to that state). Given the number of workers who position themselves in advance at the firm, and given the optimal number to be employed (and hence the probability of being hired) in each state, the firm will minimize the expected value of its wage costs while providing workers with the "competitive" level of expected utility only if it ensures the same wage across all states. The following remark may be helpful. Because the probability of being hired in each state is an independent control variable being simultaneously optimized, the problem of wage optimization is reduced, by an envelope theorem, to that of dividing up the total rent (for each state that eventuates) between the risk-averse workers who are hired and the risk-neutral firm.

Is this "wage," which is state-invariant during the contract, the money wage or the real wage? If it is supposed, as Azariadis seems to prefer, that monetary policy holds constant the price level, then the real wage is state-independent at least for that macroeconomically very special case. But, it would not do violence to the model if we stipulate, as most analysts have been inclined to do, that workers' utilities are a function of leisure and the real wage only--at least when product markets and money markets are in equilibrium. Then, stabilizing (across states) the utility from job holding entails stabilizing the real wage. It is this specialized general equilibrium version of the model that most readers have in mind when they infer from Azariadis that his theory (and that of other contract theorists) makes the real wage a "constant" over the life of the contract.

---

[7]The model is outlined in the Appendix. Perhaps the best interpretation of the postulate that workers are perfectly mobile among firms ex ante and perfectly immobile ex post is that, by assumption, every state which turns up after decisions are made is believed to be "temporary," the probability distribution of states being believed to be unchanged. Then, the failure or incapacity of a firm to offer the "competitive" level of expected utility would be a reason for workers not to join it, or to leave it if located there to begin with, if the cost of moving is not too large. But, ex post bad luck at the firm in the current period need not induce workers to leave if it is believed that next period the firm's contract will again offer the previous competitive expected utility to a pool of workers of undiminished size. Add to this the possibility that other firms will give first preference to workers who were original members of their pools.

[8]Fischer neglects this aspect of Azariadis' contracts, but his results are thereby affected only in degree, not in kind.

The fixed real wage solution takes some getting used to. If it seems riskier and therefore less attractive than the auction solution, which at least assures every worker an earning job (save in exceptional cases), then it should be noted that the level of the fixed wage may exceed the expected value of the auction wage. The firm is compensated by the resulting increase in the size of the attracted labor pool which can be employed in states requiring maximum hiring. Keep in mind also that the Azariadis firm hires beyond the cash flow maximizing level (in each state that it can do so) in order to increase the size of the labor pool attracted to it.

Nevertheless, this constancy of the real wage gives way when some of the assumptions are relaxed. The firm's neutrality toward risk is a frequently cited example. As shown by Blinder, the introduction of worker holdings of unindexed wealth would also make a difference. Azariadis himself emphasizes the strong role played by the assumption of total immobility over the life of the implicit contract--an uncomfortable assumption if it is precisely long-run contracts that are the best candidates for indexation. It would be interesting to see contingent wage commitments introduced into an intertemporal model of job search--on-the-job search or out-of-work search.

A crucial assumption is of the workers' trust that the firm will honor the contract. If the workers cannot see that the firm's state requires the number of layoffs that the firm claims, they may distrust a contract expressed in terms of such uncertifiable states. Using employment rather than the underlying state as a variable eligible for wage indexation leads to a different maximization problem. Some results concerning optimal employment contingent contracts are derived in the Appendix.

One of these is that, in cases which I believe to be normal, the real wage is lower (at any given general price level) the larger the unemployment rate at the firm.[9] It is just as we always thought--prior to the advent of state-contingent contract theory! This intuitive finding is based on the belief that the firm will hire a worker (in its predetermined labor pool) with greater probability the lower the real wage; and the proportionate increase in the employment rate induced by a one dollar concession in the real wage, hence the associated proportionate rise in the probability of being hired, is greater the larger the unemployment rate that would occur without any real wage concession.

The assumption (mine, at least) is that while sophisticated contracts will index money wage rates to the money price level (in some way), the most sophisticated of these will index the wage also to various real contingencies both within and without the firm. It is only a very rough approximation to assume,

---

[9] Another proposition, concerning "escalation," is taken up in the next section.

as Fischer does, that the money wage is indexed only to the money price level in the voluntary "indexed economy."

3.   Will equilibrium indexing (once established) nullify monetary policy?

I leave til last the perilous issue of social efficiency and the consequent role for public intervention existing in the kinds of economy under discussion. First, I simply suppose that it would be desirable to call on monetary policy to moderate the employment fluctuations that result from certain unanticipated shocks (for example, supply shocks). The question arises, however, whether monetary policy will be effective in that task when contracts are indexed in the bilaterally optimal way.

Recent discussions, including that by Fischer, presume that optimal contracts will be in "real" terms, making the money wage a linear homogeneous function of the consumer price level. The conclusion drawn from that premise is that changes in the supply of money, even unanticipated ones, will have equiproportional effects on money wages and prices and "consequently" zero effects on output and employment--at least to a satisfactory approximation. Although that thesis may turn out to be passingly accurate as an empirical prediction, it grows out of a projection of the voluntary indexed economy that seems to me to be inappropriate in important respects.

Let us tentatively accept the homogeneity premise of full escalation. It is nevertheless implausible that short-term wage commitments will be so indexed or indeed indexed at all, as I suggest above. Furthermore, many goods prices may similarly be predetermined and unindexed over the selling season to which current price lists apply.[10] Only the longer run commitments regarding wages and prices pose enough risk so that their reduction by indexing is worth the effort and complexity. One would suppose monetary policy to have some leverage over output and employment in an incompletely indexed economy if one supposes it to have such leverage in the same economy when the practice of indexation is not yet widely developed.

Another objection is that those contracts which are, in fact, indexed would be likely to make the money wage in the current quarter a function of the price level (and other nominal magnitudes) in the previous quarter, not in the current one. Most price level indices are at least a month old when first reported, and are then revised a month later. Implementing the consequent wage adjustment also takes time. Furthermore, many firms would not want to collect and process these data and to recalibrate their paychecks each month however "current" or laggard the data. Thus, an increase in the supply of money would

---

[10]This is the principal point in Phelps and Taylor (1976). Some difficulties in indexing prices to monetary conditions in a neutralizing way are implied below.

not be immediately offset, in the manner of Sargent-Wallace (1975), by an employment-preserving rise of current money wage rates and prices. For some months, wages (and perhaps prices as well) would behave predeterminedly owing to the indexation lags.

A further dispute with this thesis goes to an old theoretical issue. It seems to me that juxtaposing Phelps-Winter (1970) firms, each of which has a market limited by the size of aggregate demand, with the notion of a pool of labor to be called up or laid off at an above-market-clearing wage (indexed or not), as demand prompts, would allow unanticipated changes in the money supply to affect output and employment, despite escalation of money wage rates in proportion to the price level. In such a model, engineering a rise of output by monetary policy does not depend on a rise of money prices relative to money wage rates; it may suffice that the typical firm underestimates the rise in prices by its close competitors. (This may be a tall assumption if the rise in the general price level is immediately known.)

Another point in this brief for monetary policy is that, with workers initially unable to move between the capital goods and consumer goods industries without incurring information gathering and other frictional costs, it seems unnecessary for a rise in employment that the monetary authorities raise consumer goods prices relative to money wage rates. In an indexed economy of this frictional sort, is there any reason why an increase in the money supply (in response to an unanticipated downward shock to aggregate demand), the first impact of which is only to raise (flexible) capital goods prices and not consumer goods prices, will produce a chain effect—via indexation linkages—that raises general money wage rates and the general price level (in relation to expected future prices) by just enough as to nullify the incipient stimulus to production in the capital goods sector? I do not see how the mere escalation of money wage rates to consumer goods prices would block the desired expansion of capital goods sector employment.

I return to the homogeneity premise itself, that optimally indexed contracts will display full (100 percent) escalation to the general price level; that the contracted money wage rate is proportional to the general price level (at least at a constant general real wage level), given the real prices of outputs and inputs "facing" the firm, which are a part of the description of the individual firm's "state" (to which the money wage may also be indexed). Despite Azariadis' request that we take as given the general price level, so we may not ask what would happen if all money prices were raised, it is correctly deduced (by Fischer and others) from the Azariadis equations that if utility depends only upon the real wage and leisure (and literally nothing else), then optimal contracts will specify the real wage to be paid by the firm in each of its states (which are also expressed in real terms).

Regarding the implied escalator clause, Azariadis himself makes the point that in a more general model the expected real rate of interest would figure in the utility function; if that variable, to which the wage is not easily indexed, is positively correlated with the level of money prices, then we should expect less than full escalation to the general price level. Blinder introduces the additional factor of the workers' net position with respect to (unindexed) monetary assets and liabilities; net debtors would want less than full escalation in order to stabilize their real wage plus (expected?) net real capital gains.

There is a general point to be made against the "optimality" of full escalation if indexation must be "second-best" owing to the infeasibility of indexing the money (and therefore real) wage rate to the (real) state in all its dimensions. Suppose that, because of practical difficulties of certifying the true state of the world, money wage rates at a firm are indexable only to easily measurable variables, in particular the general price level and perhaps also the employment level at the individual firm. Then, the general price level might constitute a proxy for certain excluded variables which would call for a lower real wage were the latter indexable to them. In that case, presumably, money wage rates would not be fully escalated to the price level because on average it is desired to have a somewhat reduced real wage rate when the general price level is high.[11]

Even if the foregoing is correct, it still does not follow that monetary policy will make a difference for the fluctuation of employment in response to supply shocks (or, for that matter, to demand shocks). Might not bilaterally optimal implicit contracts index directly to indices of monetary policy in such a way that the employment effect of monetary policy reactions (at least the normal and predicted reactions) to unanticipated shocks was rendered nil?

I think it can be agreed that clever second-best indexers will devise ways to index to monetary indicators which can be seen by workers to provide more dependably the real wage, or, more accurately, the utility that the optimum implicit contract would produce in each "state" (or employment situation) in which workers and firms find themselves. But these indexers will not want to insulate totally real wages and employment from monetary policy insofar as the latter operates to signal (or proxy for) elements of the state that are not easily measured or observed.

Moreover, such neutralizing indexation of wages and prices to monetary indicators, if desired, would encounter several difficulites: the problem of temporary versus permanent changes of the money supply; the distinction

---

[11]This point is developed further in the Appendix.

between "autonomous" and "demand induced" money supply; the distinction between a change of the supply resulting from systematic policy responses and that resulting from random vicissitudes in central bank intentions; and so on. The fallacy of (misplaced) concreteness should warn us against supposing that actors in the real world will dare to experiment with such (perversely) ultra-sophisticated indexation merely because some analyst can devise the optimum contract for a model with a simple structure (M1 or maybe M2, but not more) and all probability distributions known. Therefore, I doubt that such indexing to monetary policy indicators, if it develops at all, will reduce the leverage of monetary policy over output and employment much beyond the reduction caused by (optimal) escalation.

4. Ought the central bank to moderate "contractual" layoffs in some states?

Consider first the state contingent contracts of Azariadis. If we agree to impose "imperfections" in the goods markets, such as predetermined product prices, then some states will be accompanied by layoffs (and new entrants not hired), not because of reduced productivity that might justify a general decline in employment, but, rather, because of reduced aggregate demand. Surely there will exist states in which unemployment is sufficiently large for this reason that ex post profit and expected utility would be increased by a small improvement of the state, the resultant rise of employment being effected, therefore, by monetary policy.[12] It follows, I presume, that a monetary policy which system-atically moderates deep slumps in employment attributable to unanticipated shocks to aggregate demand will secure an improvement of ex ante expected utility and expected profits.

Layoffs attributable to supply shocks present a trickier problem in the state contingent framework. Azariadis presupposes that firms (for reasons, if any, requiring examination) pay no private unemployment compensation. Yet his model, taken literally, implies that firms have sufficient incentive to establish their own private unemployment compensation programs. The firm's first-best contract offers private unemployment compensation equal to the real wage, and promises to hire the whole labor pool or to hire up to the point where marginal product of labor when multiplied by every worker's (equal) marginal utility of income equals the disutility of working instead of staying home.[13] There is, in any reasonable sense, full employment in every state; in no state is there possible a Pareto improvement. If there is a supply shock causing layoffs

---

[12]I specify "expected" utility, even ex post, because the distribution of the total layoffs over persons is determined by a random drawing.

[13]The particulars of these two results obtain if utility is additively separable in leisure and income.

157

in the contractual amount, then monetary policy would achieve nothing. Note that if leisure is preferred to working, the unemployed are the lucky ones.

These fully optimal contracts appear to be enforceable, free from moral hazard, because anyone refusing to work would be dropped from the firm's pool and would then have to incur the set-up cost of moving to another firm. ("If you were sick, you should have phoned in to relinquish your compensation claim for the day.") Yet almost nowhere do we observe contracts effectively guaranteeing income. That may be because employers have not widely perceived its advantages to them. More likely, the model is in need of extensions.

Pending these alterations, I will offer two thoughts. In the real world, unemployment produces various external diseconomies, including the public unemployment compensation intended to moderate them, while firms making hiring decisions consider mainly the private cost of hiring labor, not the (lesser) social cost. So there is a prima facie case for monetary policies that cushion unemployment from serious supply shocks. Second, is there not something disturbing about contracts which are Pareto-optimal ex ante, with regard to every worker's expected utility, if some workers will suffer unemployment and low utility ex post? Suppose the contracts are for life and the supply shock is recognized to be permanent. Should an individual be permitted to gamble his career for a sufficiently greater expected income?

Now consider the employment contingent contracts studied in the Appendix. The state is unobservable by workers. (Unemployment compensation is omitted.) Contracts index the money wage to the firm's employment rate and to the general price level. In some cases, at least, the real wage is a rising function of employment because, when the firm's demand for labor falls, a fall in the real wage serves to moderate the resulting rise in the probability of being laid off. But, this schedule shifts down with a rise in the price level because, under suitable monetary policies, such a price rise signals supply shocks which, if they had been observed by workers, would have caused them to accept a lower than usual real wage (at each level of employment) in order to moderate the greater than usual probability of being unemployed. The desirability of a monetary policy that allows a rise in the price level in response to an estimated supply shock, and the greater desirability of a policy that magnifies the price rise and thus amplifies the signal is that it accomplishes some appropriate real wage reduction directly, rather than exclusively via reduced employment, and thus it increases both profit and expected utility.

While the analysis of employment contingent contracts is very difficult, the message is simple. Sophisticated contractors will not escalate fully their money wage rates to the general price level if the monetary authorities are known to permit and to encourage a rise in prices when raw material supplies contract. Further, the central bank ought to follow that policy, if contractors will count on it, and accordingly not adopt full escalation.

There is another point that might usefully be made if it might be assumed that firms have static or dynamic monopoly power in product markets. Then, the size of the employment gain from a dollar reduction of the firm's real wage depends both on how steeply the marginal physical product of labor declines with employment and on how steeply the firm's (optimal) relative price must decline with the rise in sales. If all firms and workers were to find themselves in the same boat of high unemployment, they would, if they could, enter into a binding agreement to accept a still lower real wage than each firm's workers would agree to accept if they and the firm were acting alone. For, if they all marched in step, then, at no firm (roughly speaking) would the predictable employment effect be diminished by an associated fall in that firm's relative price. If that is correct, then it can be said that, from a social or collective viewpoint, workers are trapped (or may sometimes be trapped) in a situation of excessive unemployment because of a kind of "prisoners' dilemma" arising from the lack of opportunities for concerted wage policy. The answer to that dilemma is a decision on the part of the central bank to raise the price level in lieu of that wage policy.

These points regarding employment contingent wage behavior are strongly reminiscent of Keynes' cryptic, yet central, remark in his General Theory to the effect that there exist circumstances in which a real wage reduction that no worker nor union of workers would seek through a unilateral reduction of the money wage would be accepted knowingly and gratefully by all if there were a rise in the general price level.

APPENDIX
Employment Contingent Wage Contracts
Guillermo A. Calvo and Edmund S. Phelps

The existing theory of wage and employment contracts postulates perfect information about the possible states of nature and their probability distribution. In this note, we discuss some implications of a contrasting assumption. We show, among other things, that under imperfect information monetary policy may become an effective instrument for economic stabilization.

Let us first briefly recall the elements of Azariadis' (1975) theory. Workers are perfectly mobile between firms ex ante, i. e., before the state is known, but immobile ex post. Each worker positions himself at a firm where the wage and employment prospects give him the highest expected utility. Workers are homogeneous in all respects and the probability of employment at a firm is the same for everyone who has selected that firm. Thus, if m is the size of the firm's labor pool and n (s) is its employment when state s occurs, each worker's probability of being employed in that state is [n (s) / m]. Firms, which are price takers on the product side, offer wage and employment contracts which maximize expected profits subject to the constraint that workers' expected utility be equal to the maximum offered by other firms.

If we denote by v (s) the real wage to be paid in state s, then expected profits is given by

$$(1) \quad E_s \ f \ [\ n \ (s) \ , s] \ - v \ (s) \ n \ (s),$$

where f (·) is the firm's production function multiplied by the relative price of the firm's output in terms of wage goods. The expected utility constraint is given by

$$(2) \quad E_s \ u \ [\ v \ (s) \ ] \ \frac{n \ (s)}{m} = k \ .$$

The left side of (2) is the representative worker's expected utility under the simplifying assumption that the utility function can be scaled so that the utility derived from being unemployed is zero; function u (·) is a von Neumann-Morgenstern utility index.

If each possible s, once it has occurred, is identifiable, then it makes sense to draw contracts in terms of [n (s) , v (s)], an optimal contract being, therefore, one that maximizes (1) subject to (2), and $0 \leq n(s) \leq m$ for all s. Furthermore, if, as Azariadis assumes, there are "prohibitive" costs in breaking a contract, workers would be assured that those commitments will be honored ex post. The story is consistent.

We turn now to a case of imperfect information. Suppose that, while firms are perfectly informed about s, workers have no direct information about s--they observe only v and n--or, if w is the nominal wage and p the money price of wage goods, that workers can observe w, p, and n. (This is admittedly an extreme example of the class of situations in which the firm is "better" informed than workers.)

In such a setting, workers do not need to know the distribution of s in order to calculate their expected utility. The joint distribution of n and v will suffice; that can, in principle, be calculated once [n (s), v (s)] and m are determined. Thus, Azariadis' optimal contract for the perfect information case would, if adopted by firms, produce the same expected utility calculable on the basis of the induced distribution of n and v, as was calculable under perfect information. Moreover, that contract would be optimal in the case of imperfect information too if firms were bound to honor it ex post. It is at this point that new elements emerge.

How, in this case, would workers discover that a firm is breaking such a contract? Based on his assumptions, Azariadis showed that under perfect information an optimal contract has $v(s) = \bar{v}$, a constant, and n (s) varying with s. But, when the workers are ignorant of s, the firm can change n (s), arguing that the state is s', for example, instead of s. Would it be profitable to do so? The answer is yes, at least in the short run. To see this, let λ be the Lagrange multiplier corresponding to (2), and differentiate the Lagrangian with respect to n (s). The first order condition associated with an optimal contract is then, at an interior optimum,

$$(3) \quad f_n [n(s), s] - \bar{v} + \frac{\lambda}{m} u(\bar{v}) = 0 ,$$

where $f_n \equiv \partial f / \partial n$; in normal circumstances, $\lambda > 0$. Hence, given $\bar{v}$, the marginal productivity of labor is different ex post from the wage rate (if $u(\bar{v}) > 0$, for instance, $f_n < \bar{v}$). Thus, there is room for the firm to increase its profits by employing a different number of workers from that in Azariadis' contracts. Consequently, if workers cannot find out about s, it would be to the advantage of the firm, in general, to depart from the Azariadis contract.

This argument suggests that a contract would better be drawn up in such a way that it is possible for workers to monitor it ex post. Because they are observable by the workers in the case under analysis, w, n, and p should be the variables in terms of which a contract is expressed. Suppose, first, that the government varies the money supply to hold constant the price level. In this case, contracts might just as well be drawn in terms of v and n.[14] We will analyze the case where v is made a function of n, i. e., v = h (n) for some function h.

We will also assume that for each state s the firm maximizes profits subject to h (n). In other words, n (s) = n*(s; m, h) where[15]

(4) f [n*(s; m, h), s] - h [n*(s; m, h)] n*(s; m, h)

$$= \underset{0 \leq n \leq m}{\text{Max}} \quad [f (n, s) - h (n) n] \ .$$

This assumption would be fully justified if the firm's horizon did not extend beyond one period. With a multiperiod horizon, the impact of present policies on the estimated future joint distribution of v and n would have to be taken into account.

An optimal contract is some function h* (n) such that it solves the following problem:

(5) $\underset{s}{\text{Max E}}$ f [n*(s; m, h), s] - h [n*(s; m, h)] n*(s;m,h)

subject to

$$\underset{s}{\text{E u}} \ [h (n*(s; m, h))] \ \frac{n*(s; m, h)}{m} \ = \ k \ .$$

Thus, the function h (·) is to be optimally chosen, taking into account the firm's resulting ex post employment policy.

The full characterization of h* (·) is not a simple analytical matter. Here we will be content to show that: (i) for every (s,s') such that n*(s; m, h) >

---

[14] It is true that m, the pool of workers, can be entered into the contract, but we prefer to let it be determined by a condition like (2). That is to say, m is determined by the equilibrium condition that expected utility is equal in all firms.

[15] In order to ensure uniqueness of n*, we define it as the highest n among those that solve the maximum problem in (4). Notice that that will be the employment level chosen by the firm in any solution of problem (5) below if the utility attained when employed is always larger for the worker than that when unemployed.

$n^*(s'; m, h) > 0$, $h [n^*(s; m, h)] \geq h [n^*(s'; m, h)]$ if $\partial f_n(n,s) / \partial s \geq 0$ for all n (or $\leq$ for all n); and that (ii) there exist cases where the last inequality is strict (i. e., $>$) for optimal h (i.e., for h^*). Statement (i) says simply that for any function h a larger employment will be associated with a higher or equal real wage if a larger s always "shifts out" (or always "shifts in") the marginal labor productivity schedule. Statement (ii) is the more interesting. It asserts that one can find cases where in an optimal contract a larger employment implies a larger real wage, proving that a constant real wage contract is not optimal in general.

Statement (i) is an immediate consequence of (4). In particular, when $0 < n^* < m$, i. e., when the solution to (4) is interior and h is continuously differentiable, (i) can be verified by implicit differentiation of the first order condition involved in (4).

In order to prove (ii), let us consider the following example. Workers are risk neutral and the technology is

$$(6) \quad f(n, s) = \begin{cases} A(s) n, & 0 \leq n \leq 1 ; \\ A(s), & n \geq 1, \end{cases}$$

where $A(s)$ is positive and increasing with s. We further suppose that s can take only two values: s_1 and s_2, $s_2 \geq s_1$.

Assume now, contradicting statement (ii), that all optimal contracts have a constant $\bar{v}$, (i. e., $h^*(n) \equiv \bar{v}$). Expected utility would then be $\bar{v} \, E \, n(s)$ and, recalling that the firm maximizes ex post profits,

$$(7) \quad \text{expected utility} = \begin{cases} \bar{v} & \text{if } \bar{v} \leq A(s_1) ; \\ \bar{v} P(s_2) & \text{if } A(s_1) < \bar{v} \leq A(s_2) ; \\ 0 & \text{if } A(s_2) < \bar{v}, \end{cases}$$

where $P(s_2)$ is the probability of state s_2. Thus, if k in equation (2) is set higher than $A(s_1)$, we can ensure, by (7), that $\bar{v} > A(s_1)$; hence, (2) will read

$$(8) \quad \bar{v} P(s_2) = k .$$

Under these circumstances, the firm will be operated ($n > 0$) in state s_2 if

$$(9) \quad A(s_2) > \frac{k}{P(s_2)} .$$

Let us assume $A(s_1) < k$ and (9) hold; as argued above, the firm will be operated only if s_2 turns up. Consequently, by (8) and (9), $n = \min(m, 1)$ for $m > 0$ and

(10)   expected profit $= [A(s_2) - \dfrac{k}{P(s_2)}] \ P(s_2) \ m$ if $0 < m \leq 1$.

By (6), the maximum expected profit in this case is obtained at

(11) $m = 1$.

We will now show that there is some $\underline{v} < \bar{v}$ and $0 < n_o < 1$ such that a contract like the one depicted in Figure 1 yields higher expected utility and profit.

Taking $0 < \underline{v} < A(s_1)$, we ensure positive quasi-rents in state s_1 as long as $n_o > 0$. On the other hand, when s_2 occurs, the firm will not opt for the lower wage if n_o is such that

(12) $[A(s_2) - \underline{v}] \ n_o < A(s_2) - \bar{v}$.

Under the present assumptions, there exists $n_o > 0$ satisfying (12) because the right-hand side is positive. It is now straightforward to check that the modified contract is associated with larger expected utility and profit, which contradicts the optimality of having a constant v.

Under the assumptions of the counter example, it can also be shown that there is an optimal contract of the form indicated in Figure 1.

The supposition above is that monetary policy keeps constant the general price level p--by price stabilizing transactions in goods, if necessary. We now turn briefly to the consequences of alternative monetary policies.

It might be thought that the above monetary policy would make the "supply of money" a sufficient indicator of the state s and that, consequently, firms could and would index w (and n) by the money supply instead of by n, thus restoring Azariadis' contract.

Matters of lags and money supply measurement aside, there are two difficulties with that view. One is that, for the above analysis, the state s can be taken to be a vector of real shocks (as measured, for example, by all real materials prices and relative goods prices). Hence, the money supply would not generally disclose variations in s in a way that would reflect adequately their impacts upon every firm's f (n, s). For simplicity, however, we shall restrict the remaining discussion to an economy with a one-dimensional s (such as the real price of some material input).

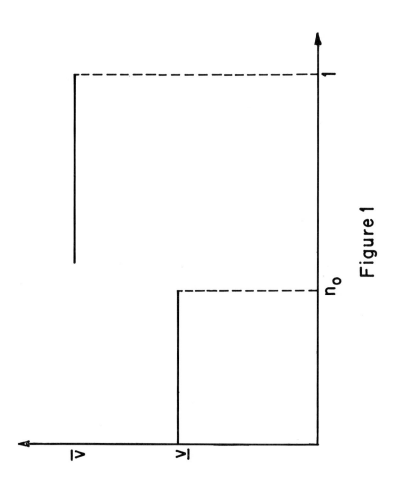

Figure 1

165

The second difficulty is that changes in the money supply may be attributable to a "velocity shock" (liquidity preference) rather than to the "real shock" measured by s. To take a simple case, let

(13a) $\quad M = p^o \, L \, [Y \, (s), s] \; z, \quad L_Y > 0, L_s > 0, z > 0 \; ;$

(14) $\quad Y \, (s) = \sum_j f^j \, [n^j \, (s), s], \quad f_n^j > 0, \; f_s^j > 0, \; s > 0 \, ,$

where z is the velocity variable and Y (s) is interpretable as aggregate output when (real) state s occurs. Then, the money supply, M, constitutes a "signal" not of s alone but, rather, of L ($\cdot$) z. The latter contains also the "noise" from z which may vary independently of s.

If money policy fixed M instead and the price level adjusted in such a way that

(13b) $\quad M^o = p \, L \, [Y \, (s), s] \; z,$

then p would constitute the same noisy signal as did M when p was fixed.

Under either policy, it is likely that contracts specifying v and n will give little weight to M, p, and M/p, as we have modeled them, if the variance of z is sufficiently large and the correlation between z and s sufficiently small.

Suppose now that the central bank can perfectly forecast z and let monetary policy make

(15) $\quad M = \beta \, z, \; \beta > 0 \, .$

If Y (s) is increasing in s, then p will be decreasing in s and will therefore constitute a perfect signal of s. Now, if s is indeed one-dimensional, firms could adopt the Azariadis contract—if they did so, no firm would find it profitable to deviate from it—and the opportunity for a welfare gain (in part from larger employment in poor states) is clear. If the state is in fact multidimensional, Azariadis' contracts are impractical (as we argued above). But, firms could write contracts indexing v by both n and p, so as to take advantage of those elements of s which are signaled by p. To illustrate the nature of this advantage, we refer to the previous two-state example. If the policy in (15) is followed, and firms index v by n in the manner previously analyzed, then p would be a decreasing function of s. Hence, the firm could index w by p instead of by n (for example, by setting $\frac{w}{p} = \bar{v}$ if s_2 and $\frac{w}{p} = \underline{v}$ if s_1) in such a way that, since this variation of v is independent of n, the firm could operate at "full employment" (n = m) in both states and thus increase both expected profits and utility. Previously, the monopsony effect of larger n upon v was a bar to full employment in the poorer state.

It is interesting to note that the usefulness of these monetary policies which (merely) neutralize z does not require that the central bank know s. Suppose now that the bank can perfectly forecast s as well as z. Then, every policy function from the class of functions M (s, z), which makes p a one-to-one function of s, performs no better or worse than the semiactivist policy described by (15). In particular, the choice among activist policy functions

(16) $M(s, z) = \beta z \mu(s)$, $\mu'(s) < 0$

makes no difference because $\mu(s)$ only introduces a monotone transformation of the one-to-one relation between p and s.

The choice among such activist monetary policy functions, however, does make a difference if the bank's estimates of z and s are subject to error. It is reasonable conjecture that if z is subject to large errors of forecast and s is not, then, when forecasting small (large) s, the central bank should increase (decrease) M relative to z so as to magnify the expected rise (fall) of p and thus strengthen the ratio of "signal to noise" conveyed by the price level.

REFERENCES

1. Arrow, K. J. Essays in the Theory of Risk-Bearing. Amsterdam: North-Holland Publishing Co., 1970.

2. Azariadis, C., "Implicit Contracts and Underemployment Equilibria," Journal of Political Economy, 83, No. 6, (December 1975), 1183-1202.

3. Baily, M. N., "Wages and Employment under Uncertain Demand," Review of Economic Studies, XLI (1), No. 125, (January 1974), 37-50.

4. Gordon, D. F., "A Neo-Classical Theory of Keynesian Unemployment," in The Phillips Curve and Labor Markets, (eds. K. Brunner and A. H. Meltzer), Carnegie-Rochester Conference Series on Public Policy, Vol. 1, Amsterdam: North-Holland, (1976), 65-97.

5. Okun, A. M., "Inflation: Its Mechanics and Welfare Costs," Brookings Papers on Economic Activity, Washington, D. C.: The Brookings Institution, 6 (1975:2), 351-401.

6. Phelps, E. S., and Taylor, J. B., "Stabilizing Powers of Monetary Policy under Rational Expectations," Journal of Political Economy, 84, No. 6, forthcoming December 1976.

7. Phelps, E. S., and Winter, S. G. Jr., "Optimal Price Policy under Atomistic Competition," in Microeconomic Foundations of Employment and Inflation Theory, (eds. E.S. Phelps, et al.), New York: W.W. Norton, 1970.

8. Sargent, T. J., and Wallace, N., "'Rational' Expectations, the Optimal Monetary Instrument, and the Optimal Money Supply Rule," Journal of Political Economy, 83, No. 2, (April 1975), 241-254.

9. Shavell, S., "Sharing Risks of Deferred Payment," Journal of Political Economy, 84, No. 1, (February 1976), 161-168.

168

INDEXING THE ECONOMY THROUGH FINANCIAL INTERMEDIATION:
A COMMENT

Michael Parkin
University of Western Ontario

Blinder's paper presents an interesting and rigorously developed analysis predicting that two types of nonexistent world will exist! It is shown that wage and bond indexation are substitutes for each other, and that we should either observe one or the other but not both and not neither. He goes on to suggest that, as there is nothing wrong with the basic idea of the simple model which leads to these predictions--namely that hedging against inflation is a sensible thing to do--it is necessary to find reasons why we observe little indexation of any kind. His essential idea is that households are interested in indexing to a broad consumer basket, while firms are interested in indexing to a basket more representative of their own output.

To overcome the problems which arise from having both sides of the market interested in indexing to different baskets, he suggests that we need to establish a National Inflation Mutual Fund (NIMF) which would be capable of providing the securities with the properties of specific indexes on the firm side and a general index on the household side.

My remarks on this paper fall into two parts. First, I want to comment on the suggested reason why we do not observe very much indexation and, secondly, to ask the question why, if an NIMF is such a good idea, has the market not produced it?

The argument that firms would like to index to a basket of commodities close to their own output while households would prefer to index to a general consumer basket is superficially attractive but I suspect wrong. The suggestion arises from a failure to distinguish between variability and predictability of prices. In general, contracts--whether to set wages, selling prices of output, or borrowing and lending of funds--typically run for a finite period. At the end of that period, all bets are off as to what the new agreed relative price will be, and a new contract is drawn up. The frequency with which contracts are renewed and relative prices adjusted is clearly a matter for optimal choice and is clearly going to depend on the relative importance and frequency of real shocks. Indexing has nothing whatsoever to do with the changes in relative prices which it becomes necessary to renegotiate from time to time as a result of real shocks. It is designed purely to ensure that, during a period for which a relative price has been agreed between two parties, inflation does not change that relative price. When seen in this way, it becomes immediately apparent that there is no point in a firm attempting to index wages or its bond yields to an output-specific price index. To do that would be to build relative price changes into a contract. Now there is no reason why economic agents should not write such contracts if they want to and if it is Pareto superior for both parties. However, that has nothing to do with the indexation issue. Indexation is designed precisely to ensure that relative prices which have been agreed at the time the contract was drawn up are maintained throughout the duration of the contract, independently of the rate of inflation. Given that that is the objective, it follows that both parties to a contract should be interested in indexing on a broad basket of consumer goods which represents generalized purchasing power.

The mystery remains as to why indexed contracts are so uncommon. Here the distinction between variability and predictability becomes critical. Presumably, agents are interested in entering into contracts which provide a formula for setting a nominal price for the item being traded which maintains a relative price as close to the equilibrium (market clearing in the case of competitive, organized markets and profit-maximizing or utility-maximizing in the case of monopolized markets) as possible. It is by no means obvious that linking a contract to a generalized price index achieves this outcome. If most firms are not pursuing such a procedure and one firm considers adopting an indexed contract, it still becomes necessary for that firm to guess what nominal prices other firms will call. It then has to set its nominal price at a level such that, when raised by what it guesses the index is going to be, its real prices are still in line with those being set by others.

If, on the other hand, most firms are entering into indexed contracts so that an individual firm knows that whatever happens to the index will be reflected in every other firm's prices (in money terms), then it will have more confidence in adopting an index itself. The central problem then is having a sufficiently large number of the firm's competitors operating the same pricing and wage setting rules. A bit more concretely and lengthily, suppose that most firms are not indexing and guess the inflation rate wrongly, thereby setting their prices too low. Suppose an individual firm that does index. It is clear that its relative price may be correct in terms of the requirements of full equilibrium but be very wrong in terms of the short-run adjustment process that results from searching individuals seeking and doing business with the lowest cost sellers (highest price buyers). The individual firm in this case would presumably attract too many workers if its wages were indexed, and sell too little output if it had entered into some kind of indexed arrangement for the price of its output. If, conversely, it had simply gone along with the market average expectation of inflation and raised its prices by roughly what others were raising

170

theirs, it would have maintained its position vis-à-vis its competitors; at the same time, it would have shared with its competitors the general excess supply (demand) situation that would have arisen from every firm's having guessed the inflation rate wrongly.

I now turn to the question why, if an NIMF is such a good idea, has the market not provided it? The basic answer to this question is not to be found in Blinder's paper. In my view it resides in the fact that during an increase in inflation neither bond yields nor equity yields rise to reflect that increase in inflation, and they fail to do so for very good reasons. The essential explanation (offered as an untested hypothesis but readily testable) is that the source of inflation is typically not simply a neutral fully anticipated rise in the rate of monetary expansion but rather a rise in the rate of monetary expansion induced by certain distorting fiscal policies which themselves mitigate against full adjustments in interest rates. The first source of the failure of interest rates to adjust fully is the very process whereby monetary control is typically exercised. Until the recent adoption of "monetarism," all countries controlled the money supply by controlling nominal interest rates and moving those nominal rates to operate on the demand for money function. Political pressure typically prevented interest rates from rising to levels sufficiently high to contain monetary expansion. Hence, nominal rates being the proximate targets of monetary policy were held down at precisely those times when inflation was becoming most troublesome.

Equity yields suffer partly from the fact that they are assets which compete in portfolios with bonds, and unattractive bond yields make the demand for equities greater than what they would otherwise have been, thereby raising their prices and depressing their market yields. However, additionally and more importantly perhaps, the fact that corporate income taxes are not indexed means that during a rise in the inflation rate corporate real net-of-tax profits take a dip. These two factors taken together constitute then a sufficient reason why asset yields will not rise to reflect inflation. They also explain why financial institutions which provide the kind of indexation that an NIMF would provide do not emerge. They also suggest that such an NIMF would, like all other nationalized industries, lose money!

ON THE INDEXATION OF CONTRACTS UNDER UNCERTAINTY:
A COMMENT ON THE BLINDER PAPER

Clifford W. Smith, Jr.*
University of Rochester

In his paper, "Indexing the Economy Through Financial Intermediation," Blinder argues that workers would demand indexed wage contracts, that firms would be willing to supply indexed contracts, and that the only problem is that workers prefer indexation based on general consumer prices while firms prefer indexation based on industry product prices. Blinder then demonstrates that indexed bonds are a substitute for indexed wage contracts and suggests a "National Inflation Mutual Fund" which would simultaneously reduce the apparent problems and satisfy the demands of workers and firms.

In this note, I would like to reformulate some of Blinder's discussion to avoid some misleading implications about the behavior of individuals and firms under uncertainty. In the process, some questions arise with respect to the conclusion that risk-averse workers will demand indexed contracts and that firms will choose to supply them.

The Supply of Indexed Wage Contracts

In his discussion of the firm, Blinder assumes that the firm is either "risk averse" or "risk neutral." This is not the most productive way to examine the behavior of the firm under uncertainty. Logically, such a statement suggests either an anthropomorphic view of the firm, or that the behavior of the firm can be associated with the preferences of a dominant individual within the firm. The first alternative seems clearly unsatisfactory, and the second presents significant conceptual difficulties, for example, which individual is dominant? Is it the president, the chairman of the board, the treasurer, or someone else? This may be an appropriate model for an owner-managed firm, but then only if the owner has no other assets.[1] However, the modern industrial company with the ownership of its shares spread across many individuals, each holding portfolios of claims, seems to require a different model.

It seems more productive to model the behavior of the firm under uncertainty by assuming that it is managed so as to maximize its market value. That is, whenever a project can be undertaken for which the market valuation is greater

---

*Assistant Professor, Graduate School of Management.

[1] If the owner/manager has other assets and is risk averse, the relevant measure of risk for the decisions regarding the firm will be his marginal risk, i.e., the effect of that decision on his total portfolio.

than the total cost, the project should be accepted since accepting the project increases the value of the firm. Because the market values of these claims result from the collective risk preferences of individuals, it is self-contradictory to assume that individuals are risk averse while assuming firms are "risk neutral" (in the sense used by Blinder).

If the typical individual, the individual whose demands determine asset prices, holds a portfolio of assets, then the appropriate measure of risk is not total risk but marginal risk. For example, given that the appropriate measure of portfolio risk is the variance of return on the portfolio, then the work of Markowitz (1959) suggests that the appropriate measure of risk for an individual security is its covariance with the return on the portfolio. This work was extended by Sharpe (1964), Lintner (1965), Treynor (1961), and Mossin (1966) to provide a general equilibrium theory of asset pricing under uncertainty. Fama and Miller (1972) employ this framework to demonstrate explicitly how value maximizing firms would behave under uncertainty. Given their assumptions of no taxes, bankruptcy costs, or other transactions costs, they show that the firm will accept all projects whose expected returns are greater than the return available in the market to an investment with the same level of marginal risk, i.e., with the same covariance with the market return. Therefore, in a Fama-Miller world, the firm will accept a project with a higher marginal risk only if its expected return is commensurately higher. Notice that the value of the firm is not affected by the level of marginal risk of the projects it accepts, but rather by the difference between the cost and valuation of the project given its marginal risk. Therefore, the firm would be "risk averse" in the sense that it requires a higher expected return to accept a higher risk project, but it is "risk neutral" in the sense that as long as it pays no more than market prices for projects, it would not prefer one level of risk over another. The firm would choose among projects (or wage contracts) based on their effect on the market value of the firm.

I believe the above analysis can replace Blinder's "risk neutral" firm discussion, and with this different interpretation, the rest of his "risk neutral" analysis will follow.

If the Fama-Miller assumptions are relaxed, the owners of the firm are not indifferent to the level of total risk of its assets. If bankruptcy costs are introduced into the model along with a tax exclusion for interest payments on debt, then for a given size firm the managers of the firm will balance the marginal benefit from the tax subsidy on debt against the marginal cost of the increased probability of bankruptcy to determine its optimal debt/equity ratio. If the firm can reduce the variability of return on its assets, thereby reducing the

174

probability of bankruptcy, then it can increase the debt in its capital structure and increase the tax subsidy it receives. In this world, the firm acts as if it were "risk averse." Not only does it, as before, require a higher expected return to accept a higher level of risk, but it is not indifferent to the total risk of its assets; it can increase its market value by reducing its total variability, increasing the debt in its capital structure, and reducing the government's tax claim against the firm.

To examine the effects of indexing wage contracts in this context, it is convenient to separate the firm's projects and contracts into two groups: the wage contract and everything else. Now consider two alternative wage contracts, both with the same expected real wage and the same covariance between the wage payment and the return to the market portfolio (the same marginal market risk). The owners of the firm may not be indifferent between these contracts. If, for one of the contracts, the covariance between the outflows required by the wage agreement are more positively correlated with the net inflows from all the other projects of the firm than for the other contract, then the total variability of the firm's cash flows associated with the acceptance of that contract would be smaller than that associated with the alternative wage contract. With smaller variability in cash flows, the probability of bankruptcy would decrease. Thus, the firm could increase the debt in its capital structure and increase the tax shelter provided through its interest payments. Therefore, the firm would choose that contract which results in the highest market value for the firm.

The question is: Which wage contract is likely to offer these advantages, a more or less indexed contract? If what Blinder calls "demand-pull" inflation occurs, then unanticipated increases in inflation rates will be generally associated with higher cash flows from the firm's nonwage contracts or projects. In this case, a value maximizing firm would prefer a more indexed to a less indexed contract. On the other hand, with "cost-push" inflation, unanticipated increases in inflation rates will be generally associated with lower cash flows from the firm's nonwage contracts or projects. In this case, a value maximizing firm would prefer a less indexed wage contract in order to minimize the variability of the firm's cash flows, reduce expected bankruptcy costs, and allow the firm to increase the debt in its capital structure, thus reducing the government's claim on the firm and increasing its market value.

The above analysis suggests that Blinder–and Shavell (1976), whose results Blinder adopts–employs incorrect variables in the analysis of the supply of indexed wage contracts by firms. The relevant variables for a value maximizing firm in the negotiation of wage contracts are the expected wage rate, the covariance between the wage payments and all other net cash flows of the firm, and the covariance between the wage payments and the market return.

The Demand for Indexed Wage Contracts

It should be noted that in a market without transactions costs, and thus one in which all assets are costlessly marketable, individuals would be indifferent between two wage contracts with the same expected return and marginal risk, even if one contract were indexed more than the other. This is because the individual can enter the capital markets and hedge away this diversifiable risk himself. And, if this transaction is (by assumption) costless, he will be indifferent between reducing the risk through the capital markets and having the firm offer him a contract in which it has reduced some of the residual variation.

If individuals are specifically to demand indexed contracts, they must face positive transactions costs in some market.[2] However, since transactions costs must provide the rationale for the existence of these contracts, some very difficult questions follow. How expensive is it to enforce these contracts? What alternative methods achieve these same ends? What are the costs associated with each alternative?

I believe that indexed wage contracts could be more expensive to enforce than unindexed contracts. This is because (1) the rate of inflation is not directly observable and thus there are expenses incurred in monitoring its estimation,[3] and (2) there is a systematic change engendered in the distribution of nominal wages if contracts are indexed.

Blinder generally considers contracts with a given expected real wage without examining the relationship between the expected nominal wage and expected real wage for different degrees of indexation. Long (1974) has demonstrated that if the marginal distributions of nominal wealth (or of its associated flow, income) and the price level are taken as given, and indexation simply changes the correlation coefficient between nominal wealth and the price level, then indexation not only decreases the variance of real wealth but also decreases expected real wealth.[4] Thus, the existence of two contracts with the same expected real wage, with the first more indexed than the second, implies that the first contract will also have a higher expected nominal wage.

---

[2] A special case which includes sufficient conditions for indexation has been analyzed by Mayers (1972). He considers a market in which assets can be segregated into two exhaustive sets, one containing costlessly marketable assets and the other containing totally nonmarketable assets (i.e., transactions costs in that market are infinite). For example, a contract to sell a worker's claim to his future wage income is unenforceable.

[3] Whether the allegations are true or not, the suggestion that manipulation of the estimates of the rate of inflation by the Federal government for political purposes occurs suggests that the costs of using government figures is not zero.

[4] See also Fama (1972).

This relationship illustrates that there are nonobvious implications of indexation of wage contracts and suggests that an indexed contract with a specified expected real wage is likely to be a very sophisticated instrument. Furthermore, more complex contracts entail higher negotiation costs and generally entail higher enforcement costs; these are costs which both the employer and employee wish to minimize. However, if a simpler instrument is written which specifies the expected nominal wage, then a risk-averse worker may rationally reject the contract if greater indexation is offered. Since this results in a lower expected real wage and a lower variance of the real wage, a worker's preference for the contract would depend on the degree of his risk aversion.

There is one final point affecting both the supply of and demand for indexed wage contracts which I believe has received too little attention. The magnitude of costs, in real terms, which an unindexed contract can impose on either party is directly related to the length of time between recontracting dates. Since there seems to be no externally imposed contract length, the parties involved should change the contract length until the marginal costs of recontracting sooner equal the marginal benefits. Therefore, shortening the length of the contract may be cheaper than incurring those costs imposed by indexation.[5]

Thus, questions involving indexation of wage contracts are essentially empirical, and empirical questions cannot be resolved without empirical evidence. However, there is one observation which is striking—indexation is not prohibited institutionally, yet we do not observe contracts written containing these provisions. This suggests that the costs exceed the benefits.

The Demand for Indexed Bonds

Blinder suggests that indexed bonds are a substitute for indexed wages. However, if the capital market imperfection which leads to the demand for indexed wages is that contracts to sell an individual's claim on future wages are not enforceable (if slavery is illegal), then the presence of a market for indexed bonds provides little aid in removing the residual variation in the individual's portfolio of assets resulting from the unindexed wage contract when his non-human capital is small.

Even if indexed bonds would meet the demand by individuals for risk reduction, the question must be asked: Is the creation of an indexed bond fund the lowest cost way to achieve these ends? The answer to this question is not clear, although Blinder's analysis suggests that an individual's ability to hedge

---

[5] It has been reported that during the German hyperinflation in 1923 some workers were paid twice per day. Presumably the wage rate was changed almost as frequently.

against price level changes is limited; Long (1974) has shown that, using existing assets, these risks can be partially hedged. He analyzes a multi-period world in which there are many consumption goods whose future prices are uncertain, and consumer's investment opportunities include both common stocks and default free bills of different maturities. He demonstrates that, in maximizing the expected utility of consumption over time, an individual forms a portfolio which can be conceptually separated into various funds. In equilibrium, each consumer allocates his wealth among (1) default free bills of every maturity, (2) the "stock market portfolio," and (3) a set of portfolios representing the "closest available substitutes" for claims to future delivery of each of the various consumption goods.[6] Using these funds, the consumer can hedge against price changes in his individual market basket of consumption goods.[7]

Thus, the benefits which would be derived from the creation of an indexed bond mutual fund are similar to the benefits derived from currently available common stock mutual funds. For some investors, such an indexed bond mutual fund would lower the transactions costs of hedging certain risks.

Therefore, the reason why this market for indexed bonds is not currently "open" may be the same reason why so many other conceivable markets are "closed"–the costs of maintaining the market exceed the benefits.

---

[6] Long calls these portfolios "quasi" futures contracts. Note that this result does not depend on the existence of "true" futures contracts. However, if true futures contracts do not exist, the consumer's ability to hedge against changes in any specific commodity price will generally be less than complete.

[7] Note that Blinder's "National Inflation Mutual Fund" does not allow the consumer to hedge against price changes in his specific market basket of goods; NIMF offers a hedge only against price changes in those industries which sold bonds to the fund.

REFERENCES

1. Fama, E. F., "Ordinal and Measurable Utility," in <u>Studies in the Theory of Capital Markets</u>, (ed. M. C. Jensen), New York: Praeger, 1972.

2. Fama, E. F., and Miller, M. <u>The Theory of Finance</u>. New York: Holt, Rinehart and Winston, 1972.

3. Lintner, J., "Securities Prices, Risk, and Maximal Gains from Diversification," <u>Journal of Finance</u>, XX, No. 4, (December 1965), 587-616.

4. Long, J. B., "Stock Prices, Inflation, and the Term Structure of Interest Rates," <u>Journal of Financial Economics</u>, 1, No. 2, (July 1974), 131-170.

5. Markowitz, H. M. <u>Portfolio Selection: Efficient Diversification of Investments</u>. New York: Wiley, 1959.

6. Mayers, D., "Non-Marketable Assets and Capital Market Equilibrium Under Uncertainty," in <u>Studies in the Theory of Capital Markets</u>, (ed. M. C. Jensen), New York: Praeger, 1972.

7. Mossin, J., "Equilibrium in a Capital Asset Market," <u>Econometrica</u>, 34, No. 4, (October 1966), 768-783.

8. Sharpe, W. F., "Capital Asset Prices: A Theory of Market Equilibrium Under Conditions of Risk," <u>Journal of Finance</u>, XIX, No. 3, (September 1964), 425-442.

9. Shavell, S., "Sharing Risks of Deferred Payment," <u>Journal of Political Economy</u>, 84, No. 1, (February 1976), 161-168.

10. Treynor, J. L., "Toward a Theory of Market Value of Risky Assets," unpublished manuscript, 1961.

STRUCTURAL UNEMPLOYMENT AND
THE PRODUCTIVITY OF WOMEN*

Robert J. Gordon
Northwestern University

I. INTRODUCTION

During the past decade the framework of macroeconomic policymaking in the U.S. has been altered by two major developments, both of which appear revolutionary when viewed in the context of policy analyses written in the 1964-66 era. First, the economics profession has been almost universally converted to the "Natural Rate Hypothesis" (NRH), which states that macro policy cannot permanently "buy" lower unemployment and higher output by generating a higher inflation rate. Instead, the unemployment rate is independent of the inflation rate in the long run, and any employment stimulus associated with faster inflation is purely transitory (there remains strong disagreement over the length of the transition). The NRH introduces caution as a new ingredient in policy recommendations, since unemployment cannot be pushed below the natural rate of unemployment without creating an acceleration in the rate of inflation.

The second development, originally proposed by Perry (1970) in a wage equation which denied the NRH, and since then accepted as well by most proponents of the NRH, is a "structural shift" in unemployment, which has caused a rightward shift in the long-run Phillips curve (whether negatively sloped or vertical). Wage change, given expected inflation, appears to display much more stable behavior relative to the unemployment rate of prime-age adult males than to the broader official unemployment rate, which includes teenagers and adult women as well. In a recent test by Wachter (1976), a stable relationship is assumed between wage change and the unemployment rate of males aged 25 to 54; since the assumed (2.9 percent) natural unemployment rate of these prime-age adult males was achieved in both 1956 and 1974, the natural unemployment rate for the aggregate unemployment concept shifted upwards from 4.1 percent, the total rate actually achieved in 1956, to 5.6 percent, the total rate achieved in 1974.

The implications of the "Structural Shift Hypothesis" (SSH) are per-

*A revised (September 1976) version of the paper originally presented at the Conference. The research was supported by the National Science Foundation and benefited from the suggestions and comments of G. Goldstein, D.F. Gordon, Z. Griliches, R.E. Hall, R.E. Lipsey, D.T. Mortensen, A.M. Okun, M. Reder, and M.L. Wachter.

181

vasive. Combining NRH and SSH, one concludes that the U.S. economy could have been safely pushed to an aggregate unemployment rate of 4.1 percent in 1956 without an acceleration in inflation, whereas in 1974 any attempt to stimulate the economy and push the aggregate unemployment rate below 5.6 percent would have accelerated the inflation rate. As long as NRH is valid, unemployment rates below the natural rate cannot be maintained for more than a transition period, implying that published official estimates of the nation's "potential" output at an assumed 4 percent unemployment rate should be scrapped as unrealistic, along with the associated "full employment surplus" series based on hypothetical government revenues and expenditures at 4 percent unemployment.[1] Also rejected as unrealistic are legislative proposals like the 1976 "Humphrey-Hawkins Bill," which proclaims a goal of 3.0 percent unemployment for adults aged 20 and over, far below the 4.5 percent unemployment rate for this group achieved in 1972 and 1974 when prime-age male unemployment was approximately at its "natural rate."

This paper assesses the "welfare cost" of the 1956-1974 structural shift in unemployment. In a previous paper (Gordon, 1973), I evaluated the loss of welfare resulting from a hypothetical increase in the unemployment rate caused by a decline in aggregate demand, taking account not only of the resulting decline in the value of market output but also of the partially offsetting increase in the value of nonmarket activity. A 1 percentage point temporary demand-induced increase in the unemployment rate was estimated to cause a substantial 2.3 percent reduction in the value of total market and nonmarket welfare, but a much smaller 0.7 percent reduction when the 1 percentage point increase in unemployment was assumed to be permanent. The simple "Okun's Law" technique, which associates a 1 percentage point increase in the unemployment rate with a 3.0 percent decline in output, very seriously exaggerates the welfare cost of a permanent shift in unemployment caused by lower aggregate demand.

The welfare effects of a structural unemployment shift depend on the causes of the shift. High unemployment groups--teenagers and women--have substantially increased their share in the labor force at the expense of adult men. The added number of teenagers reflects the "hump" in the U.S. age distribution caused by a high fertility rate between the mid-1940s and early 1960s. If fertility decisions are assumed to be voluntary, and if by the "welfare" of society is meant that of the individuals which comprise it, then a mere change

---

[1] Applying Okun's Law that a 1.5 percentage point increase in the unemployment rate is associated with a 4.5 percent drop in output, the economy's "natural output rate" lies 4.5 percent below the official "potential output" series. The growth rate of "natural output" between 1955 and 1974 is only 3.49 percent per annum, compared to the 3.74 percent annual growth rate of potential output. Similarly, the government's "natural employment surplus" is about $20 billion below the "full employment surplus" and was in deficit continuously throughout the 1970-76 period.

in the age distribution has no welfare consequences, holding constant the wage rate, hours worked, and unemployment rate of each age group. Under these assumptions, the lower per capita income of society during the period when the "hump" cohort is young is a mere phenomenon of aggregation, since the welfare of each individual is unchanged.

The higher number of women in the labor force reflects the voluntary response of women to a variety of stimuli, including technical improvements in contraception, technological innovations which have reduced the time needed to perform a given amount of housework, increased social acceptance of working women, and the substitution effect of higher real wages. Even if each working woman earns less than each man, causing the average wage rate per employee to decline as the share of women in the labor force increases, society may nevertheless benefit if the marginal product of an extra woman (net of the capital investment required to equip her) exceeds the value of her previous home activity. A major task of this paper is to measure the marginal product of market work by females. Do women really produce less than men by a proportion equal to the female-male wage differential, or are female wages held below the "true" female marginal product by economic discrimination?

If the unemployment and wage rates of teenagers, women, and men had all remained unaffected by their increasing shares in the labor force, then social welfare might actually have increased as the result of an upward structural shift in unemployment. Men would be just as well off as before; teenagers would be greater in numbers but individually unaffected; women would have gained by their voluntary shift into market work, and, in addition, their additional woman-hours would have generated government tax revenues which would have allowed tax reductions for those previously in the labor force.

Thus, the case for an adverse welfare effect of an upward structural shift in unemployment rests on the fact that between the mid-1950s and early 1970s, the unemployment rates of teenagers and women have not remained constant, as assumed above, but have increased relative to adult men. Today's teenager is worse off than the teenager of the mid-1950s if there has been a decline in the sum of his "full income" from market work, unemployed time, and home time (including school). The case for an adverse effect of the higher relative unemployment rate of women is less clear, however. The fact that extra women have chosen voluntarily to enter the labor force indicates that the market wage rate, adjusted for the probability of unemployment, still outweighs the value of time at home, leaving intact the deduction that women must have achieved an improvement in welfare by their voluntary shift into market activity.

My basic task is an assessment of the welfare cost (or benefit) of the structural shift which occurred in the U.S. between 1956 and 1974, as a result of the increased labor-force shares of teenagers and women–groups with higher unemployment rates than adult men–and also as a result of a further increase in the teenage and female unemployment rates relative to men. Most of the discussion is conceptual, and the empirical estimates of the welfare cost attempt only to produce suggestive orders of magnitude. As I show, precise calculations are impossible on several issues for which the data do not give strong signals, and on which previous papers have been unable to reach definitive conclusions. For instance, the benefit to society of the shift of one woman from housework to market work requires an estimate of the woman's market productivity, requiring in turn the difficult and controversial allocation of the female-male earnings differential between economic discrimination and "true" differences in productivity. Similarly, the cost to teenagers of higher unemployment depends on the value of learning inherent in experimentation as teenagers shift from job to job.

The policy implications of this study of structural unemployment are less obvious than those of my previous paper (Gordon, 1973) on the welfare costs of a reduction in aggregate demand. In that study, the numerical estimates of the costs of a temporary increase in unemployment were directly relevant to the perpetual debate about the costs of creating a temporary recession in order to achieve the benefits of a lower future inflation rate.[2] The conclusions of the present paper are relevant for the evaluation of two types of policy proposals.

(1)   Some economists still do not believe that the NRH is valid and believe that the costs of the 1956-1974 increase in unemployment from 4.1 to 5.6 percent are sufficiently high to warrant risking a demand stimulus which would push the unemployment rate below 5.6 percent. A demonstration below that the welfare costs of the 1956-1974 structural shift have been negligible or minor could be used as an argument against such a demand stimulus.

(2)   Numerous plans, e. g., manpower training, a better employment service, and public-service employment, have been proposed as uses of government funds which might reduce the natural rate of unemployment. The impetus for these plans comes partly from the widespread feeling that the 1956-1974 increase in the total natural unemployment rate must have imposed substantial costs on society. If the benefits of reversing the structural unemployment shift are judged in what follows to be minor, then the benefit/cost ratio of some or all of the proposed programs may be small.

---

[2] Since the earlier paper was written, James Tobin has pointed out to me my omission of the future welfare loss resulting from the reduction in capital investment which occurs during a temporary recession.

II. THE ANATOMY OF THE STRUCTURAL SHIFT

Table 1 displays the main ingredients of the structural shift which occurred between 1956 and 1974. The labor force is divided by age and sex into four groups. The dividing line by age is set at 25 years, rather than at the traditional boundary of 20 years, because the behavior of the relative unemployment rates and labor-force shares of the group aged 20-24 followed patterns much closer to those of the teenagers than to those of the adults aged 25 years and over.[3]

The contrast in the group unemployment rates is especially interesting, because in each of the two years the unemployment rate of the "super-prime-aged" 35-44 year male group was identical at 2.6 percent. The overall unemployment rate of men 25 years and over fell slightly from 3.07 to 2.98 percent (Table 1, line 1a). Nevertheless, the total unemployment rate rose from 4.13 to 5.58 percent, as a result both of an increase in the unemployment rates and labor-force shares of adult women and young people. The labor-force share of adult women resulted entirely from an increase in their labor-force participation rate (line 2b); the population share of adult women declined as a result of the shift in the age distribution caused by the "hump" in the fertility rate. Young males increased their labor-force share entirely as a result of a higher share of the population (line 3c), while their labor-force participation rate declined slightly (line 2c). The labor-force share of young women was boosted by a substantially higher labor-force participation rate and by a higher population share.

The number of unemployed individuals in a labor-force group (X_i) can be rewritten as the product of the group's unemployment rate (u_i), the ratio of the number of unemployed to the group labor force ($u_i = X_i/F_i$) times the group's labor-force participation rate as a ratio to group population ($f_i = F_i/P_i$) times the group's population (P_i):

$$(1) \quad X_i = \frac{X_i F_i P_i}{F_i P_i} = u_i f_i P_i .$$

The total unemployment rate is the sum of the unemployed individuals in each group ($\sum_i X_i$) divided by the total labor force ($F = fP$):

---

[3]In fact, the 1956-1974 increase in the unemployment rate of women aged 20-24 (51 percent) exceeded the increase for women aged 16-17 (35 percent). For men, the increase in the 20-24 year group (26 percent) was almost identical to that in the 18-19 year group (27 percent). The labor-force shares of both men and women aged 20-24 increased more between 1956 and 1974 (41 and 74 percent, respectively) than did the shares of men and women aged 16-17 (36 and 64 percent, respectively).

Table 1

Unemployment Rates, Labor-Force Participation Rates,
and Population Shares of Major Groups, 1956 and 1974

		1956	1974
1.	**Unemployment Rates (u_i)**		
	a. Males 25+	3.07	2.98
	b. Females 25+	3.95	4.60
	c. Males 16-24	8.60	11.44
	d. Females 16-24	8.43	12.34
	Total	4.13	5.58
2.	**Labor-Force Participation Rates (f_i)**		
	a. Males 25+	.876	.803
	b. Females 25+	.353	.425
	c. Males 16-24	.741	.737
	d. Females 16-24	.444	.564
	Total	.600	.613
3.	**Population Shares (P_i/P)**		
	a. Males 25+	.403	.361
	b. Females 25+	.437	.411
	c. Males 16-24	.072	.110
	d. Females 16-24	.088	.117
	Total	1.000	.999

Source: Calculated from **Handbook of Labor Statistics, 1975**, Tables 3, 4, 61.

$$(2) \quad u = \frac{\sum_i X_i}{F} = \frac{\sum_i u_i f_i P_i}{f\, P}\ .$$

A structural shift in unemployment (ds) is defined as a change in the total unemployment rate when the unemployment rate of a given group, for example u_1, remains fixed. When we differentiate (2) totally, and measure the change in each group unemployment rate (u_i) relative to the employment rate of the base group (u_1), we obtain the following decomposition of the structural shift:

$$(3) \quad ds = \sum_{i=2}^{n} \frac{f_i P_i}{f\, P} u_1\, d\left(\frac{u_i}{u_1}\right) + \sum_{i=1}^{n} \left[\frac{u_i P_i}{P}\, d\left(\frac{f_i}{f}\right) + \frac{u_i f_i}{f}\, d\left(\frac{P_i}{P}\right)\right]\ .$$

Numerical values for each of the terms in (3) for the 1956-1974 structural shift are presented in Table 2. If the unemployment rate of males 25 years and over had remained constant at 3.07 percent between 1956 and 1974, instead of falling from 3.07 to 2.98 percent, and if the relative unemployment rates (u_i/u_1) had retained their 1974 values, the overall unemployment rate in 1974 would have been 5.70 percent, instead of the actual 5.58 percent. This structural shift of 1.57 percentage points (1.57 = 5.70 - 4.13) is decomposed in Table 2 into the contribution of higher group relative unemployment rates (0.92 points, or 58.6 percent of the structural shift); the contribution of the shift in labor-force participation rates towards higher unemployment groups (0.18 points, or 11.5 percent of the shift); and the contribution of the shift in population shares towards higher unemployment groups (0.47 points, or 30.0 percent of the shift).

When we add the contribution to the three terms of each of the four separate demographic groups, we can attribute responsibility to the groups as follows:

	Percentage Points	Share of Structural Shift
Males 25+	-0.36	-22.9
Females 25+	0.35	22.3
Males 16-24	0.77	49.0
Females 16-24	0.81	51.6
	1.57	100.0

Table 2

Decomposition of Sources of Structural Shift in Unemployment, 1956-1974

(All figures are percentages)

1.   1956 Total Unemployment Rate   4.13

2.   Contribution to Higher Unemployment Rate of Increased Group Unemployment Rates Relative to Unemployment Rate of Males 25+:

$$\frac{f_i P_i u_1}{f P} \; d\frac{(u_i)}{u_1'}$$

a.	Males 25+	0.00
b.	Females 25+	0.23
c.	Males 16-24	0.34
d.	Females 16-24	0.35

    0.92

3.   Contribution to Higher Unemployment Rate of Changed Group Labor-Force Participation Rates Relative to Average Labor-Force Participation Rate:

$$\frac{u_i P_i}{P} \; d\frac{(f_i)}{f}$$

a.	Males 25+	-0.18
b.	Females 25+	0.19
c.	Males 16-24	-0.03
d.	Females 16-24	0.20

    0.18

4.   Contribution to Higher Unemployment Rate of Changed Group Population Shares:

$$\frac{u_i f_i}{f} \; d\frac{(P_i)}{P}$$

a.	Males 25+	-0.18
b.	Females 25+	-0.07
c.	Males 16-24	0.46
d.	Females 16-24	0.26

    0.47

5.   Hypothetical 1974 Unemployment Rate with Actual 1974 Values of u_i/u_1, f_i/f, and P_i/P, but 1956 value of u_1 5.70

6.   Actual 1974 Unemployment Rate   5.58

Source: Calculated from Table 1.

188

I conclude that the structural shift has been predominately a phenomenon attributable to the 16-24 year group, with approximately equal contributions within that group of young men and young women. The contribution of adult women has been relatively minor.

III. HOW ROBUST IS THE CONCLUSION THAT THE NATURAL RATE OF UNEMPLOYMENT HAS SHIFTED?

The decomposition of the structural shift in Table 2 does not in itself identify the extent of the increase in the natural unemployment rate (u^N) over the 1956-1974 period. A three-step procedure is required to estimate u^N. First, the rate of growth of the wage rate (w_t) relative to expected inflation (p_t^e) must be tied to a particular unemployment concept (u_{jt}):

$$(4) \quad w_t = a_0 + a_1 u_{jt}^{-1} + p_t^e .$$

Note that in (4) the coefficient on p_t^e is <u>assumed</u> to be unity, thus embodying the NRH. Second, the natural unemployment rate for that group unemployment rate (u_j^N) is calculated from the estimated coefficients of (4):

$$(5) \quad \hat{u}_j^N = \frac{\hat{a}_1}{q^* - \hat{a}_0}$$

where q^* is the long-run productivity trend, the extent to which wage growth can exceed expected inflation without causing the rate of inflation to accelerate. Finally, the natural rate for the total unemployment concept must be calculated by estimating the value of the other group unemployment rates (u_k, $k \neq j$) relative to u_j:

$$(6) \quad u_{kt} = u_{kt}(u_{jt}, S_{kt}),$$

where S_{kt} is a structural variable, e.g., the relative labor-force share of the kth group, which explains secular movements of u_{kt} relative to u_{jt}. The aggregate natural rate ($\hat{u}_t^N$) is then:

$$(7) \quad \hat{u}_t^N = \frac{\hat{u}_j^N F_{jt}}{F_t} + \sum_k \frac{\hat{u}_{kt}^N F_{kt}}{F_t} \quad ,$$

where $\hat{u}_{kt}^N$ is calculated by computing the predicted value of (6) for $\hat{u}_j^N$ and S_{kt}.

The estimated 1956-1974 increase in $\hat{u}_t^N$ is very sensitive to the particular choice of the unemployment concept "j." For instance, at one extreme the choice of the aggregate unemployment rate as u_{jt} in (4) eliminates the other "k" groups, leading to the conclusion that the aggregate natural unemployment rate has remained constant as the solution to (5). This result is illustrated in Table 3, line 8, for two different estimates of the rate of expected inflation based on different speeds of adjustment of adaptive expectations. The standard errors of the two estimates are displayed in columns 1 and 2, and the estimated natural unemployment rates ($\hat{u}^N$) of about 4.8 percent are exhibited in columns 3 and 4. According to the equation estimated for the aggregate unemployment concept reported on line 8, actual aggregate unemployment was 0.6 percentage points below the natural rate in 1956, but 0.8 percentage points above the natural rate in 1974.

At the other extreme is the estimate, line 4, in which group "j" is chosen to be males aged 25 and over. Now the economy is estimated to have been roughly at the group natural rate $\hat{u}_j^N$ in 1956, but about 0.1 percentage points below $\hat{u}_j^N$ in 1974. The resulting estimate of the aggregate natural rate thus rises more than the actual total, from 4.11 to 5.72 percent. Limitation of group "j" to the relatively narrow over-25 male group thus provides the pessimistic conclusion that the total natural rate has shifted up a great deal, and that prudent policymakers cannot allow the aggregate unemployment rate to fall below 5.7 percent without running the risk of an accelerating rate of inflation. The same pessimistic conclusion that the natural rate has risen by more than 1.5 percentage points was reached recently by Wachter (1976).

But other less pessimistic conclusions are possible. Several investigations have followed Perry's (1970) lead by measuring unemployment concept "j" as a "weighted unemployment rate," with the unemployment rate of each demographic subgroup weighted by its wage rate and weekly hours relative to prime-age males, on the ground that the contribution to effective labor supply of one unemployed member of each group is proportional to the average productivity and hours of that group. Since teenagers and women are given

190

Table 3
Phillips Curves Estimated for Alternative Unemployment Definitions, Annual Observations, 1954-1971

Group J	Standard Errors		Estimated $\hat{u}_j^N$		Actual u_{jt}		Estimated $\hat{u}_t^N$ (for p^e Long)		$\hat{u}^N$ 1974 / $\hat{u}^N$ 1956
	p^e Short	p^e Long	p^e Short	p^e Long	1956	1974	1956	1974	
	(1)	(2)	(3)	(4)	(5)	(6)	(7)	(8)	(9)
1. Males 35-44	.475	.414	2.69	2.70	2.60	2.55	4.18	5.71	1.53
2. Males 25-54	.458	.404	2.95	2.96	2.97	3.05	4.13	5.42	1.29
3. All 25-54	.451	.405	3.53	3.54	3.31	3.76	4.36	5.25	0.89
4. Males 25+	.471	.413	3.06	3.07	3.09	2.99	4.11	5.72	1.61
5. All 25+	.462	.406	3.49	3.50	3.34	3.60	4.28	5.43	1.15
6. All 20+	.456	.427	3.97	3.99	3.65	4.47	4.43	5.01	0.58
7. Perry Weighted	.457	.426	3.92	3.93	3.60	4.37	4.43	5.06	0.63
8. All	.474	.491	4.76	4.77	4.13	5.59	4.77	4.77	0.00

Extrapolation of lines 2 and 3, p^e long equation, 1972-76

	1972	1973	1974	1975	1976^e	Total 72 - 76
9. Actual w	6.68	6.62	9.11	8.14	6.87	37.42
10. Predicted, Males 25-54, line 2	5.62	6.97	8.74	9.37	7.53	38.23
11. Predicted, All 25-54, line 3	5.54	6.92	8.66	9.16	7.30	37.58
12. Actual Minus Predicted, line 2	1.06	-0.35	0.37	-1.23	-.66	- 0.81
13. Actual Minus Predicted, line 3	1.14	-0.30	0.45	-1.02	-.43	- 0.16

Sources and methods:

1. All unemployment rates are annual averages.

2. Wage change (w_t) is the total of the quarterly percentage changes over the four quarters of each calendar year of the hourly earnings index for the private nonfarm economy, adjusted for changes in overtime and the interindustry employment mix, pre-1964 from Gordon (1971) and post-1964 from the Bureau of Labor Statistics.

3. Expected price change (p_t^e): A quarterly polynomial distributed lag regression of the Moody's Aaa bond rate on the quarterly rate of change in Gordon's (1975b) "nonfood net-of-energy" deflator for the period 1953:I to 1975:IV yielded a set of lag coefficients, which were then constrained to sum to 1.0 and subtracted from the left-hand side of (4) to form the dependent variable ($w - p^e$). Two versions were used, one from a 10-quarter estimated lag distribution in the interest rate equation (column labelled "p^e Short") and another from a 20-quarter estimated lag distribution (column labelled "p^e Long"). The respective mean lags are 2.8 and 5.3 quarters.

4. Predictions were estimated using a price deflator both net and gross of energy and food prices to calculate p^e, using the lag distribution described in note 3. The gross deflator worked considerably better and was used to calculate the predicted values listed in lines 10 and 11 of the table. Estimated 1976 annual values were based on: annual rate of change between August 1975 and May 1976 for wages; annual rate of change between 1975:III and 1976:II for prices; March values of unemployment (when the aggregate unemployment rate was 7.5 percent).

5. q^* in (5), needed for the calculation of $\hat{u}_{jt}^N$, is the average of $w_t - p_t^e$ over the entire sample period.

much lower weights than adult men, the Perry weighted unemployment rate rises by only 0.77 percentage points between 1956 and 1974, compared to the 1.45 increase in the aggregate rate. The actual aggregate rate thus shifts up much less relative to the Perry weighted rate than relative to the over-25 male rate, and so the estimated aggregate natural rate ($\hat{u}_t^N$) shifts up by less (only 0.63 points) on line 7 when group "j" is Perry's weighted rate than does the 1.61 aggregate natural rate shift on line 4 when group "j" is defined as males 25 years and over.

Previous studies of the upward shift in the natural rate have erred by assuming a particular definition of group "j" without testing for the ability of the data to discriminate among different definitions. Perry's estimated upward shift is much less than Wachter's, because Perry assumed the weighted unemployment concept as group "j" while Wachter assumed a prime-age male concept. The remaining lines in Table 3 demonstrate that the data cannot find a statistically significant difference between several widely varying estimates of the natural rate shift. If we concentrate on the standard errors in column 2 for the better-fitting "long lag" version of expected inflation ("p^e long"), we note that the evidence for special treatment of prime-age males is very weak. For the age group 25-54 years, the standard errors for the male (line 2) and "all" (line 3) equations are almost identical. For the age group 25 years and over, the inclusion of females in line 5 actually improves the fit over the male-only version in line 4, although not significantly. In fact, the only difference in Table 3 which is statistically signifiant is between lines 1-7, on the one hand, and the aggregate equation in line 8, on the other.

When we examine only the best-fitting equations on lines 1-5, we may conclude that the aggregate natural rate has shifted up by as much as 1.61 points on line 4, a figure roughly equal to Wachter's, or we may choose the much smaller figure of 0.89 points on line 3. The inclusion of adult females, as on lines 3 and 5, may be supported for at least two reasons beyond the normal claims of equal opportunity for females. First, the equations on lines 3 and 5 suggest that the economy was operating below its natural rate in 1956, whereas the male-only equations on lines 2 and 4 do not. The male-only equations leave us with the puzzle as to why wage and price increases accelerated in 1956. Second, 1972-76 postsample extrapolations for the male-only equation on line 2 and the "all" equation on line 3 yield better results for the latter.

The results in Table 3 were tested for their sensitivity to several other variations. The lagged effect of unemployment on wages, emphasized by Wachter, was tested by adding a lagged value of u_{jt}^{-1} to all equations, but in no case were the lagged variables significant. Second, separate versions were tested for the 1954-1975 sample period, including as extra variables a wage-control dummy and/or a trend term (the latter as a test of the hypothesis that even the natural rate for prime-age males may have shifted up as a consequence of liberalized unemployment compensation). No significant coefficients could be found for the extra variables.[4] Extra versions were also fitted with the coefficient on p_t^e estimated freely, rather than constrained to equal unity. The results (for p^e long) were almost identical, with estimates of the p_t^e coefficient ranging from 0.95 to 1.05.

IV. THE WELFARE COST OF A STRUCTURAL SHIFT IN UNEMPLOYMENT

As in my earlier paper (1973) on aggregate demand unemployment, I assume here that the aggregate welfare of households depends on their total output of "final commodities" (Z), which they produce by combining goods purchased on the market (Q), together with their own hours of time spent searching for new jobs while unemployed (U), and hours spent on "home activity" (N), which includes time devoted to consumption, household production, and sleep:

(8) $Z = Z(Q,U,N)$.

The production of a meal, for example, requires purchased groceries (part of Q) and hours spent in shopping and cooking (part of N). The search time of unemployed individuals (U) is also productive in raising future income, monetary or psychic.

Since the aim is to measure the effect of a structural shift which involves differences among family members in labor-force behavior, I shall define the output of "final commodities" of the members of a particular demographic group as depending only on market goods purchased with their own wage income, and on their hours spent in nonmarket activity:

(9) $Z_i = Z_i(Q_i, U_i, N_i)$.

The form of (9) embodies the important simplification that there are no intra-family interdependencies of household production and consumption, e.g., that

---

[4] An important and totally unexpected conclusion, but one with implications outside the scope of this paper, is that wage changes during 1972-75 are far better explained by an expected inflation concept which includes food and energy prices than by one which excludes them. This implies, in the context of Gordon (1975a), that an attempt by the Federal Reserve to "accomodate" the supply shocks of 1973-74 would have made the inflation substantially worse.

there is no reduction in the value of a husband's home time when his wife takes a job and forces him to spend more hours feeding the dog and washing dishes, nor is there any increase enjoyed by the husband when his wife's extra income allows the family to purchase a second TV set or a new car.

Market output (Q_i) is assumed to be produced by "market manhours" (M_i) and capital (K_i):

$$(10) \quad Q_i = Q_i(M_i, K_i).$$

Substituting (10) into (9), we can write:

$$(11) \quad Z_i = Z_i [Q_i(M_i, K_i), U_i, N_i] .$$

The effect on group welfare of a specified structural shift in unemployment (ds_i) depends on the change in the group output of "final commodities":

$$(12) \quad \frac{dZ_i}{ds_i} = Z_{Q_i} \, Q_{M_i} \left(\frac{dM_i}{ds_i}\right) + Z_{U_i} \left(\frac{dU_i}{ds_i}\right) + Z_{N_i} \left(\frac{dN_i}{ds_i}\right),$$

where Z_{Q_i}, Z_{U_i}, and Z_{N_i} are the group marginal products of market goods, unemployed time, and home time, respectively, in producing final commodities. Q_{M_i} is the group marginal product of market manhours in producing market output. The effect of the structural unemployment shift on the capital stock (K_i) is ignored. The economy's group market production functions are assumed to exhibit constant returns; the average productivity of a group's market manhours is a function of the ratio of manhours to capital, but not of the scale of operations. Additional labor input when a structural shift increases the market manhours of, for instance, women or teenagers, is assumed to stimulate investment until the capital stock is raised sufficiently to equip the new workers in the group with the same capital/labor ratio as those working previously. Since the higher capital stock must be maintained by larger depreciation deductions and returns to owners of capital, the marginal product of the extra capital stimulated by the structural shift is unavailable for consumption and hence is not a net social benefit.[5]

In equilibrium the three marginal products in the production of final commodities are equal to, respectively, the price of market goods relative to final commodities (P_Q/P_Z), and the relative "shadow wages" per unit of unemployed time (W_{U_i}/P_Z) and home time (W_{N_i}/P_Z):

$$(13) \quad Z_{Q_i} = \frac{P_Q}{P_Z}; \quad Z_{U_i} = \frac{W_{U_i}}{P_Z}; \quad Z_{N_i} = \frac{W_{N_i}}{P_Z}.$$

The term W_{N_i} is sometimes called "the price of time" or "the price of home time," and its determinants have been explored by Becker (1965) and others. I do not at this stage assume that the market for final output is in equilibrium with the marginal product of manhours equal to the real wage rate, since the validity of this assumption is a matter to be investigated. When the relative prices in (13) are substituted into (12), we obtain:

$$(14) \quad \frac{dZ_i}{ds_i} = \frac{P_Q}{P_Z} \left[Q_{M_i} \left(\frac{dM_i}{ds_i} \right) + \frac{W_{U_i}}{P_Q} \left(\frac{dU_i}{ds_i} \right) + \frac{W_{N_i}}{P_Q} \left(\frac{dN_i}{ds_i} \right) \right].$$

What changes in market manhours (M_i), unemployed time (U_i), and home time (N_i) have been caused by the 1956-1974 structural shift of unemployment in the U.S.? The welfare concept is the change in the consumption of final commodities per member of a given demographic group (Z_i/P_i). Thus, I ignore the portion of the structural shift directly attributable in Table 2, line 4, to changes in group populations. If the "fertility hump" had simply caused an increased population of teenagers in the 1960s and 1970s without any resulting changes in unemployment, wage rates, or labor-force participation, then the welfare of each individual teenager would have been unaffected. I shall also simplify the discussion by ignoring the declining labor-force participation of adult men, due primarily to earlier retirement. Thus, the analysis will be limited to the effects of, first, the increasing labor-force participation rates of a given population of young females and adult females, and second, the higher relative unemployment rates of females and young males relative to adult males.

---

[5]This treatment of capital is the same as in the case of a permanent shift in aggregate unemployment caused by a change in aggregate demand, as examined in Gordon (1973).

Since the population of each demographic group is held constant, we can make use of the identity that the total time spent in market and nonmarket activity exhausts the total time available, and thus an increase in the time spent in any one activity must be balanced by a decrease in one or both of the other activities:

$$(15) \quad dM_i + dU_i + dN_i \equiv 0 .$$

The substitution of (15) into (14) allows the group change in welfare to be written in the following simple form:

$$(16) \quad \frac{dZ_i}{ds_i} = \frac{P_Q}{P_Z} \left[\left(\frac{Q_{M_i} - W_{N_i}}{P_Q} \right) \left(\frac{dM_i}{ds_i} \right) + \left(\frac{W_{U_i} - W_{N_i}}{P_Q} \right) \left(\frac{dU_i}{ds_i} \right) \right] .$$

The total effect of the structural shift within a demographic group (ds_i) is divided into two parts. The first term inside the brackets represents the change in market manhours (dM_i), valued at the difference between the group's marginal product (Q_{M_i}) minus the shadow price (W_{N_i}) attached to the off-setting change in home time. The second term represents the change in hours spent in job search (dU_i), valued at the difference between the shadow price of unemployed time (W_{U_i}) minus the shadow price of home time (W_{N_i}).

As an example of the operation of (16) in an artificial case, imagine that an increase in labor-force participation raised the market manhours of adult females (dM_i) by 1 billion manhours annually, and hours spent in job search by 50 million, while reducing home time by 1.05 billion. If the marginal product of women in market activity was $4.00, the shadow price of time spent in job search was $1.00, and the shadow price of home time was $2.00, then the effect on the "full income" of women (dZ_i) would be:[6]

$$(\$4 - \$2) (1.0) + (\$0 - \$2) (0.05) = \$1.9 \text{ billion}.$$

---

[6] The P_Q and P_Z terms can be ignored, since these price indices can be arbitrarily set equal to 1.0 for the year in question.

In the example, the structural shift in unemployment caused by the flow of women into the labor force actually makes women better off, not worse off, by a total of $1.9 billion.

The estimation of the components of (16) for the actual 1956-1974 U.S. structural unemployment shift involves two basic tasks, one easy and one difficult. First, the observed changes in labor-force participation rates (df_i) and relative unemployment rates $[d(u_i/u_1)]$, quantified in Table 1 must be translated into changes in manhours of market and nonmarket activity. The translation is relatively straightforward, requiring only estimates of average annual hours spent by the demographic groups on the job and in job search, since the changes in participation and unemployment rates are taken as basic data and need not be estimated.

The manhour estimates are presented in Table 4. For each demographic group four numbers are calculated: the effect on market and unemployed manhours of changes in labor-force participation $(dM_i/df_i$ and $dU_i/df_i)$; and the effect on market and unemployed manhours of changes in unemployment rates of the demographic groups relative to adult males $(dM_i/du_i^*$ and $dU_i/du_i^*)$.[7] The only surprising ingredient of Table 4 is the estimate, based on a U.S. government survey conducted in 1973, that men spend only eight hours per week on average in job search activity while unemployed, and women spend only six hours. The remainder of the time of unemployed individuals is counted as "home time." Thus, the increase in the relative unemployment rates in the right column of Table 4 had the effect mainly of shifting hours away from market work into home time. But the effects of du^* are swamped by the shift of hours from home time to market work activity caused by the substantial increase in the labor-force participation rates of women in both the 16-24 year and 25 years and over groups.

The second and more difficult portion of the calculation of the elements of (16) requires estimates of the group marginal products of market activity and of the shadow prices of unemployed and home time, raising the following issues for discussion.

1. What is the value of the <u>extra</u> search engaged in by young workers and adult women as a consequence of their higher relative unemployment rates (du_i^*)? An answer requires an interpretation of the cause of du_i^*. The value of the extra hours may have been substantial if they resulted from a voluntary decision responding to a change in the benefits and costs of search; on the other

---

[7] $du_i^* = u_1 d(u_i/u_1)$, the same term as that used in (3) and in Table 2 to compute the decomposition of the 1956-1974 structural shift.

Table 4

Estimated Change in Manhours, 1974,

Attributable to 1956-1974 Change in Group

Labor-Force Participation Rate (df_i)

and in Group Relative Unemployment Rates (du_i^*)

(billions of manhours annually)

		Effect of df_i	Effect of du_i^*
1.	Males 16-24		
	a. dM_i	- .250	- .592
	b. dU_i	- .009	.155
	c. dN_i (= - dM_i - dU_i)	.259	.437
2.	Females 16-24		
	a. dM_i	2.772	- .646
	b. dU_i	.077	.127
	c. dN_i (= -dM_i - dU_i)	-2.849	.519
3.	Females 25+		
	a. dM_i	7.718	- .311
	b. dU_i	.072	.060
	c. dN_i (= -dM_i - dU_i)	-7.790	.251

Sources and methods:

1. dM_i was calculated starting from the identity that $M \equiv EH \equiv (1\text{-}u)$ fPH, where E is employed workers, H is annual hours of work, the other symbols are the same as before, and the "i" subscripts are dropped for convenience. The total change in manhours resulting from a change in labor-force participation (df) and in relative unemployment rates (du*) is dM = (1-u) PHdf -- fPHdu*. Sources are as follows. P, f, and u are actual 1974 figures from the Handbook of Labor Statistics, 1975--Reference Edition (Washington, 1975) and from the Manpower Report of the President (Washington, 1975). df and du* are from Table 2. H is calculated as wH2000/w, where 2000 is the assumed annual hours for prime-age males; wH is Perry's (1970, Appendix A) set of weights of demographic group wages times hours relative to prime-age adult males; and w is the 1974 relative median full-time year-round wage of each demographic group relative to prime-age adult males, from the Current Population Survey, Series P-60. The resulting estimates of H are 1542 for males aged 16-24, 1501 for females aged 16-24, and 1534 for females aged 25 and over.

2. dU_i was calculated starting from the identity that $U \equiv XH_U \equiv ufPH_U$, where the only new symbol is H_U, annual hours of search per unemployed worker, and where the "i" subscripts are again dropped for convenience. The total change in search manhours resulting from a change in labor-force participation (df) and in relative unemployment rates (du*) is $dU = uPH_U df + fPH_U du*$. Data for u, P, f, dF, and du* are from the same sources as in note 1. Weekly hours of search are taken to be 8.1 for men and 5.9 for women, based on the evidence compiled in U.S. Bureau of Labor Statistics, Jobseeking Methods Used by American Workers, BLS Bulletin 1886 (Washington, 1975, p. 51, Table H-2). This source reports that hours of search do not vary appreciably with age.

hand, the value of the extra hours may have been zero if the extra unemployment was totally involuntary.

    2.   On what basis can a value be placed on a marginal hour of home time? Is the "waiting time" of the unemployed as valuable as other uses of home time?

    3. Is the marginal product of young workers and adult women accurately measured by their gross before-tax wage? If there is economic discrimination, then wage rates may be held moderately or substantially below marginal products.

V. INTERPRETATIONS OF THE SHIFT IN RELATIVE UNEMPLOYMENT RATES

    The idea that there is a positive value attributable to at least a part of the time of an unemployed worker, introduced by Mortensen (1970) and others in the late 1960s as an ingredient in the "new microeconomics of unemployment," seemed a novelty to a generation raised on the idea of involuntary Keynesian unemployment as a pure waste of time. Workers and jobs are assumed to differ in their characteristics, and much unemployment involves a search by workers for a job possessing the best possible combination of pecuniary and nonpecuniary rewards. Workers will not necessarily accept the first job offer they receive if they judge that the present value of the return to further search, including expected future wage increments and unemployment benefits, net of the cost of search, outweighs the return of accepting a job now, net of taxes and commuting expenses.

    Figure 1 is designed to examine the consequences of an upward shift in the supply of labor of a given demographic group relative to a "base" group, for example prime-age males, on the assumption that the groups are imperfect substitutes in production. The horizontal axis is the M_i/M_1 ratio, and the vertical axis is w_i/w_1; the variables on both axes are measured as natural logs; all of the supply curves are drawn to have constant elasticities. The initial situation in 1956 is described by the two left-hand curves. S_{56}^{M+V} is the group's relative supply of manhours to labor-force activity, and S_{56}^{M} is the supply of employed manhours. The horizontal distance between the two curves represents the supply of "voluntary search manhours" (V), the outcome of the worker's rational balancing of the marginal benefits and costs of search. As a point of reference, it is assumed that all 1956 unemployment is voluntary, and that point A represents an equilibrium position at the crossing point of S_{56}^{M} with D^{M}, the

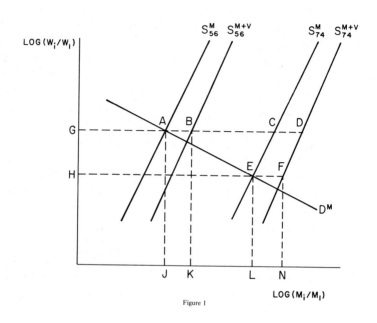

Figure 1

demand curve for group manhour input.[8] Note that the two supply curves are drawn so that the percentage unemployment rate (for instance, the ratio AB at the initial 1956 wage rate OG) depends inversely on the wage rate. Although most determinants of the benefits and costs of search should be unit-elastic functions of the wage rate in the long run (unemployment compensation, taxes, bus fares, pay telephone charges), nevertheless a permanent wage reduction could cause a substitution away from market work toward the joint activity of "searching and waiting."[9] Another possibility, not drawn in Figure 1, would be a reduction in both employed and unemployed hours in response to a lower wage.

Now, I examine the effects of an increase in the relative group supply of labor, shown as a shift to the new pair of supply curves, S_{74}^M and S_{74}^{M+V}. The new curves are drawn to exhibit the same voluntary unemployment rate as in 1956 at the initial 1956 wage rate (CD = AB on the logarithmic scale). Two extreme possibilities are suggested as the net effect of the labor supply shift, on the assumption that there has been no change in the relative demand for labor. First, the relative wage might drop from G to H, stimulating an increase in the demand for manhours from J to L. The decline in the wage rate, relative to the value of home time, could induce an increase in the voluntary unemployment rate (EF > AB). The second extreme case would occur if the relative group wage were fixed at G, for instance by a minimum wage with universal coverage set by the legislature as a constant fraction of the prime-age group wage rate. The relative demand for group manhour input would remain fixed at A, creating a new higher unemployment rate AD, consisting of the voluntary segment CD (=AB) and the involuntary segment AC.

If the first case were correct, we should observe a negative statistical correlation between the change in group relative wage rates between 1956 and 1974 and the change in group shares in the labor force. As the curves are drawn, we should also observe a positive correlation between the change in the relative unemployment rates and change in group shares in the labor force. The extra unemployment, as noted above, is purely voluntary and stems from the assumption that the market wage declines relative to the value of home time,

---

[8]The device of two supply curves, with the supply of unemployment as the distance between them, was introduced by Hall (1975, p. 322).

[9]See the expression for the marginal revenue from additional job search in Gordon (1973, p. 179, equation A-2). Since the shadow price of home time (W_N) appears only as a component of marginal revenue, and not as a component of marginal cost, a reduction in the market wage relative to W_N will raise marginal revenue relative to marginal cost, and thus extend the duration of job search. If this approach predicts correctly, a labor-force group with an increasing share of supply should experience a higher duration of unemployment.

which the unemployed enjoy during the "waiting period" of their unemployment. If the second case were correct, we should observe the same positive correlation between group rates and labor-force shares.

A preview of these findings is displayed in Figures 2 and 3, depicting the changes between 1956 and 1974 of relative unemployment rates and wage rates by age-sex group. Between these years, the labor-force shares of each adult male group (25-34, 35-44, etc.) declined, while the share of every other group increased with the two exceptions of females 35-44 years (the Depression babies), and females 65 and over. In Figure 2, actual 1974 unemployment rates appear to have increased in every female age group except the 55-64 year group, whereas the males display a systematic increase in the young age groups (16-34), and a decrease in the 45-64 year groups. A regression equation indicates a strong positive correlation between the unemployment and labor-force share changes :

(17) $LRU_i = .104 + .463 LRS_i$; $R^2 = .412$; $SEE = .194$.
$[2.058]$ $[8.129]$

The numbers in brackets are t-statistics;

$$LRU_i = Log \left(\frac{u_{i74}}{u_{i56}} \right); \text{ and } LRS_i = Log \left(\frac{f_{i74}/f_{74}}{f_{i56}/f_{56}} \right).$$

As an example, the labor-force share of male youth aged 20-24 increased by 51.0 percent. Equation (17) predicts an increase in the group unemployment rate of 23.6 percent, as compared to the actual increase of 26.1 percent (from an actual figure in 1956 of 6.9 percent to 8.7 percent in 1974).

The behavior of relative wage rates is illustrated in Figure 3. Relative wage rates increased for exactly those male groups whose unemployment rates decreased. For females, the relationship is almost as systematic, with relative wage rates dropping for all female groups aged 16-64, whereas unemployment rates increased for all female groups except for the 55-64 group. A regression equation indicates a strong negative correlation between the relative wage rate and labor-force share changes.

(18) $LRW_i = -.088 - .355 LRS_i$; $R^2 = .504$; $SEE = .124$.
$[-2.721]$ $[-3.768]$

The symbol LRS_i is the same variable as in (17); and

$$LRW_i = \text{Log}\left(\frac{W_{i74}/W_{174}}{W_{i56}/W_{156}}\right), \quad \text{where group "1" is males aged 35-44.}$$

As an example, the labor-force share of male youth aged 20-24 increased by 51.0 percent. The equation predicts a decrease in the relative wage rate of 18.1 percent, as compared to the actual decrease of 20.4 percent (from an actual ratio in 1956 of 71.2 percent of the male 35-44 years wage to 56.7 percent in 1974).

The decline in relative wage rates in the context of Figure 1 rules out the second extreme case, that of completely inflexible relative wage rates. But, how close to validity is the first extreme case, in which relative wages decline sufficiently to clear the market, and all unemployment is voluntary? The positive correlation between changes in relative shares and unemployment rates in (17) could describe the substitution between market and search hours caused by a lower wage rate, but one would expect this substitution to be accompanied by a reduction in the intensity of search and by an increase in the duration of a spell of unemployment. Perry's (1972) evidence, however, indicates exactly the opposite. The average duration of an unemployment spell fell between 1956 and 1972 (a year almost identical to 1974 in its labor market characteristics) for all the groups which experienced higher unemployment rates between 1956 and 1974.[10] The higher 1972 unemployment rates of young people and women were entirely attributable to more spells of unemployment per year, with a 1956-1972 increase in annual spells of 50, 29, 73, and 43 percent, respectively, for males 16-19 years, males 20-24 years, females 16-19 years, and females 20-24 years.

The fact that higher youth and adult female unemployment was caused by more annual spells, not by the same number of longer lasting spells, does not by itself demonstrate that the extra unemployment was involuntary rather than by voluntary choice. Much has been made of the prominent role of labor-force entry and reentry as the source of high relative teenage and adult female unemployment rates. More than two-thirds of teenage unemployment and more

---

[10]A single exception to the statement is males 20-24 years, who experienced a minor increase in duration from 4.6 to 4.8 weeks. The statement also refers to the groups defined by Perry's aggregated age definitions (duration decreased for males 16-19 years and for females 16-19, 20-24, 25-44, and 45-64 years).

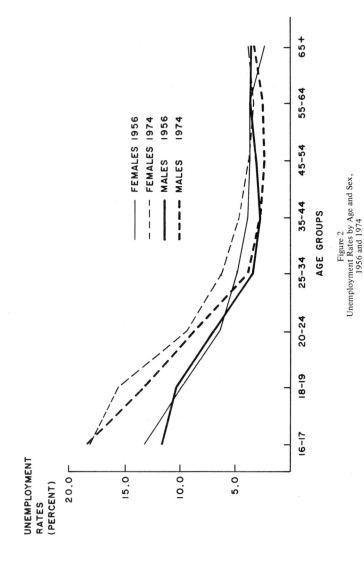

Figure 2
Unemployment Rates by Age and Sex,
1956 and 1974

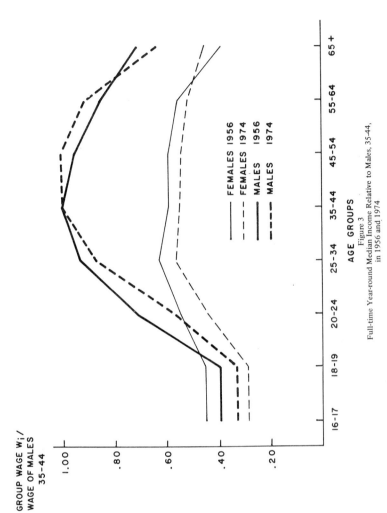

GROUP WAGE W_i /
WAGE OF MALES
35-44

Figure 3
Full-time Year-round Median Income Relative to Males, 35-44,
in 1956 and 1974

205

than 40 percent of adult female unemployment occurs for the "reason" of entry or reentry.[11] The 1956-1972 (or 1974) increase in teenage relative unemployment rates could have been entirely due to the voluntary choice by teenagers of more frequent spells of unemployment to pursue schooling or traveling opportunities made possible by growing affluence.

Nevertheless, several pieces of evidence dispute the interpretation of the extra unemployment as purely voluntary. First, exit from the labor force and subsequent reentry need not be voluntary. Perry's data suggest that a substantial number of labor-force dropouts was previously unemployed; the sequence employment-to-dropout becomes less common than the sequence employment-to-unemployment-to-dropout as age increases for both men and women. In fact, the monthly probability for an unemployed person of dropping out of the labor force is greater than the probability of being hired for males 16-19 years and for females 16-19 and 25-59 years.

> Once these reasons [school enrollment and having babies] are allowed for, most people plainly leave the work force only after first becoming unemployed. Rather than being an important cause of unemployment, such transitions appear to result from it.[12]

In Figure 1, I assumed that all unemployment of group "i" in 1956 was voluntary, and that extra involuntary unemployment in 1974 could have occurred if the group "i" wage rate had been held up by some institutional barrier which prevented the group relative wage from falling sufficiently. A considerable literature has developed on the effect of higher minimum wages on teenage unemployment.[13] Unfortunately, while most recent studies agree that teenage employment is reduced by increases in the minimum wage rate, the quantitative estimates of the total effect vary widely.

A set of strong conclusions is implied by Mincer's (1976) results. He finds that the elasticity of the employment/population ratio of teenagers to an increase in the effective ratio of the minimum wage to hourly earnings is -.24; for males aged 20-24, it is -.21. Although Mincer's sample period extends only through 1969, and thus does not apply directly to the 1956-1974 comparison,

---

[11] Averages for the years 1968 through 1971 are from Perry (1972, p. 272, Table 6).

[12] Perry (1972, pp. 270-271).

[13] See especially Goldfarb (1974) and Welch (1974).

a rough comparison can be made by calculating an effective minimum wage ratio for 1974.[14] Calculations on this basis are presented in Table 5 for two labor-force groups, all teenagers 16-19 years and males 20-24 years, the groups for which Mincer found significant coefficients on the minimum wage elasticity. For both groups the estimated elasticities are high enough to overexplain slightly the actual 1956-1974 change in unemployment rates. With 1956 values of the minimum wage ratio, the 1974 unemployment rates of both teenagers 16-19 years and males 20-24 years would have been below actual 1956 values. Softening the conclusion slightly to allow for time lags in the effect of the May 1974 minimum wage increase, I derive from Mincer the conclusion that the 1956-1974 minimum wage increase is sufficient at least to explain fully the 1956-1974 increase in the unemployment of teenagers 16-19 years and males 20-24 years.

Unfortunately, some studies find much weaker effects than Mincer's, whose teenage elasticity of -.24 is on the high end of the results surveyed by Goldfarb (1974). In a recent study covering quarterly data over the entire postwar period, 1948-1975, Gramlich (1976) finds an elasticity of only -.10. More important, Gramlich concludes that only changes in the basic minimum wage rate influence employment, and that changes in coverage do not matter. The elimination of the coverage effect destroys completely the conclusion of Table 5. Between 1956 and 1974, the ratio of the basic minimum wage to teenage full-time median earnings (converted to an hourly basis) fell from 103 to 96 percent, and should have stimulated rather than depressed teenage employment. Gramlich concludes from additional regression equations that the major impact of the minimum wage has been to shift teenagers from full-time to part-time employment, with little effect on the total number employed.

Can Gramlich's conclusion denying any effect for coverage increases be believed? Part of the problem may be multicollinearity in the particular specification of Gramlich's regressions. The effect of the basic minimum wage (MW) is measured as a ratio to average hourly earnings (AHE). The MW/AHE ratio has a "sawtooth" appearance, increasing sharply in years of minimum wage increases, and declining thereafter as AHE grows. The effect of coverage changes is represented by a set of "0-1" dummy variables, equal to 0 before the date

---

[14]The basic minimum wage remained at $1.60 between February 1968 and May 1974, and fell substantially over the interval as a share of average hourly earnings from an average of 55.6 percent in 1968 to 44.8 percent in 1974. Two partially offsetting factors were an increase in coverage in 1974 and a smaller rate of increase of average teenage earnings. Gramlich (1976) estimates that coverage for teenagers (C_T) increased from 46.1 percent in 1973 (assumed equal to 1968) to 57.6 percent in 1975, or a 52.8 percent average rate for 1974 (when, on May 1, coverage changed). Multiplying by the ratio of the basic minimum wage to average hourly earnings (MW/AHE) produces: 1968, C_TMW/AHE = .256; 1974, C_TMW/AHE = .236, or a decline of 7.5 percent. The same factor was applied to males 20-24 years.

of the coverage change and 1 thereafter. The three coverage dummies, stacked on top of each other, represent a "step" variable:

$$0\ 0\ 0\ 0\ 0\ 0\ 1\ 1\ 1$$
$$0\ 0\ 0\ 0\ 1\ 1\ 1\ 1\ 1$$
$$0\ 0\ 1\ 1\ 1\ 1\ 1\ 1\ 1\ .$$

Since the dates of most of the coverage changes coincide with the dates of the minimum wage changes, the net effect of the coverage variable may be approximated by a linear combination of the MW/AHE ratio and a time trend, both of which are included as right-hand variables in Gramlich's regressions.[15] Because of this multicollinearity, it may be impossible to obtain a significant estimate of the separate effect of coverage, and it may be necessary to assume, as did Mincer, that the proper minimum wage variable is the product of the coverage ratio and MW/AHE. Overall, I lean toward acceptance of the Mincer results as summarized in Table 5, because I fail to see any a priori reason why changes in the MW/AHE ratio within a given industry should have a strong effect, whereas an extension of minimum wage coverage to a new industry should have no effect on the employment of low-wage workers in that industry.

The strong adverse effect on teenage employment of increasing minimum wage coverage estimated by Mincer, and the defects in Gramlich's tests for the coverage effect, point toward acceptance of the conclusion, from Table 5, that the entire increase in teenage unemployment between 1956 and 1974 was involuntary. This conclusion might overstate the involuntary portion of the increase if Mincer's elasticities are too high, a possibility raised by lower estimates produced in some other studies, as summarized in Goldfarb's survey. On the other hand, Table 5 disguises the additional deterioration in teenage welfare as teenagers have been pushed by the higher minimum wage from full-time into part-time work, a conclusion of Gramlich's study which appears relatively robust. Since my interest is in order-of-magnitude estimates, I shall assume that the possible upward bias in Mincer's elasticities is just balanced by the consequences of the full-time to part-time shift.

As a result, the full 1956-1974 increase in the teenage relative unemployment rate will be taken to be involuntary. Because the minimum wage prevents employers from offering young workers the opportunity to "buy" specific human capital by working for a very low wage during a training period, a substantial number of teenagers are pushed against their will into "dead-end"

---

[15]Gramlich's equations suffer from several trend-related misspecifications. He uses the ratio of MW to a price deflator, not MW/AHE, and his left-hand variable is total employment (E_i), not the ratio (E_i/P_i).

Table 5

Actual 1956-1974 Changes
in Unemployment, Employment, and Labor-Force Ratios,
and Changes Attributable to Increase in Effective Minimum Wage Ratio

		u_i	f_i	E_i/P_i
1.	Teenagers, 16-19			
	a. Actual 1956	11.5%	50.9%	45.1%
	b. Actual 1974	16.0	55.2	46.4
	c. Calculated 1974 with 1956 Minimum Wage Ratio[1]	11.0	65.2	58.2
2.	Males, 20-24			
	a. Actual 1956	6.9	87.8	81.8
	b. Actual 1974	8.7	86.0	78.5
	c. Calculated 1974 with 1956 Minimum Wage Ratio[2]	6.6	89.5	83.7

---

[1]Uses 90.9 percent 1956-1968 increase in BLS teenage effective minimum wage ratio, from Mincer (1976, p. S102, Table 2, column 4), multiplied by .925 factor for 1968-1974 derived in text footnote.

[2]Uses 30.7 percent 1956-1968 increase in BLS total effective minimum wage ratio, from Mincer (1976, p. S102, Table 2, column 3), multiplied by .925 factor for 1968-74 derived in text footnote.

jobs without any concomitant training or promotion possibilities. Since there is no incentive to remain on a single job, teenagers have a strong incentive to change jobs frequently and to drop out of the labor force frequently to enjoy spells of leisure between spells of employment.

Recall that an estimate of the value of hours spent in job search is required for the estimation of the term $(W_{U_i} - W_{N_i})$ in (16) below, because the shift of an hour into search time from home time changes welfare by the difference between the value per hour of the two activities. Since I assume from the above analysis that all the increase in teenage job search is involuntary, W_{U_i} for both males and females aged 16-24 is set equal to zero.

On the other hand, previous studies have found little, if any, adverse effect of the minimum wage on adult female employment, and so I shall treat the additional hours of adult female job search time (Table 4, line 3b) as voluntary. This is a corollary of the basic assumption that the 1956-1974 increase in adult female labor-force participation was voluntary. Female entrants and reentrants chose to spend time searching for the best possible job, given the costs of search, rather than to accept the unsatisfactory low-paying jobs which in many cases may have been immediately available (e.g., waitress in the neighborhood coffee shop).

In an earlier paper, I noted that for married women with no access to welfare payments or unemployment benefits, the price of home time at the margin would equal the value of search time and would be equal in turn to the value of average gross hourly earnings, less taxes, commuting costs, and search costs. A review of the evidence yielded a deduction of about 50 percent for these three items.[16] Thus, in the final calculations, I shall take the value of the difference between the value of search time and home time for adult females $(W_{U_i} - W_{N_i})$ to be zero, and the value of home time itself to be $.5W_i$, where W_i is average adult female hourly earnings.

VI. A MODEL OF "RATIONAL" OCCUPATIONAL CROWDING

The final ingredient required for insertion in (16) is the marginal product of women and teenagers. Without further investigation this cannot be proxied by before-tax group average hourly earnings, because a number of writers have suggested that, at least in the case of adult females, earnings are held below marginal products by pure economic discrimination. I shall attempt to determine where the truth lies between the two extremes: first, that the entire male-female

[16]See Gordon (1973, p. 158, n. 40). The combined deduction for taxes and commuting costs of 37.7 percent is derived in n. 33 of that paper. The deduction for search costs is a further 19.4 percent of the net wage, based on an estimate of the ratio of the acceptance wage to the previous wage for adult women cited in n. 40 of that paper.

earnings differential reflects discrimination, in which case the female marginal product should be measured by the male wage; and, second, that females produce at a rate equivalent only to what they are paid, so that their marginal product should be measured not by the male wage but by the female wage.

Two basic classes of models have been developed to explain why the ratio of female to male wage rates is so low, below 60 percent for the age group 35-54 (see Figure 2 above). Becker's (1971) classic analysis is the starting point for the first class of models which attempts to explain the wage differential between two groups (blacks vs. whites, females vs. males) which are <u>assumed</u> to have equal productivities. The second class of models attributes the wage differential not to pure economic discrimination but rather to a "real" difference in productivity between males and females, due to the higher turn-over and shorter expected job tenure of females. Discrimination may still exist in the second class of models but takes the form of "social discrimination," which forces females to drop out of the labor force and take care of children, rather than "economic discrimination," which holds wage rates below productivity.

The Becker framework explains low female wages by the male "taste for discrimination," a desire to minimize economic transactions with women. Efficient production requires that the marginal products of males and females be equated to their marginal cost, consisting for females of a pecuniary wage and a nonpecuniary cost imposed on female-averse males. If the discriminatory "wedge" between male and female wage rates is proportional rather than absolute, the female/male wage ratio is unaffected by a shift in the demand for labor.[17] At one semantic level, the Becker approach implies that the female marginal product should be measured by the male wage. But, at a deeper level, the female marginal product should be reduced by the nonpecuniary cost females impose on males. This cost is just as "real" as any other cost, for other-wise nondiscriminating firms could drive discriminating firms out of business.[18] The only argument for excluding it is that the national accounts at present exclude other nonpecuniary costs, e.g., pollution and congestion. But, in principle, the welfare measure in (16) is based on "full income," including both pecuniary and nonpecuniary benefits net of costs, and should be adjusted for the nonpecuniary costs imposed by the presence of females.

---

[17]This differs from the analysis of Arrow (1973, pp. 7-13) and Freeman (1973, pp. 92-96), where the discrimination coefficient is <u>absolute</u>, an assumption which implies that the <u>relative</u> discrimination coefficient will automatically be reduced toward zero by the process of real economic growth.

[18]Freeman (1973) points out that discriminatory wage differentials can be maintained only if (a) there are no nondiscriminating firms, (b) u-shaped cost curves set a limit on the expansion of nondiscriminating firms, or (c) external costs (e.g., social pressure) prevent nondiscriminatory behavior.

The phrase "female-averse males" has a false ring, and indeed there is little to recommend the Becker-type theories as an explanation of low female earnings. The most important flaw is the absence of any explanation of the decline with age of the female/male wage ratio depicted in Figure 2. Why should the male aversion to adult females be so marked, but the male aversion to teenage females relative to teenage males so minor? To explain Figure 2, Becker would have to argue that adult males are averse not only to adult females but to all teenagers.

A weaker version of the Becker approach is taken by Arrow (1972) and Phelps (1972), both of whom invoke imperfect information to explain why employers, who are deterred by the high cost of direct measurement, classify as inferior all members of a group (blacks, women) despite the fact that only some members are actually less productive than the members of the favored group. This theory, which Phelps calls the "statistical theory of sexual discrimination," can be regarded as describing "partial economic discrimination." The members of the subordinate group who are actually inferior are paid at a rate equivalent to their marginal product; economic discrimination only affects the subgroup which is not inferior. This approach is incomplete, lacking an explanation of the "true inferiority" of the workers who give their non-inferior groupmates a bad name.

This paper amalgamates two strands in the literature on female earnings. The first is associated with Bergmann (1974), who specializes the Becker approach by introducing the idea that men "crowd" women into a small number of occupations, driving down the wage of those occupations relative to those dominated by men. Weisskoff (1972, p. 163) has calculated that, ". . .well over half of all working women in both 1900 and 1960 were employed in jobs in which 70 percent or more of the workers were female." The second strand is the application of human capital theory to the explanation of low relative female earnings. Mincer and Polachek (1974) have explained the flat age-earnings profile of women relative to men as a result of the smaller accumulation by women of on-the-job training, caused by short spells in the labor force followed by the depreciation of skills during spells out of the labor force. Polachek (1975) has extended this idea by classifying occupations on the basis of their "expected rate of atrophy," i.e., the expected rate of depreciation of market skills during periods of nonparticipation in the labor force. Women choose to enter into occupations which allow acquired skills to be remembered rather than lost.

Both the Bergmann (1974) and Polachek (1975) contributions are incomplete. Bergmann follows Becker by assuming either that employers push the less favored group into lower-paying occupations because of pure prejudice or because they may be loyal ". . .to the employers' group which may be making a good thing financially out of discrimination."[19] There is nothing in the Bergmann model which would explain why the female/male wage ratios of Figure 2 are inversely proportional to age. Polachek's model describes the maximization problem which leads employees with expectations of intermittent labor-force behavior to avoid jobs with rapid "atrophy," but does not explain the sources of the differential atrophy rates nor the general equilibrium response of relative wages across occupations to employee occupational choices.

The model below describes an economy of many firms and workers in which only two occupations exist, differing from each other in the process by which knowledge and skills are acquired. In the "firm specific human capital" (FSHC) occupation, skills are unique to each firm, must be learned on-the-job, and cannot be transferred to other firms. The marginal product (θ) of all workers, whether male or female, rises with job tenure (τ) as more on-the-job skills are acquired. When other factors of production are held fixed, an increase in the share (ρ) of the labor force working in the occupation reduces the marginal product of labor:

(19) $\quad \theta = \theta\,(\tau,\rho)\,,\theta_{\tau}>0,\theta_{\rho}<0.$

In the "general human capital" (GHC) occupation, workers must make an initial investment (I_0) to obtain a wage $W_0(1-\rho)$, which is fixed for any given participating share ($1-\rho$) of the labor force. Both men and women are perfect substitutes in production in both occupations and receive the same wage in GHC, and the same wage for any given tenure in FSHC. The only difference between the sexes is an expected tenure $\tau = 1$ in both occupations for men, and a shorter expected tenure $\tau = \gamma$ ($\gamma<1$) for women. A complete model would specify productivity functions for successive spells of labor-force participation by women, allowing for the depreciation of skills between spells. To simplify the exposition, I assume that women experience a single spell of participation for the period γ, and then leave the labor force for the remaining period $1-\gamma$. This abstraction does not alter the qualitative results if future spells of participation provide the same choices as the first spell. In particular, I assume implicitly that women cannot retain their accumulated skills and seniority in FSHC. Instead, skills depreciate with sufficient rapidity for firms to treat a female labor-force reentrant as identical to any other job applicant, even if she has previous experience with the firm. This is quite realistic for the straightforward reason

---

[19]Bergmann (1974, n. 6).

that the woman's previous job slot will have been occupied in the interim by a new employee who will have acquired her former skills, and in many cases the woman will have to take a job in a new firm. GHC skills do not depreciate, however. If, upon reentry, females can resume their previous GHC job without repeating the initial investment in skill accumulation (I_0), then the following one-spell analysis understates the attraction for women of the GHC occupation.

Figure 4(a) contrasts the flat relationship between the wage rate (productivity) and tenure in GHC with the positively sloped θ (τ,ρ) schedule in FSHC for an assumed value of $\rho = 1$. The present value of future wage income available to men in GHC is:

$$(20) \quad \eta_m = \eta(I_0,1,\rho,r) = -I_0 + \int_{\tau=0}^{1} W_0 (1-\rho) e^{-r\tau} d\tau .$$

For women GHC offers:

$$(21) \quad \eta_w = \eta(I_0,\gamma,\rho,r) = -I_0 + \int_{\tau=0}^{\gamma} W_0 (1-\rho) e^{-r\tau} d\tau .$$

The present value of the marginal product of men in FSHC is:

$$(22) \quad \lambda_m = \lambda(\theta,1,\rho,r) = \int_{\tau=0}^{1} \theta(\tau,\rho) e^{-r\tau} d\tau .$$

As I show, there is nothing to keep λ_m from exceeding the return to the alternative occupation η_m once males are completely concentrated in FSHC. If so, the excess of λ_m over η_m is a rent which is divided between FSHC workers and firms in a proportion β and $(1-\beta)$, respectively. The value of β is indeterminate in the present model and is determined as the outcome of a process of bilateral bargaining. A more complex model can provide enough structure to allow a determinate solution for β. For instance, Mortensen (1976) analyzes a labor market in which firms face a distribution of native ability across present and prospective employees, and employees face a distribution of nonpecuniary job attractiveness across present and prospective employers. A high value of β gives firms the incentive to fire present employees and search for more able replacements, whereas the firm is deterred from pushing β too low in order to deter employees from quitting to search for a more attractive job.

In the present model, I take β to be predetermined and fixed, since the basic conclusions are not sensitive to the particular process by which β is set.

The present value of FSHC wage income of men can be written:

$$(23) \quad \mu_m = \mu(I_0,\theta,1,\rho,r,\beta) = \eta_m + \beta(\lambda_m - \eta_m)$$

$$= \int_{\tau=0}^{1} \phi(\tau,\rho)e^{-r\tau} \, d\tau \,.$$

In (23) the present value (μ_m) depends on the determinants of the GHC wage, since this is the alternative occupation, and in addition on the determinants of productivity θ, and on β, the surplus-dividing proportion. $\phi(\tau,\rho)$ is the wage schedule which satisfies (23) and is drawn as the lower line in the right frame of Figure 4(a).

If firms pay men and women the same wage for any level of tenure, then the wage available to women in FSHC is the value of (23) for the shorter tenure length γ:

$$(24) \quad \mu_w = \mu(I_0,\theta,\gamma,\rho,r,\beta).$$

Equilibrium in the economy occurs when the present value of future wage income for women in the two occupations is equal:

$$(25) \quad \eta(I_0,\gamma,\rho,r) = \mu(I_0,\theta,\gamma,\rho,r,\beta).$$

Figure 4(b) depicts a situation in which the economy is out of equilibrium when all workers are in the FSHC occupation. Women will shift out of FSHC into GHC, reducing ρ until (25) is satisfied at the equilibrium value $\rho*$:

$$(26) \quad \rho* = \rho(I_0,\theta,\gamma,r,\beta) \,.$$

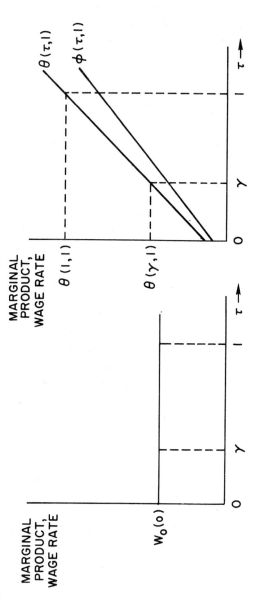

Figure 4 (a)

216

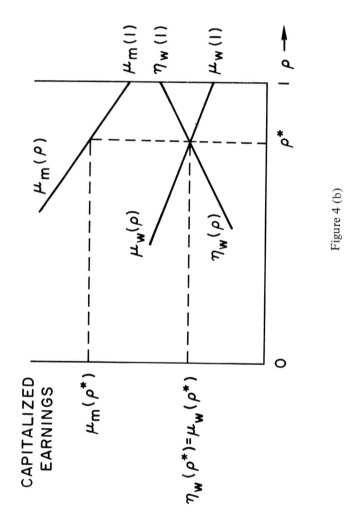

Figure 4 (b)

217

Figure 4(b) is drawn for the special case where the GHC occupation is sufficiently unattractive to result in complete specialization of men within FSHC. Because of longer tenure of men in GHC, the present value of their GHC wage in (20) is higher than η_w for women in (21), and so it is possible that male as well as female employment will be divided between the two occupations. The positive slope of the wage function in FSHC guarantees, however, that the share of female employees in GHC will always be greater than that of males.

In reality, females are not all "crowded" into a single occupation. Instead, there is a hierarchy of occupations into which females have been crowded and in which the overwhelming share of employees is female. Examples, in roughly ascending order of wage rates and GHC skill requirements, are household domestic workers, retail sales clerks, typists, secretaries, elementary school teachers, and registered nurses. All of these occupations share the common feature of general skills which can be transferred from firm to firm. The model would predict that females whose expected job tenure is relatively long and who plan only short spells of nonparticipation would be willing to make a greater initial investment (I_0) in skill acquisition. A full explanation of female occupational choice would have to take account as well of native intelligence and schooling attainment, since individuals lacking minimum requirements cannot voluntarily choose to train for the better female occupations, even if they plan on permanent labor-force attachment.

Up to this point the model has no place for pure economic discrimination. Females in GHC occupations are paid at a rate equal to their marginal products; the excess of productivity over the wage in FSHC occupations is not the result of discrimination but, rather, is a rent which firms earn on the specific human capital of all employees, both men and women. But, an amalgam of the model with Phelpsian (1972) "statistical discrimination" is more realistic. If there are positive costs to turnover, firms may calculate that women with low expected tenure should not be hired for the FSHC occupation. They may thereby overlook the minority of women who participate without any interruption in tenure, screening them out simply because it is too expensive to try to predict tenure in advance. These high tenure women are then the victims of pure economic discrimination, rejected at the job window simply because their female identity labels them with the low expected tenure of the majority of women.

VII.   EVIDENCE ON THE SOURCES OF
THE MALE-FEMALE WAGE DIFFERENTIAL

A study of the association between female earnings and on-the-job experience has recently been completed by Mincer and Polachek (1974). They test a human capital model in which current earnings (W_t) depend on the earnings of "brute force" labor with no education or experience (W_0), years of schooling (s), and the duration of i separate segments of experience (e_i):

$$(27) \quad \ln W_t = \ln W_0 + rs + \sum_i (rk_i^* - \delta_i)e_i \,,$$

where k_i is the ratio of on-the-job investment expenditures to gross earnings during the ith segment; r is the rate of return; and δ_i is the rate of depreciation. During periods of work experience, investment is relatively high compared to depreciation, and earnings tend to grow. Current earnings are reduced, however, by spells of nonparticipation in the labor force, when net investment is negative.

Although Mincer and Polachek cannot identify the separate contributions of investment and depreciation for spells of work experience, they estimate the depreciation rate during spells of nonparticipation (when k_i^* is assumed zero) to be about 1.5 percent per year for married women.[20] Table 6 illustrates the net contribution of experience to the white male-female "wage gap" for the age group 30-44, which was 34.3 percent of male wages in 1966 for white married women and 14.2 percent for white single women. Both female groups had less work experience than the males, only about half as much in the case of married women. Line 4 indicates the wage rates which women would have earned if their shortfall in experience is evaluated by the male coefficient on experience in the estimated version of (27). The wage gap for both groups is reduced to about 10 percent of male earnings, which can be considered an upper limit on the extent of "direct" discrimination (paying different wages to individuals with identical endowments). To the extent that the remaining 10 percent gap is caused by other objective determinants of productivity omitted from the equation, the extent of direct discrimination may be smaller.

The extent of direct discrimination is larger in the Mincer-Polachek sample when the net contribution of experience is estimated from the female coefficients on experience. This occurs as a result of the relatively flat

---

[20]In the context of my model, this is the weighted average of the high depreciation rates in FSHC occupations and the low depreciation rates in GHC occupations.

age-earnings profiles for women, as illustrated in Figure 3. The choice between the male and female coefficients on experience for the calculation of the extent of discrimination depends on the underlying causes of the relatively flat female profile. Bergmann's approach treats the lower female experience coefficients as entirely caused by discrimination which takes the form of occupational crowding into occupations which provide little reward for experience. An alternative interpretation is provided by my model; a substantial number of women prefer to work in GHC occupations which do not provide a markedly higher wage for more' experienced workers. The small male-female earnings differential of unmarried white females in Table 6 supports the second interpretation, and suggests that the low return to experience of married females is caused by their own rational choice, and rational choices by firms, in response to their low expected job tenure, and is not caused by discrimination against all females.

In a study of the same data used in the Mincer-Polachek paper, Oaxaca (1973) arrives at a completely different conclusion--that 78 percent of the raw male-female wage differential is caused by direct discrimination, as compared to the 29 percent found by Mincer-Polachek. The conflict between the cross-section wage equations of the respective studies appears to center on their divergent estimates of the effect of experience on male earnings. Only 2.1 percent of the raw differential is due to differences in the experience of males and females in the white subsample when calculated with the white male experience coefficients in the Oaxaca paper (1973, p. 144, Table 4), as opposed to about 70 percent in the Mincer-Polachek study. The discrepancy appears to be explained by a simple mistake made by Oaxaca. Lacking the separate "spells of experience" variables used by Mincer-Polachek, Oaxaca estimates the effect of experience by two variables: (1) age minus school years; and, (2) number of children. But, in calculating the difference in experience to be multiplied by the male weights, Oaxaca takes account only of (1), i.e., he essentially measures differences in age rather than in experience, and he neglects to compute the gap between male and female levels of experience attributable to years spent raising children. I speculate that a proper recalculation of direct discrimination from the Oaxaca regressions would yield results similar to those of Mincer-Polachek.

Other cross-section studies are less systematic than the two just cited. Cohen (1971) reaches a finding of no direct discrimination in a sample of 900 individuals questioned in 1969 by the Michigan Survey Research Center, in the sense that there were no significant wage differences ". . .between men and women with the same job." About half of the raw earnings differential was explained by differences in personal characteristics, the remaining half

Table 6

Contribution of Job Experience
to the Wage Differential Between
Men and Women, Aged 30-44

(Data: 1966 Survey of Economic Opportunity)

	White Married Males	White Married Females	White Unmarried Females
1. Average Hourly Wage Rate	$3.18	$2.09	$2.73
2. Line (1), percent of males	1.000	0.657	0.858
3. Years of Job Experience Since Completion of School	19.4	9.6	15.6
4. Wage Rate Calculated with Male Years of Job Experience and Male Coefficients on Experience	$3.18	$2.85	$2.91
5. Line (4), percent of males	1.000	0.896	0.915

Source: Computed from Mincer and Polachek (1974, pp. 590-593).

by "...the presence of women in lower-paying occupations for whatever causes: less on-the-job training than men, the lesser choice of women as to geographic area of job, greater desire of women for specific hours, and more physical dangers or unhealthy conditions in the male jobs"(p. 446). One notes that all of the reasons for occupational crowding cited by Cohen refer to male-female differences in productivity. Similarly Sanborn concludes that,"...within a wide range of occupations, market discrimination against women, if it exists at all, is under 10 percent" (1964, p. 546). Unlike Cohen, Sanborn provides no explanation of the occupational distribution of women; in my model, the occupational distribution of women results from low expected tenure and reflects social rather than economic discrimination.

Malkiel and Malkiel (1973) study data for a group of professionals (employees of the Educational Testing Service). The unadjusted wage rate of females is 66.3 percent of males, almost the same as the relative wage rate of married females in the Mincer-Polachek sample in Table 6. The regression coefficients from equations explaining earnings are used to calculate the wages of women on the condition that their endowments of schooling, experience, and other characteristics were equal to those of men. There is an "area of study" variable, roughly equivalent to a control for occupation. The conclusion is that the relative wage rates of women would have risen from 66.3 percent to 88.8 percent if they had been endowed with the same characteristics as males, leaving a difference of 11.2 percent as attributable to pure discrimination. This is similar to the Mincer-Polachek estimate of 10.4 percent for pure discrimination for the married women in their more comprehensive sample.

Other studies of individual occupations are mainly limited to teachers (a comment on the ethnocentricity of academic research). In a sample of public school teachers taken from the 1965 Coleman Report, Antos and Rosen (1974) find a relatively small gross differential between men and women of only 13 percent, an unsurprising result as this is an occupation into which women are "crowded." Careful adjustment for a very extensive set of teacher and student characteristics accounts for about 60 percent of the gross differential, reducing the coefficient of direct discrimination to about 5 percent. Gordon, Morton, and Braden (1974) find a discrimination factor of 9.5 percent for the faculty of a single unidentified university, but one of the right-hand regression variables is faculty rank. The authors do not rule out the possibility of additional discrimination in the promotion of faculty, which would raise the discrimination estimate, although, in the context of my model, the failure of women to reach the higher faculty ranks could by and large reflect their weaker level of labor-force attachment. Finally, Johnson and Stafford (1974) estimate an average "salary disadvantage" for women faculty members in a 1970 NSF sample as only 6.9 percent, based on the female relative wage of newly hired inexperienced faculty. Their study raises the same question as that of Gordon, Morton, and Braden--does the decline in the female/male wage ratio with experience occur because discrimination increases with experience, or because women fail to stay in the labor force regularly enough to accumulate experience. The latter interpretation is consistent with the model and with most of the evidence examined here.

VIII. CONCLUSION

Most of the evidence in the previous section is consistent with the conclusion that pure economic discrimination against women reduces the female wage about 10 percent below the male wage. The rest of the female-male wage differential is due to numerous factors, but most particularly to the low return to added years of experience for females. The overriding fact limiting females to a flat experience-earnings profile is the expectation by employers, correct for most females but incorrect for a substantial and growing minority, that females will have a shorter job tenure than a man of the same age hired at the same time, as well as the realistic expectation by female employees that they are not likely to hold FSHC-type jobs long enough to acquire as much on-the-job training as men. Females choose jobs which require general training and may give a higher wage early in the job tenure, and firms prefer to hire and promote males in FSHC-type occupations if there are positive costs of turnover. The simple model emphasized the possibility of "voluntary occupational crowding" by females making their own optimal choices and abstracted from the costs of turnover. A more complex model including the costs of turnover would lead firms to behave in a manner frequently observed in the real world, refusing female applications from the beginning, and refusing to promote existing female employees.

The estimate that "pure economic discrimination" amounts to "only" 10 percent of the male wage leaves the majority of the male-female wage differential to be explained by lower female productivity, due primarily to the economic consequences of shorter job tenure. This conclusion does not mean that women have not been the victims of discrimination, but merely shifts the majority of the blame from economic to social discrimination which is responsible for the weak attachment of women to the labor force. Among the social factors which limit female economic opportunity are the absence of government-subsidized maternity leaves and child care for small children, and the inability or unwillingness of most wives to convince their husbands to contribute half of the time input required to raise children.

Table 7 completes the process of calculating the components of (16) above, the total effect on the consumption of "final commodities" of the 1956-1974 structural shift in unemployment. The top portion of the Table inserts the results of sections V and VII. In line 1a the relative female marginal product is taken to be the ratio of the female to the male wage, plus 10 percent for pure economic discrimination. The productivity of teenagers is arbitrarily set equal to their wage, in the absence of any evidence of pure economic discrimination against teenagers. Lines 1b and 1c reflect the conclusions of section V, that the value of extra search time of teenagers is zero, and that the value of extra search time by adult women is equal to the value of their home time.

The bottom portion of Table 7 provides the estimates of the separate components of (16). The results are dominated by the large positive contributions of the movement of both young women and adult women from the home into employment. Society gains because the tax system and pure economic discrimination both insert a "wedge" between the productivity of women and the value of their home time. The basic assumption is that women found it possible to enter the labor force as the result of improved contraceptive technology and of the time released by the presence of modern consumer durables. If women previously spent their workhours in "involuntary household captivity," taking care of children they did not want, and performing household chores now made unnecessary by better appliances, then the benefits of the structural shift may have been grossly understated above. Instead of the procedure in Table 7 of valuing female released home time at the margin, as equal to the net-of-tax acceptance wage, a case can be made for valuing the home time at zero, or even a negative number, if the household drudgery was sufficiently "more unpleasant" than work activity.

Table 7, line 2b, measures the social cost (negative benefits) of the higher relative unemployment rates of young people and adult females. Partly because an unemployed teenager works fewer hours than an adult male, and partly because home time can still be enjoyed while 5-10 hours per week are devoted to search, the overall social cost of the higher relative unemployment rates is amazingly small. The total of line 2b for both groups is only $2.8 billion, or 0.2 percent of GNP. Thus, the welfare cost of the structural shift in unemployment between 1956 and 1974 is not 4.5 percent of GNP, as a crude Okun's Law calculation would conclude, but rather only a tiny fraction of that amount, even if the benefits of the increased female participation rate are ignored. The total impact of the structural shift, netting out the cost of the increased relative unemployment rates against the benefits of increasing participation, amounts to $18.2 billion, or 1.4 percent of GNP, in improved welfare.

Table 7

Values Attached to Changes
in Employed, Unemployed, and Home Time
Caused by the
1956-1974 Structural Shift in Unemployment

	Males and Females 16-24	Adult Females 25+
1. Fraction of Wage of Males 35-44		
a. Q_{M_i} (Marginal Product of Work)	$W_i/W_1 = .433$	$.10 + W_i/W_1 = .667$
b. W_{U_i} (Value of Search Time)	0	$0.5(W_i/W_1) = .284$
c. W_{N_i} (Value of Home Time)	$0.5(W_i/W_1) = .217$	$0.5(W_i/W_1) = .284$
2. Value of Shifts ($ Billion) Due to:		
a. Change in Participation		
i. Movement into Work	3.253	17.736
ii. Movement into Unemployment	- 0.112	0.000
b. Change in Relative Unemployment Rates		
i. Loss of Work	- 1.597	- 0.714
ii. Increased Unemployment	- 0.367	0.000
c. Total of 2a and 2b	1.177	17.022

Sources:

1. W_i/W_1 is based on the ratios of group full-time earnings to those of males 35-44, from Figure 3, which is based on the Current Population Survey, Series P-60.

2. The dollar values are calculated by multiplying the values of Q_{M_i}, W_{U_i}, and W_{N_i} from the top of this Table by the appropriate changes in manhours, from Table 4, according to (16) in the text. The value of W_1 is taken to be $6.00, the annual earnings of males aged 35-44 in 1974 divided by 2000 annual hours.

I conclude that, if policymakers were satisfied with a 4.1 percent unemployment rate in 1956, then they should be even more satisfied with 5.6 percent unemployment as of 1974. This does not mean, however, that there is no case for considering government action to try to narrow the differential of unemployment rates between the secondary groups and prime-age adult males. This analysis provides an estimate that the increase in relative unemployment rates taken by itself, without counting the effects of higher female participation, has cost society at least $2.8 billion, omitting any costs of increased crime caused by unemployed youth. This measure of the benefits of reducing relative unemployment rates to 1956 levels should be set against the costs of proposed programs. If the analysis of section V is to be believed, however, the unemployment rates of teenagers and males aged 20-24 could be reduced to 1956 levels if the teenage minimum wage were set at a level equal to 54 percent of its 1974 value (see Table 5).

REFERENCES

1. Antos, J. R., and Rosen, S. N., "Discrimination in the Market for Public School Teachers," University of Rochester working paper 74-14, June 1974.

2. Arrow, K., "Models of Job Discrimination," in Racial Discrimination in Economic Life, (ed. A. H. Pascal), Lexington, Mass.: Heath Lexington, 1972.

3. _____, "The Theory of Discrimination," in Discrimination in Labor Markets, (eds. O. Ashenfelter and A. Rees), Princeton: Princeton University Press, 1973.

4. Becker, G. S., "A Theory of the Allocation of Time," Economic Journal, LXXV, No. 299, (September 1965), 493-517.

5. _____. The Economics of Discrimination, 2nd edition. Chicago: University of Chicago Press, 1971.

6. Bergmann, B., "Occupational Segregation, Wages and Profits When Employers Discriminate by Race or Sex," Eastern Economic Journal, 1, No. 2, (April /July 1974), 103-10.

7. Cohen, M. S., "Sex Differences in Compensation," Journal of Human Resources, VI, No. 4, (Fall 1971), 434-47.

8. Freeman, R. B., "Changes in the Labor Market for Black Americans, 1948-72," Brookings Papers on Economic Activity, Washington, D. C.: The Brookings Institution, 4 (1973: 1), 67-120.

9. Goldfarb, R. S., "The Policy Content of Quantitative Minimum Wage Research," Proceedings of IRRA Winter Meetings, San Francisco: Industrial Relations Research Association, 1974.

10. Gordon, N., Morton, T., and Braden, I., "Faculty Salaries: Is There Discrimination by Sex, Race, and Discipline?" American Economic Review, LXIV, No. 3, (June 1974), 419-27.

11. Gordon, R. J., "Inflation in Recession and Recovery," <u>Brookings Papers on Economic Activity</u>, Washington, D. C.: The Brookings Institution, 2 (1971: 1), 105-66.

12. _____, "The Welfare Cost of Higher Unemployment," <u>Brookings Papers on Economic Activity</u>, Washington, D. C.: The Brookings Institution, 4 (1973: 1), 133-95.

13. _____, "Alternative Responses of Policy to External Supply Shocks," <u>Brookings Papers on Economic Activity</u>, Washington, D.C.: The Brookings Institution, 6 (1975: 1), 183-206 (a).

14. _____, "The Impact of Aggregate Demand on Prices," <u>Brookings Papers on Economic Activity</u>, Washington, D. C.: The Brookings Institution, 6 (1975: 3),613-62 (b).

15. Gramlich, E. M., "The Impact of Minimum Wages on Other Wages, Employment and Family Incomes," <u>Brookings Papers on Economic Activity</u>, Washington, D. C.: The Brookings Institution,forthcoming 1976.

16. Hall, R. E., "The Rigidity of Wages and the Persistence of Unemployment," <u>Brookings Papers on Economic Activity</u>, Washington, D. C.: The Brookings Institution, 6 (1975: 2), 301-35.

17. Johnson, G. E., and Stafford, F. P., "The Earnings and Promotion of Women Faculty," <u>American Economic Review</u>, LXIV, No. 6, (December 1974), 888-903.

18. Malkiel, B. G., and Malkiel, J. A., "Male-Female Pay Differentials in Professional Employment," <u>American Economic Review</u>, LXIII, No. 4, (September 1973), 693-705.

19. Mincer, J., "Unemployment Effects of Minimum Wages," <u>Journal of Political Economy</u>, 84, No. 4, II, (August 1976), S87-S104.

20. Mincer, J., and Polachek, S. W., "Family Investments in Human Capital: Earnings of Women," <u>Journal of Political Economy</u>, 82, No. 2, II, (March/April 1974), S76-S108.

21. Mortensen, D. T., "Job Search, the Duration of Unemployment, and the Phillips Curve," American Economic Review, LX, No. 5, (December 1970), 847-62.

22. _____, "Specific Skills, Search, and Separations," Northwestern University working paper, August 1976.

23. Oaxaca, R., "Sex Discrimination in Wages," in Discrimination in Labor Markets, (eds. O. Ashenfelter and A. Rees), Princeton: Princeton University Press, 1973.

24. Perry, G. L., "Changing Labor Markets and Inflation," Brookings Papers on Economic Activity, Washington, D. C.: The Brookings Institution, 1 (1970: 3), 411-41.

25. _____, "Unemployment Flows in the U.S. Labor Market," Brookings Papers on Economic Activity, Washington, D. C.: The Brookings Institution, 3 (1972: 2), 245-78.

26. Phelps, E. S., "The Statistical Theory of Racism and Sexism," American Economic Review, LXII, No. 4, (September 1972), 659-61.

27. Polachek, S. W., "Occupational Segregation Among Women: A Human Capital Approach," unpublished, presented at Third World Congress of the Econometric Society, Toronto, August 1975.

28. Sanborn, H., "Pay Differences Between Men and Women," Industrial and Labor Relations Review, 17, No. 4, (July 1964), 534-50.

29. Wachter, M. L., "The Changing Cyclical Responsiveness of Wage Inflation," Brookings Papers on Economic Activity, Washington, D. C.: The Brookings Institution, 7 (1976: 1), 115-19.

30. Weisskoff, F. B., "'Women's Place' in the Labor Market," American Economic Review, LXII, No. 2, (May 1972), 161-66.

31. Welch, F., "Minimum Wage Legislation in the United States," Economic Inquiry, 12, No. 3, (September 1974), 285-318.

STRUCTURAL UNEMPLOYMENT
AND THE PRODUCTIVITY OF WOMEN: A COMMENT

Robert E. Hall
Massachusetts Institute of Technology

In his paper, Gordon's basic idea is to price out the changes in the pattern of activities of young people and women during the period 1956 to 1974. In this period, young people have come to spend much more of their time unemployed, and older women have come to spend much more time working. Gordon tries to give an economic appraisal of these structural changes.

Now, in an ideal economy with no taxes on earnings, no minimum wage, no unemployment compensation or other stimulus to unemployment, and no discrimination, individuals allocate their time to equate its marginal value in all uses, and Gordon's technique would give a net value of zero to any structural change. The interest in this paper, as in his companion paper (Gordon, 1973) on the welfare implications of cyclical changes in unemployment, arises from his discussion and measurements of the various wedges and externalities that make the modern U.S. economy so different from the ideal economy. His conclusion is exactly the same as in the earlier paper, and exactly correct and important, in my view: The wedge imposed by the heavy taxation of earnings is totally dominant, and any change in the economy, either structural or cyclical, which moves people into employment and out of time spent at home, has a tremendous social benefit. With respect to the structural shift of the past 20 years, the message of the paper is very clear that the social benefits of increased employment far outweigh the costs of any increase in unemployment that attended the increase in employment.

Though I consider it to have only limited practical importance, there is a serious theoretical shortcoming to this technique. Gordon is vague about why the structural change took place, yet surely in principle the pricing out of the change depends on the source of the movement. My impression is that only part of the movement of women into the labor force can be explained by quantifiable economic forces. For the rest, one can only appeal to the notion that preferences have changed, resulting in a lower valuation of home time (in the sense of a shift in the demand function for that time). But economists are incapable of pricing out the effects of a change in preferences. Gordon is careful not to rest his case on shifting preferences, however; he focuses instead on calculating the social value of improved contraception in an economy with huge wedges between social and private trade-offs. The paper would be improved if it were clearer on this point, but I would guess that the empirical results would be much the same regardless what assumptions were made, because the numbers are totally dominated by the extra social value of additional market work.

Gordon carries over from his earlier work the assumption that the wedge between the marginal product of labor and the net wage is 50 percent, and that individuals equate the value of time at home to the net wage. He is concerned in this paper with estimating the marginal product of labor and the marginal social value of unemployment. For young workers, he accepts the observed gross wage as the appropriate measure of the marginal product of labor. For adult women, he presents a detailed survey of recent investigations of the degree of discrimination against women which takes the form of being paid a wage less than their marginal product. He concludes that discrimination in this sense does not exceed 10 percent, and in fact uses the wage plus 10 percent as his measure of the marginal product of the labor of adult women. However, the issue of discrimination against women arises here only in its narrowest sense. Women suffer serious discrimination if they are excluded from occupations in which their marginal products would be higher, yet this form of discrimination is irrelevant for Gordon's calculations. Only a measure of the gap between the marginal product and the wage for the occupations that women actually entered is necessary for his argument. Much of the discussion in section VI concerning occupational crowding as the result of rational behavior on the part of employers, rather than of discrimination, is off the point. The results of the paper do not change if pure discrimination is blamed for crowding instead. The most relevant evidence on this point is the research on particular occupations cited by Gordon at the end of section VII. The rest of the discussion of discrimination could be abbreviated.

Gordon takes the general view that the marginal social product of unemployment is fairly low, though his numerical results would not change very much if he took a more favorable view of the value of unemployment. For young workers, he attributes all of the increase in unemployment to the increasing impact of the minimum wage, and expresses the opinion that the marginal social product of this kind of unemployment is zero. On this point, he is surely very close to being correct, though it is remarkable that he can discuss such a cruelly perverse institution as the minimum wage so dispassionately. For adult women, he assumes equality of the marginal social product of unemployment and the net private value of home time. In principle, he disagrees on this point with much recent thought about the determinants of unemployment, which accepts the equality of the private marginal benefits of search and time at home, but blames various forces for creating private returns to unemployment that do not correspond to any social returns. Feldstein's (1975) work on temporary layoffs and the fairly extensive literature on the influence of wage differentials both support such an externality. However, none of these considerations would make any appreciable difference in Gordon's calculations, because unemployment occupies almost none of an unemployed woman's time--most of each week of unemployment is allocated to time at home in his calculations.

Gordon's discussion of the treatment of unemployment is marred by his dogged insistence on the use of Keynes' distinction between voluntary and involuntary unemployment. Gordon seeks to distinguish between unemployment with a social value and unemployment without it, but he needlessly involves the paper in the running feud between orthodox Keynesian and modern classical interpretations of the cyclical movements in unemployment. In this dispute, orthodox Keynesians have drawn the caricature of the search theory (in which mistaken expectations cause workers to quit to become unemployed) so often that they have convinced themselves that some economists actually believe that unemployment is a voluntary activity in this sense. Nothing in this paper rests on settling this argument. Economists of all persuasions can agree to discuss the issue of the social benefit of unemployment without reliance on the controversial vocabulary of that feud.

REFERENCES

1. Feldstein, M., "The Importance of Temporary Layoffs: An Empirical Analysis," Brookings Papers on Economic Activity, Washington, D.C.: The Brookings Institution, 6 (1975:3), 725-44.

2. Gordon, R.J., "The Welfare Cost of Higher Unemployment," Brookings Papers on Economic Activity, Washington, D.C.: The Brookings Institution, 4 (1973:1), 133-95.

AN EMPIRICAL STUDY OF RISK
UNDER FIXED AND FLEXIBLE EXCHANGE *

André Farber
Université Libre de Bruxelles and
the Center for Operations Research and Econometrics

Richard Roll **
University of California, Los Angeles

and Bruno Solnik
Centre d'Enseignement Supérieur des Affaires and
the European Institute for Advanced Studies in Management

I. INTRODUCTION

The shift in the international monetary system from pegged to flexible exchange rates[1] has finally provided scholars with empirical material to arbitrate their welfare arguments in favor of or against a floating exchange regime. Since Friedman's celebrated paper (1953) pleading the case for flexible exchange rates, the arguments advanced to support one or another system have been primarily theoretical. Experiences with floating exchange rates were restricted to Canada from 1950 to 1962, to European countries just after World War I, and to smaller countries such as Peru or Thailand which were less familiar to American and European scholars. New material could only be found by going back to the nineteenth century when Austria, Russia, and the United States experienced (although not simultaneously) unregulated exchange rates. Given the importance of the controversy, such data were insufficient. The new empirical evidence which begins to be available is welcome; see Aliber (1975) and Whitman (1975) for surveys of recent empirical work.

---

*
We wish to thank the participants at the Carnegie-Rochester conference on monetary economics for a lively discussion and many useful suggestions. The comments of Eugene Fama were also very helpful. Any remaining errors are, of course, our responsibility.

**
At the time of the meeting, Roll was at the Centre d'Enseignement Supérieur des Affaires and the European Institute for Advanced Studies in Management.

[1] It is difficult to give a name to the present system. It is a far cry from the pure floating exchange rates referred to in the literature since some European currencies participate in a joint float and central banks intervene on the market but without any coordination. The term "flexible" will be used to refer to the present system. Other nomenclatures are "managed floating" system or "dirty floating" system.

Uncertainty has been a recurrent theme of discussion. Two worries about free exchange rates have been expressed: (1) that speculation could destabilize exchange markets; and (2) that exchange risk could be an obstacle to international trade and investment.

These two related contentions, advanced by Nurske (1944), were later criticized by Friedman (1953), Aliber (1972), and others. It is our purpose to analyze the uncertainty problem using recent data.

The stability issue is ambiguous. There does not seem to exist a general agreement on the definition of destabilizing speculation. Implicit to any reasoning is the assumption that there exists a "normal" price in the exchange market, possibly different from the observed rate, and generally defined as the price that brings purchasing power parity (Yeager, 1966). Speculators are defined as persons with open exchange positions. Speculative functions are separated from trade functions. The scenario then runs as follows--in the absence of speculation (i.e., if all transactors cover their exchange positions), realized exchange rates will be identical to their normal values. The existence of speculators in the market will create disparities between normal and realized values. Speculators will accentuate any movement in exchange rates, buying when they notice an increase of exchange rates and selling when they notice a decrease.

This argument has been questioned by Friedman (1953), who doubts the profitability of the behavior assumed for speculators, and is thus reluctant to admit its existence. Moreover, as noted by Farrell (1966), the credibility of this scenario is not high because it lacks a theory of speculation. Indeed, models starting with individual preferences to support the theory are not numerous. Finally, the scenario implicitly assumes imperfect exchange markets. A well-functioning market would be characterized by available information being reflected in prices (Fama, 1970); and a divergence between the observed exchange rate and some knowable "normal" price would imply inefficiency. This is contrary to the wide belief that foreign exchange markets are very efficient, at least for the major trading nations. This belief is shared even by dealers, which is indeed a rare fact for speculative assets.

The second general worry is that uncertainty would increase under a floating exchange rate regime, and that this would impede international trade.

Thus stated, this argument is somewhat simplistic and several objections can be raised. First, as noted by Friedman (1953), the possibility of hedging in the forward market should be considered. If traders consider it optimal to hedge completely their exchange positions, they will not be in a less favorable position under floating exchange rates unless the forward exchange premium is greater. Second, an increase in uncertainty could be accompanied by an increase in expected return such that some individuals would prefer the more uncertain but also more rewarding situation.

This paper intends to provide some empirical evidence with respect to the questions just raised. In section II, the distribution functions of exchange rate fluctuations will be examined. The objective is to present a record of the experience of each individual currency. However, the study of currencies fluctuating on an individual basis does not give complete information about the evolution of risk. In order to analyze this question, section III of the paper examines the risk-return relation for portfolios of currencies. If the exchange market is dominated by risk-averse participants, they will diversify their risk and hold such currency portfolios.

Solnik (1973) and Farber (1975) have given more theoretical content to this idea. Basically, the argument can be stated as follows. (a) It can be shown that a risk-averting trader facing assets or liabilities in foreign countries will choose a completely hedged position if, and only if, he expects that future spot exchange rates will equal the current forward exchange rates (Farber, 1975). Otherwise, he will assume a partially unhedged position in foreign currencies. For example, a Canadian exporter to France will completely hedge his franc-denominated accounts receivable only when his subjective expectation of the future spot franc/dollar rate equals the current forward franc/dollar rate for the term of his receivable. (b) Solnik (1973) has shown that rational investors will choose portfolios of foreign-denominated assets and will be able to diversify away any independent random variations in exchange rates. In other words, traders facing foreign positions will not hedge perfectly, and prices will be set based on portfolio risk rather than on individual risk.

This last point is critical for our definition of risk. Many traders may occupy themselves with one or only a few foreign countries. Exporters and importers might fall into this group. However, if enough rational risk-averse investors exist, equilibrium exchange rates will be established on the basis of variations in a diversified portfolio of foreign assets. Portfolio risk would depend upon co-movements in exchange rates, and equilibrium forward premia would be determined by the risk-bearing attitudes of portfolio diversifiers. The flexible rate period might have witnessed a great increase in individual exchange variation; but it might also have witnessed a reduction in co-variation, and portfolio risk might actually have decreased as a result. The next two sections present what actually happened.

II. THE DISTRIBUTION OF INDIVIDUAL EXCHANGE RATES

In this section, we report on the forms of distributions of individual rates of change in exchange rates. The basic random variable under study is

$$R_{j,t} = \frac{(S_{j,t} - S_{j,t-1})}{S_{j,t-1}} \quad ,$$

where $S_{j,t}$ is the exchange rate of U. S. dollars per currency j at the end of period t. This exchange rate return is the fundamental building block in the study of risk, speculation, and other attributes of the world foreign exchange system. The market sets the forward discount or premium as some function of the distribution of this variable including, perhaps, its co-movements with other exchange rate returns.

We might have defined exchange risk as the variance of the individual R_j, but this would have been an incomplete definition of risk for the portfolio reasons given above. Nevertheless, an examination of individual distributions sets the stage for a correct analysis and also gives some historical insight into the intertemporal evolution of the basic variables.

The Data

The data consist of two independently collected samples of spot exchange rates, a sample of three-month forward exchange rates, and a sample of short-term interest rates. The basic data characteristics are given in Table 1. There are 17 countries with at least some available data, but not all of these have full records. The maximum sample periods for weekly spot rates and for interest rates apply to all indicated countries. For monthly spot rates, however, the Australian sample begins in October 1961, and the Brazilian sample in February 1967. There are no large gaps in the forward rate series, but a few observations are missing.

We made an effort to discover data errors by employing various filter programs. Large absolute values of exchange rate returns and unusual sequences (large positive return followed by large negative return, or vice versa) were examined and corrected. For the spot exchange rates, the two independent samples were compared during their overlapping period. Several additional errors were found in this way. The resulting spot exchange rate series should be relatively error-free. The forward rate series is probably less clean, simply because two independent samples were not available.

Table 1

Data Definitions and Sources

Variable	Source	Frequency of Observations	Maximum Sample Period	Maximum Sample Size	Countries Available
Spot Exchange Rate	International Financial Statistics	Monthly (end-of-month)	Jan. 1957 -Jan. 1975	217	17
Spot Exchange Rate	National Bank of Belgium	Weekly (end-of-week)	Jan. 1965 -May 1975	541	8
Three-month Forward Exchange Rate	International Financial Statistics	Monthly (end-of-month)	July 1960 -Jan. 1975	175	7
Short-term Interest Rate	International Financial Statistics	Monthly (end-of-month)	Jan. 1964 -Jan. 1975	133	17

Countries for which all series are available:

   Belgium, Canada, France, Germany, Great Britain, Netherlands, Switzerland

Country which lacks forward rate series:

   Italy

Other countries (which lack forward rates and weekly data):

   Australia, Austria, Brazil, Denmark, Japan, Norway, South Africa, Spain, Sweden

For Belgium, which maintains a two-tier system, the weekly data are "free market" rates, and the monthly data are "regulated" rates. The two series are highly co-linear, but there is usually about a 2 percent difference in their levels.

The interest rate series does not contain many data errors, but it suffers from a more troubling characteristic. Not all countries have available free market short-term interest rates, and those that are available do not all have the same characteristics. When a treasury bill rate was available, we used it: Canada, Great Britain, The Netherlands, South Africa, U.S. The next most preferred series was a "short-term government": Australia; then the call money rate: Belgium, France, Germany, Japan; and finally, the rediscount rate: Austria, Brazil, Denmark, Italy, Norway, Spain, Sweden, Switzerland. There is no doubt that some measurement error is induced by these differences among the interest rate series. However, it is probably not very significant because the variability in interest rates is only about one-tenth the variability in exchange rate changes. (The measured variance is only about one-one hundredth as great.) Furthermore, an examination of the interest rate series shows that even the rediscount rates vary to a certain extent, and that they follow market-determined rates over long periods.

Empirical Distributions of Exchange Rate Returns

Since our basic objective is to analyze the results of the flexible rate system, we had to determine dates when the fixed rate regimes were abandoned by each country. This is the least solvable problem of all because (a) some monetary authorities made no announcement; (b) some evidently abandoned first and announced they would abandon later; (c) others announced the cessation of fixed rate maintenance while continuing to support their currencies; and (d) some countries maintained fixed rates with certain trading partners while allowing their currency to float with others.

In addition, the portfolio work of section III requires concurrent observations since empirical estimates of covariation are calculated. Thus, we felt it best to select a single date near the beginning of the transition period, and to use it as the cutoff point between fixed and flexible rate analysis for all countries. The date chosen was the end of March 1971. At that time, some countries had already announced their intention to abandon the fixed system and other countries were clearly about to follow. The U. S. would release the gold price of dollars on August 15, 1971.

The choice of date is admittedly subjective. We can only defend it by stating a lack of intention on our part to affect the results one way or the other. In addition, we examined the effect of our choice for a few countries that announced a clear policy and did not lie about it. For example, West Germany actually allowed the mark to float on May 9, 1971. Using this date, rather than the end of March 1971, results in only a trivial change in the estimates.

240

Table 2 gives empirical estimates for the monthly and weekly spot exchange rate returns. In addition to the familiar statistics such as mean, standard deviation, skewness, and kurtosis,[2] we have calculated several other statistics in order to better describe the shapes of these distributions. One fact which is immediately evident is that the two periods displayed quite different distributions in almost every attribute.

For example, let us take the dollar return on French francs in the two periods. Using monthly data, the average arithmetic return was -2.975 percent per annum from January 1957 through March 1971, and the standard error of this number was $22.26/\sqrt{170} = 1.71$. From April 1971 through January 1975, a position in French currency would have earned 6.941 percent, with a standard error of $37.6/\sqrt{46} = 5.54$. If the two distributions were random Gaussian samples, these mean returns would be different at any commonly used significance level. Of course, not all countries were strong vis-à-vis the dollar in the second period. Italy, for example, had virtually the same average return in both periods, but its standard deviation was much larger in the second period. Brazilian currency was weak in both periods, and so on.

Of the 17 countries, only three (Canada, Spain, and Brazil) had larger standard deviations in the "fixed rate period." Canada is no surprise since it had actually floated long before the other countries and then went back to fixed rates. Brazil was effectively floating prior to 1971 since it had such a

---

[2]Let X_i (i=1,...,N) be a sample of the random variable X. The kth central sample moment is

$$m_k = \frac{1}{N} \sum_i (X_i - \sum_i X_i /N)^k .$$

The sample standard deviation is $[(N/N-1)m_2]^{1/2}$. Sample skewness is given by $m_3/m_2^{3/2}$, kurtosis by m_4/m_2^2. As a benchmark, random samples from a normal distribution have expected skewness of zero and expected kurtosis of 3.0.

Approximate sampling variances for the skewness and kurtosis statistics are given by 6/N and 24/N, respectively, for a Gaussian population (see Cramer, 1945, p. 357). For the sample sizes that appear in our tables, the following approximate 95 percent acceptance intervals can be applied.

Sample Size	Skewness	Kurtosis*
	95 percent Acceptance Intervals	
46	±.708	4.42
86	±.518	4.03
135	±.413	3.83
170	±.368	3.74
213	±.329	3.66
328	±.265	3.53

*For the kurtosis, only the upper limit of the acceptance interval is given because all the observed values are larger than 3.0.

Table 2

Distributional Characteristics of Exchange Rate Returns (Dollar/Other), 1957 - 1975 [1]

Country	Means (% / annum)	Standard deviations (% / annum)[4]	Skewnesses	Kurtoses	Studentized Ranges	Scales (% / annum)	Characteristic Exponents	Coefficients of Variation	Sample Sizes
					Monthly data[2]				
Australia	- .0270 / 4.96	2.86 / 33.0	2.42 / .267	15.8 / 15.0	8.29 / 8.41	.975 / N.C.[3]	1.40 / N.C.	- 106. / 6.64	113 / 46
Austria	.044 / 12.4	1.45 / 36.8	1.33 / .856	11.4 / 5.19	9.58 / 5.66	.560 / 15.7	1.18 / 1.13	32.7 / 2.97	170 / 46
Belgium	.0897 / 9.63	2.21 / 35.0	1.26 / .605	11.9 / 5.53	9.13 / 6.08	.438 / 20.3	~.9 / 1.45	24.7 / 3.64	170 / 46
Brazil	-14.9 / -10.4	32.9 / 13.4	- 4.10 / .355	20.2 / 5.32	5.72 / 6.17	11.4 / 11.1	1.11 / 2.0	- 2.21 / - 1.39	49 / 44
Canada	- .331 / .260	8.33 / 7.56	- 1.81 / .515	22.2 / 3.65	13.1 / 5.00	2.56 / 5.76	1.27 / 1.82	- 25.1 / 29.1	170 / 46
Denmark	- 5.36 / 8.10	6.60 / 33.1	-11.7 / .548	147. / 6.31	14.0 / 6.35	.943 / 10.6	1.51 / 1.03	- 12.3 / 4.08	170 / 46
France	- 2.98 / 6.94	22.3 / 37.6	- 7.65 / .507	61.3 / 5.21	9.21 / 5.95	.296 / 15.7	~.8 / 1.14	- 7.48 / 5.42	170 / 46
Germany	1.06 / 12.12	8.69 / 39.6	8.17 / 1.13	76.9 / 6.38	11.3 / 5.82	.564 / 19.5	~.8 / 1.14	8.18 / 3.26	170 / 46
Great Britain	- .964 / - .203	12.4 / 23.0	-11.6 / - .623	146. / 4.92	14.5 / 5.74	1.14 / 8.02	1.25 / 1.06	- 12.9 / -113.	170 / 46
Italy	.0361 / - .509	1.74 / 23.6	.743 / -1.53	13.6 / 8.06	10.1 / 6.04	.186 / 6.84	~.70 / ~.90	48.1 / - 46.3	170 / 46

Table 2 (continued)

Country	Means (% / annum)	Standard deviations (% / annum)[4]	Skewnesses	Kurtoses	Studentized Ranges	Scales (% / annum)	Characteristic Exponents	Coefficients of Variation	Sample Sizes
Japan	.0484 / 5.16	2.72 / 31.3	- 5.73 / 1.30	22.4 / 9.38	8.82 / 6.87	.602 / 8.98	~.90 / ~.95	56.2 / 6.06	170 / 46
Netherlands	.458 / 10.8	5.71 / 36.7	9.97 / .618	119. / 5.76	12.9 / 6.32	1.21 / 17.5	1.45 / 1.40	12.5 / 3.41	170 / 46
Norway	.000470 / 9.37	1.06 / 28.3	.423 / 1.05	6.49 / 5.64	7.91 / 5.71	N.C. / 9.70	N.C. / 2.03	2260. / 3.02	170 / 46
South Africa	.0606 / 1.53	2.49 / 28.5	2.42 / 1.46	18.3 / 13.1	9.70 / 7.75	1.04 / .517	1.46 / ~.1	41.1 / 18.6	170 / 46
Spain	-3.79 / 5.76	25.8 / 19.6	- 7.20 / 2.77	56.5 / 16.4	9.34 / 7.69	N.C. / 2.74	N.C. / ~.6	- 6.80 / 3.40	170 / 46
Sweden	.00534 / 6.96	1.73 / 27.8	- .550 / .0812	6.89 / 3.67	8.18 / 4.66	.701 / 8.78	1.40 / ~.95	324. / 4.00	170 / 46
Switzerland	-.0222 / 14.7	5.98 / 40.2	.529 / 1.76	5.12 / 8.98	6.91 / 6.33	1.34 / 23.4	1.73 / 1.70	- 269. / 2.73	170 / 45

Weekly Data [2]

Country	Means (% / annum)	Standard deviations (% / annum)[4]	Skewnesses	Kurtoses	Studentized Ranges	Scales (% / annum)	Characteristic Exponents	Coefficients of Variation	Sample Sizes
Belgium	.0315 / 6.27	20.6 / 65.8	- 1.77 / .538	26.9 / 7.21	13.9 / 8.51	5.65 / 25.6	1.17 / 1.17	654. / 10.5	328 / 213
Canada	1.07 / .0627	24.1 / 38.1	2.12 / - 1.12	29.9 / 21.8	14.4 / 12.4	5.42 / 10.3	1.20 / 1.32	22.5 / 608.	328 / 213
France	- 1.75 / 7.18	33.8 / 74.2	-12.6 / .964	206. / 7.39	20.7 / 7.31	3.73 / 22.2	1.30 / 1.07	- 19.3 / 10.3	378 / 213
Germany (F.R.)	1.45 / 10.0	20.0 / 76.7	1.55 / 1.13	38.7 / 9.21	15.7 / 8.72	4.38 / 26.5	1.24 / 1.14	13.8 / 7.67	328 / 213
Great Britain	- 2.09 / - 2.66	40.9 / 51.8	-14.0 / - 1.12	234. / 12.4	19.8 / 10.0	3.04 / 17.0	1.07 / 1.07	- 19.5 / - 19.5	328 / 213

Table 2 (continued)

Country	Means (% / annum)	Standard deviations (% / annum)[4]	Skewnesses	Kurtoses	Studentized Ranges	Scales (% / annum)	Characteristic Exponents	Coefficients of Variation	Sample Sizes
Italy	.0956 .0553	16.3 78.1	.444 .460	30.7 9.81	16.1 9.78	4.05 23.0	1.13 1.04	171. 1414.	328 213
Netherlands	.0046 9.63	16.5 67.2	.642 .960	35.9 7.47	16.2 7.99	4.06 22.9	1.29 1.09	3560. 6.98	328 213
Switzerland	.0706 12.9	16.2 78.4	.541 1.02	29.2 6.94	16.1 7.65	5.00 27.1	1.19 1.08	229. 6.08	328 213

[1]Two samples, divided by the end of March 1971, are given for each country.

[2]See Table 1 for data sources and dates. The weekly data do not cover the same period as the monthly data.

[3]N.C. means that the middle 44 percent of all sample values were identical, thus precluding the calculation of this statistic (see text).

[4]If a comparison is made between weekly and monthly standard deviations, the units must be altered. To obtain percentages per annum, the raw returns were multiplied by 5200 for weekly data and by 1200 for monthly data. Thus, the computed standard deviations of these converted numbers may seem quite different even when the standard errors are rather close. For example, the standard errors of the mean for Belgium in period 2 are $35.0/\sqrt{46} = 5.16$, and $65.8/\sqrt{213} = 4.51$, for monthly and weekly data, respectively.

large inflation rate that it was forced to devalue every two to three months. Only Spain can be considered the exception to the rule that standard deviation increased with floating rates.

Unfortunately, we cannot stop the empirical analysis with the fact of increasing standard deviations. The distributions have also changed in other ways, one of the most striking being in the measured kurtosis. If the distributions were normal, the expected value of this statistic is 3.0. In both periods, measured kurtosis is significantly different from 3.0, indicating some non-Gaussian properties of both empirical frequencies. In every case but one, the kurtosis was larger under fixed rates, and in most cases it was an order of magnitude larger.

Intuitively, this means that the fixed rate period was characterized by larger probabilities of extreme changes; this is quite in accord with the characteristics of fixed rates - - periods of zero variability in exchange rates exhibit increasing pressure for an exchange rate change if there is an imbalance of payments. Finally, the disequilibruim becomes insupportable and leads to a central bank decision to revalue or devalue. We see in these data the essence of the two systems. There is no such thing as a truly fixed rate. Instead, there is a modification of the form of the distribution. Instead of a sequence of small changes under flexible rates, fixed rates bring a sequence of even smaller changes interspersed with extremely large changes. The two sequences might happen to cumulate by exactly the same amount ex post. But which prospective sequence would investors regard as the more risky?

It is already evident that the empirical distributions are poorly characterized by a Gaussian model. A formal test of nonnormality is provided by the sample studentized ranges.[3] Under a normal null hypothesis, the .90 fractiles of the distribution of the studentized range for the sample sizes of Tables 1 and 2 are given approximately by:

Sample Size	Approximate Null .90 Fractile of Studentized Range
46	5.0
170	4.9
213	4.8
328	4.8

---

[3]The studentized range is the difference between the largest and smallest sample values divided by the sample standard deviation.

245

Since all but one of the observed values exceed their 90th null fractiles, the general impression is that the data are not very well described by a Gaussian process.

A rough idea of how far from normal these distributions deviate can be obtained from a simple order statistic estimator of the characteristic exponent of the distribution.[4] The characteristic exponent measures the type of distribution within the broader class of stable distributions of which the Gaussian is a member (with characteristic exponent equal to 2.0). Roughly speaking, the smaller the estimated characteristic exponent, the more nonnormal the distribution. A characteristic exponent of 1.0, for example, corresponds to a Cauchy distribution which has no finite first- or higher-order moments. We wish to emphasize that this particular statistic is presented only for descriptive purposes; we are not hypothesizing that these distributions are actually members of the stable class. Also, the statistic has very poor properties in small samples and should not be taken too seriously in the period 2 monthly sample.

Given the apparent nonnormality of the empirical observations, the sample standard deviation may be a poor measure of dispersion. Therefore, we also provide a nonparametric measure of dispersion (labelled "scale"). This measure, a constant times the sample 44 percent interfractile range, has been shown to be relatively robust to wide departures from normality.[5] It does have one problem, however. If 44 percent or more of the sample observations of returns are zero, the statistic is undefined. This has actually happened in the monthly sample for Norway and Spain during the first period, and for Australia during the second period. For these countries, the exchange rate remained unchanged from one month to the next in at least 44 percent of the observations (e.g., for 75 pairs of months during period 1 and 20 pairs of months during period 2).

Under the fixed system, long sequences of unchanged rates are to be expected; but how can the Australian result be explained? It turns out to be quite easy. Australia did not institute a floating system when the others did, but instead revalued periodically.[6] Thus, it is our choice of cutoff date

---

[4]The sample measure used here was derived in Fama and Roll (1968). It is actually a function of the sample interfractile 90 percent range divided by the sample interfractile 44 percent range.

[5]See Fama and Roll (1971).

[6]From December 1971 through November 1972 the Australian/U.S. exchange rate did not vary. This is also true of December 1973 through August 1974.

which is at fault. This led us to the observation that the sample kurtosis was relatively constant for Australia too, as it should have been. On the other hand, the sample standard deviation has increased by a factor of 10.

In other words, it would appear that Australia stayed with fixed rates; that the kurtosis remained unchanged; but that the standard deviation increased in proportion to the mean return. This would suggest that the increase in standard deviation from the first to the second period is more a consequence of the dollar's weakness than a consequence of floating rates.

Canada's case seems to be a confirmation of this hypothesis. During part of the earlier period, the Canadian dollar was fixed. The mean returns are roughly the same (in absolute magnitude) in the two periods, and so are the standard deviations. The kurtosis, however, has decreased greatly under the flexible system. France and Great Britain appear to be less striking examples of the same phenomenon.

This implies that we should be able to detect countries which stayed on a fixed rate system by looking for constant sample kurtoses and changes in sample standard deviation (if the mean has also changed). Possible cases, in addition to Australia, would appear to be Switzerland, Norway, Japan, and South Africa. Sweden is less clear cut, and Italy does not have enough of a change in mean. From the raw data, we determined that South Africa has clearly not abandoned a fixed rate with the dollar since there are still long sequences of no change. Japan did not abandon before December 1972, if then. Switzerland and Norway seem to be exceptions. For them, there are no long sequences of unchanged rates as for Australia, Japan, and South Africa, but it is still possible that the Norwegian and Swiss central banks were trading "to stabilize the market."

The main point to emphasize is not that our cutoff date is subject to error, but that the standard deviation may not adequately measure the uncertainty in the series. In fact, the coefficient of variation (standard deviation relative to the mean) is <u>smaller</u> during the second period for 15 of 17 countries with monthly data, and for five of eight countries with weekly data. The distribution of this statistic does not have good properties, however, and it would not be wise to place too much significance on the possibility that standard deviations were relatively smaller in period 2.

A Sample Measure of Changing Individual Risk

Since the distributions are generally shaped differently before and after the fixed-flexible cutoff date, it would be quite unlikely to find that <u>all</u> investors regard one or the other periods as more risky. Instead, one should expect that

247

some investors would consider the standard deviation to be of overriding importance and thus assign more risk to the recent period, whereas other investors with differently shaped utility functions would have the opposite opinion.

To make this notion more precise, we have recourse to a sample analog of first-order stochastic dominance.[7] Stochastic dominance has the following intuitive definition-- distribution A is dominant over distribution B if, when confronted by a choice of A or B, all individuals would prefer A. For example, if A and B were distributions of wealth across states of nature, all individuals would prefer A if it had more wealth than B in every state. First-order stochastic dominance is defined in the same way but with the additional assumption that investors are risk averse (i.e., have strictly concave utility functions). Thus, if A and B are normal distributions of wealth with equal means, A is preferred to B by all risk averters if the standard deviation of B is larger. In general, for arbitrary distribution functions $F_A(w)$ and $F_B(w)$ on stochastic wealth, w, A is first-order stochastically dominant if, and only if,

$$ \int_{-\infty}^{k} [F_A(w) - F_B(w)] \, dw \leq 0 $$

for all k, with a strict inequality for some k; whereas B is dominant if the inequality is reversed.

If the integral is positive for some value of k and negative for some other value, risk averters will not be unanimous in their preferences for A and B.

In principle, this should provide the ability to ascertain whether the fixed system of exchange rate returns (distribution A) is less or more risky than the floating system (distribution B) for all or for only some investors. The advantage of the technique is that no presumption is necessary about the forms of the distributions. They can be (and in our case are) different.

Unfortunately, there is a difficulty caused by the fact that F_A and F_B are not known with certainty but can only be estimated. The order statistics of the sample are usually taken to be estimators of the corresponding population fractiles. Thus, if $R_{j,(\tau)}$ is the τth largest exchange return in a given period, it is an estimate of the $\tau/(N + 1)$'st sample fractile (where N is the total sample size); it has a known asymptotic distribution; and it is unbiased.[8] This suggests as a sample counterpart of the stochastic dominance integral

---

[7]See Hadar and Russell (1969) and Hanoch and Levy (1969). Levy and Sarnat (1972) give a lucid summary of the basic result and its extensions.

[8]See Cramer (1945, ch. 28). The distribution of $R_{j,(\tau)}$ is asymptotically normal under mildly restrictive conditions.

$$D_k \equiv \frac{1}{N+1} \left(\sum_{\substack{\tau \\ R_{A,(\tau)} < k}} - \sum_{\substack{\tau \\ R_{B,(\tau)} < k}} \right)$$

for k equal to some real number. If D_k is nonpositive for all values of k, then A would be judged stochastically dominant, and vice versa if D_k is always nonnegative. Due to sampling variation, however, we should expect some differences in sign for D_k's within a given sample even if the populations have a dominance relation.

To ascertain the likely error caused by sampling, we conducted some Monte Carlo experiments for known dominantly related populations. Table 3 gives the results. In all cases the parent populations are Gaussian, and the number of different D_k's computed for each replication was equal to the larger of the two sample sizes (N). k was varied in equal increments, where the increment size was

$$\Delta = [\max (R_{A,(N_A)}, R_{B,(N_B)}) - \min (R_{A,(1)}, R_{B,(1)})] / (N + 1).$$

The final statistic was the percentage of positive values of D_k. Thus, A is stochastically dominant if this percentage is zero, and B is dominant if the percentage is 100.

Table 3 indicates that the test statistic has quite good discriminatory power for normal distributions that differ in the mean by one-half standard deviation. In the last case, for example, when the two populations had equal standard deviations but population A's mean was $\sigma/2$ larger than population B's, the mean percentage of positive test D_k's was only 2.41 and 90 percent of the Monte Carlo sampling observations had percentages of positive D_k's less than 10.0.

Sample stochastic dominance statistics are presented in Table 4 for all 17 countries. The sample sizes of the two distributions are given in Table 2. A low value of the statistic corresponds to the fixed rate period being stochastically dominant over the flexible period. Italy is the only country for which this seems to be unquestionably true. It appears that the flexible rate period would have been preferred by all risk-averse investors in the cases of Canada, Spain, and Brazil. For the other countries, the statistic is not sufficiently far from 50 percent to permit a judgment that either period would have been uniformly preferred.

Table 3

Monte Carlo Experiments for Sample Stochastic Dominance
with Gaussian Population

Population				Monte Carlo Results			
A	B	A	B	$\bar{D}_k$	$\sigma(D_k)$	Fractiles	
Mean		Standard Deviations				.1	.9
0.	0.	1.0	1.	56.6	39.6	0.	100.
0.	0.	1.1	1.	61.3	38.0	0.	100.
0.	0.	1.5	1.	75.3	24.6	40.	100.
0.1	0.	1.0	1.	31.6	34.6	0.	88.
0.5	0.	1.0	1.	2.41	7.15	0.	10.

Number of replications is 49.
Sample sizes are 49.

Correcting for Nominal Interest and Inflation

Until now, we have presented descriptive statistics for pure exchange rate returns without bothering to recognize that few investors would actually hold a noninterest-earning position in foreign currency. Their positions are usually taken in an earning asset of some kind[9] and we may suppose that the nominal certainty equivalent on this position is a positive interest rate. Furthermore, by forgoing current consumption, investors assume risky real positions in their own currency which is subject to unpredictable changes in purchasing power.

It is possible to calculate the ex post real return on a foreign position in an earning asset. The rate of exchange of home currency per foreign currency is S_t in period t, and the foreign nominal interest rate is i_F. The

---

[9]The earning asset could be a financial asset or anything else. For example, the exporter who extends foreign credit must think that he earns a goodwill rate of interest by doing so.

Table 4

Sample Stochastic Dominance Statistics[1]

for Exchange Rate Nominal Returns

Before and After Floating

(1957 - 1975)[2]

(Monthly observations)

Country	Dominance Statistic[1]		Country	Dominance Statistic
Australia	44.7		Italy	5.85
Austria	59.7		Japan	55.0
Belgium	54.4		Netherlands	52.6
Brazil	100.		Norway	63.2
Canada	91.8		South Africa	40.9
Denmark	55.0		Spain	100.
France	83.6		Sweden	41.5
Germany (F.R.)	59.1		Switzerland	70.2
Great Britain	64.9			

[1] A low number corresponds to the fixed rate period being stochastically dominant, and vice versa. (A value of 100 means that all risk-averse investors would have preferred the flexible rate period.)

[2] See Table 1 for data sources.

251

domestic ex post real rate of interest is r_H and the domestic price level $p_{H,t}$. An investor who places W foreign units in a foreign asset receives $(1 + i_F)$ W at the end of the period $t + 1$. In his own currency, this is worth in purchasing power S_{t+1} $(p_{H,t} / p_{H,t+1})$ $(1 + i_F)$ W. The present value of this sum in period t would have been S_{t+1} $(p_{H,t} / p_{H,t+1})$ $(1 + i_F)$ $W/(1 + r_H)$. At time t, the home-currency value of the investment was WS_t. Thus, his relative real rate of windfall return (above and beyond the real rate of domestic interest) was

$$r_{t+1} = \{[(S_{t+1}/S_t)\, (p_{H,t}/p_{H,t+1})\, (1+i_F)] / (1+r_H)\} - 1.$$

In fact, if purchasing power parity and the Irving Fisher relations are valid ex post, and ex post real interest rates are equal in both countries, this return must be zero.[10] The ex post domestic real rate is given by the Irving Fisher relation as $(1 + r_H) = (1 + i_H)\, (p_{H,t}/p_{H,t+1})$. Thus,

$$(1) \quad r_{t+1} = (S_{t+1}/S_t)\, [(1 + i_F) / (1 + i_H)] - 1$$

should give an estimate of the real rent from foreign investment positions. If the interest rate parity arbitrage condition is valid, then $(1+i_F)/(1+i_H) = S_t/F_t$, where F_t is the forward exchange rate of domestic per foreign currency for the same term as the interest rates. In this case, the real rent has an even simpler form:

$$(2) \quad r_{t+1} = (S_{t+1}/F_t) - 1 .$$

---

[10] Purchasing power parity means that the relative change in exchange rates must equal the relative change in the price levels of goods, or $(S_{t+1}/S_t)\, (p_{H,t}/p_{H,t+1}) = p_{F,t}/p_{F,t+1}$ where F and H denote foreign and home, respectively. Thus, $r_{t+1} = \{[(1+i_F)\, (p_{F,t}/p_{F,t+1})] / (1+r_H) \} - 1$. But, if the Irving Fisher relation is valid, the first two terms in parentheses equal $1 + r_F$. This proves that real rents are zero if real interest rates are the same in both countries and if the parity relations have held ex post.

Using either equation (1) or (2) as a definition of real profit, we avoid price index measurement problems. Equation (2) has the extra advantage that the interest rates also need not be measurable.

Table 5 gives a summary of the most important real rent statistics for the monthly data. (Neither weekly interest rates nor weekly forward rates are available.) For seven countries, forward rates of exchange were available and equation (2) was used. For all other countries, equation (1) was used with the nominal interest rate series specified in Table 1.

Unfortunately, because interest rates and forward rates were not as available as spot exchange rates (see Table 1), the earlier fixed rate period has a smaller sample size. In some cases, the sample size is only about half as large. We have repeated the calculation of Table 2 for this restricted period. The results are very similar except for one country, and this exception is discussed in the footnote.[11]

The general impression of the real rents is that they are somewhat less bizarre statistically than the nominal returns. The mean returns are more uniform across countries, and the distributions for the fixed rate period are closer to the Gaussian. This latter is indicated by the studentized ranges which are similar during the flexible period to those computed for nominal returns (see Table 1), but which are smaller for 15 of 17 countries during the fixed period.[12]

---

[11] A table with the results for nominal returns on all currencies over the 1964-1971 period is available on request. The exceptional case is Canada. For all other countries, stochastic dominance statistics computed for 1964-1971/1971-75 were only a few percentage points from the same statistics computed with data covering the entire fixed rate period (1957-1971/1971-75). Eleven of 17 differed by less than two percentage points. For Canada, however, the statistic was 91.8 for 1957-1971/1971-75, and zero for 1964-1971/1971-75! This means that all investors would have preferred 1964-1971 to 1971-75 for Canada, but that nearly all would have preferred 1971-75 to 1957-1971 taken as a whole. Canada floated against the U. S. dollar in the 1950s and early sixties, reintroducing fixed rates in January 1963. Thus, our selected fixed period from 1957- March 1971 actually was partly floating, whereas the 1964-1971 period was indeed fixed. (This is so except for the last four months; the Canadian dollar recommenced to float in 1970.)

[12] Of course, the sample sizes differ, and this could be responsible. In other words, the period before 1964 might be different, and less Gaussian, than the period from 1964 through March 1971.

Table 5

Distributional Characteristics for Real Excess Returns (Rents)
from Foreign Interest-earning Positions (1964-1975)
(Monthly data in dollars)

Country	Means (%/annum)	Standard Deviations (%/annum)	Kurtoses	Studentized Ranges	Coefficients of Variation	Dominance Statistics[2]	Sample Sizes
Australia	.112	3.36	11.8	7.23	30.1	44.8	86
	5.73	32.6	15.1	8.43	5.69		46
Austria	-.636	1.72	3.20	5.11	-2.71	59.8	86
	11.6	35.8	5.26	5.70	3.09		46
Belgium[1]	.290	3.45	5.09	6.75	11.9	47.5	138
	7.29	38.0	4.32	5.61	5.21	(41.9)	46
Brazil	.372	33.4	19.5	5.76	89.7	100.	49
	2.09	13.9	5.20	6.12	6.67		44
Canada[1]	.837	8.32	24.4	11.8	9.94	42.7	142
	-1.62	8.75	3.56	4.73	-5.40	(55.8)	39
Denmark	1.02	9.24	74.9	10.1	9.10	56.3	86
	10.4	33.1	6.32	6.38	3.18		46
France[1]	-.593	11.1	114.	11.8	-18.7	65.2	134
	6.92	38.1	5.06	5.81	5.51	(33.3)	46
Germany (F.R.)[1]	-1.72	8.10	28.5	10.4	-4.72	52.5	139
	6.00	39.3	5.36	5.41	6.55	(52.5)	44
Great Britain[1]	5.13	5.51	5.33	5.43	1.07	34.1	128
	8.75	25.5	5.05	5.91	2.92		46
Italy	-1.15	2.60	7.28	7.74	-2.26	11.5	86
	-.891	23.7	8.04	6.03	-26.5		46
Japan	2.76	2.92	8.57	6.04	1.06	52.9	86
	6.98	31.1	9.13	6.81	4.45		46
Netherlands[1]	-1.67	6.53	68.9	11.4	-3.91	47.9	139
	5.04	37.7	4.96	5.94	7.50	(48.8)	44
Norway	-1.23	1.43	3.95	5.28	-1.16	63.2	86
	8.19	28.4	5.69	5.79	3.47		46
South Africa	-.594	3.19	15.6	7.60	-5.36	35.6	86
	.363	28.5	12.9	7.65	78.5		45
Spain	-1.86	17.9	83.2	9.46	-9.51	100.	86
	5.53	19.7	16.0	7.69	3.57		46
Sweden	1.52	2.26	6.47	7.43	1.49	41.4	86
	8.50	28.0	3.72	4.66	3.29		46
Switzerland[1]	-3.02	4.02	3.71	5.45	-1.34	56.3	134
	4.68	41.8	8.42	6.59	8.94	(55.8)	45

[1]Equation (2) with forward exchange rates was used for this country, while equation (1) with interest rates was used for others.

[2]Dominance statistics in parentheses were computed with quarterly data.

The stochastic dominance statistics have changed little. They still indicate that there is no uniform preference for one period or the other, except for the same three countries: Brazil and Spain for which the flexible rate period would have been preferred; and Italy with a fixed rate period preference.

The mean real returns, however, are quite different from the nominal returns. This is illustrated best by extreme cases such as Brazil. For Brazil, the nominal returns on pure currency positions were about -15 and -10 percent in the two periods, whereas the mean real rents were .372 and 2.09 percent, respectively. Thus, the real returns (in dollars) to a Brazilian interest-bearing asset was on the same order of magnitude as similar positions in stronger currencies. This was possible because the Brazilian nominal rate of interest was much higher.

One should presume that the mean returns of Table 5 reflect unanticipated exchange rate changes. (Remember that these returns would be zero if investors could forecast perfectly, and if real interest rates were the same in the U. S. and in each country.) It would appear, for example, that the decline of the pound was actually overestimated in both periods because the mean real returns are positive in both periods.[13] The same conclusion can be deduced for Japan.

Except for two countries (Canada and Italy), the mean return was positive and between 1 and 2 times its standard error during the period of flexible rates. This uniformity leads directly to the conclusion that the base currency's strength was overestimated. The dollar was not expected to fall by as much as it did. For the Scandinavian countries, the forecasting error appears to have been particularly large.

As with any empirical study, there are many caveats that could be offered to qualify the results. We feel that only two problems might have been important: (a) the definitions of interest rates; and (b) the duration of the forward rates. The measurement error in interest rates arises because rediscount rates do not respond completely to market rates, and because none of the rates are for one-month durations. Treasury bill rates are for three months, and call money has an undefined maturity.

A similar maturity problem arises for countries where forward exchange rates were available. In these cases, the forward exchange rate was for three months hence. At the expense of a reduction in sample size, this particular difficulty can be surmounted, for equation (2) can be estimated with quarterly data. That is, the real rent over three months can be defined exactly as

---

[13] In the floating rate period, however, the mean may not be significantly positive or may be only marginally so.

$$(3) \quad r_t = (S_{t+3}/F_t) - 1 \, ,$$

where the spot rate is now observed three months after the forward rate. Distributional statistics have been calculated for this variable too, and a full table is available upon request. In Table 5, there was room to include the stochastic dominance statistic for quarterly data using the real rent defined by (3). These numbers are given in parentheses in the "dominance statistics" column. Except for France, there were only trivial differences, and the larger French statistic based on quarterly data still cannot be judged significant. In all cases, the quarterly mean returns and standard deviations have the same magnitudes and patterns. The kurtoses are also very close, with the exception of Switzerland which has a smaller kurtosis during the flexible rate period using quarterly data. This is without doubt attributable to the Swiss Central Bank's penchant for smoothing short-run changes in exchange, while allowing a true market equilibrium to obtain over long periods. (The Swiss kurtosis falls from 8.4 for monthly data to 2.6 for quarterly data during the floating rate period.)

III. PORTFOLIO RISK AND FOREIGN EXCHANGE

Although the previous analysis has been conducted for individual currencies, portfolio theory teaches that individual risks should not be measured independently. Because of diversification, the risk of a portfolio composed of various currencies is not equal to the sum of the risks of each currency.

Markowitz (1959), Sharpe (1964), Lintner (1965), and others have developed a risk-return analysis which has been applied to asset pricing in various markets. In an efficient exchange market, only the contribution of the currency to the total risk of a portfolio should influence the value of the currency (risk premium). All other risks can be eliminated by holding a diversified portfolio. It is not necessary that every individual and business firm engaging in exchange transactions hold a diversified portfolio. The sole requirement is the existence of rational, risk-averse financial investors who will price currencies and risk in a portfolio context.

Unfortunately, this portfolio diversification model relies on variance as a risk measure. We have already seen that this measure is inadequate as a full description of the probabilities observed for individual currencies. In fact, the fixed rate period is characterized by much smaller individual variances. Thus, if the covariances have not changed drastically between the two periods, we should also find a smaller variance for a portfolio of currencies during the fixed period. As a consequence, the use of a Markowitz-style mean-variance analysis is biased a priori against the flexible rate system, since it is likely to have missed other important changes in the multivariate probability distribution.[14] Nevertheless, the absence of a more sophisticated portfolio risk measure obliges us to use the standard mean-variance methodology. As we shall show, the bias against flexible rates induced by this necessity is not of overwhelming importance because a dominant period does not emerge.

Consider an investment in nominally riskless short-term foreign-denominated bonds. The nominal return will be the quoted interest rate plus (or minus) any exchange rate fluctuation over the period, and the risk will be pure exchange risk for investors of a specific country. For any sample period, we can calculate the portfolio which, for a given sample mean return, would have minimized the intertemporal variance of that return. One can show that minimum variance portfolios lie on an "efficient frontier" of the shape represented in Figure 1.[15] Given a desired level of variance, an investor maximizes his expected wealth by picking a currency portfolio[16] lying on this boundary. Individual currencies are generally "inefficient" and located inside the frontier, such as at point j. Even in risky speculation, a mix of currencies will provide the same return with less variance. No combination of foreign currencies could provide a lower variance than the minimum σ_0^2 .

If one considers the more general case of constructing portfolios by investing both in the domestic, risk-free interest rate (i_H) and in foreign nominally riskless bonds, the efficient set of portfolios is the line $i_H M$ in Figure 2, which is tangent at M to the former efficient frontier drawn in the mean standard deviation space. The composition of portfolio M is very important, since all optimal investments will be linear combinations of that portfolio and the domestic risk-free asset. The "price of exchange risk" can be thought of as the slope of $i_H M$, the marginal return from bearing an additional unit of exchange standard deviation.

---

[14] As shown above, the distributions of individual exchange rate fluctuations are closer to normal under flexible rates; and the distribution of a portfolio's return is likely to be even closer. We cannot maintain, however, that a mean-variance analysis is unbiased with respect to a judgment on differential risk in the two periods.

[15] The efficient frontier is a sample statistic derived from the sample means and sample covariances of individual currencies. See Merton (1972). We are well aware of the econometric problems associated with this calculation, and the reader is warned to regard the results as merely descriptive. For a full discussion, see Roll (1976, Section III.B).

[16] By currency investment, we mean nominally riskless short-term obligations denominated in the foreign currency.

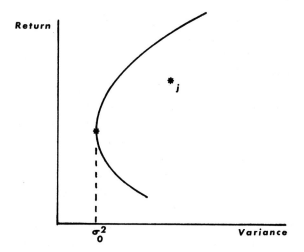

Figure 1
The Mean-Variance Efficient Frontier

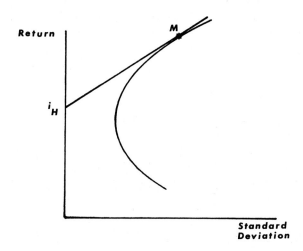

Figure 2
The Mean-Standard Deviation Efficient Frontier and the Price of Risk

258

For the two subperiods previously described, we have computed ex post efficient frontiers as viewed by investors in each country. Taking Belgium and the U.S. as examples, their efficient frontiers are shown in Figure 3 for Belgium, and in Figure 4 for the U. S. (I and II refer to the first and second periods, respectively.) Using the (arithmetic) mean of nominal short-term rates as the intercept, a tangent efficient line is drawn in for Belgium, and equations of such lines for all countries are given in Table 6. The sample mean returns and standard deviations of the minimum variance portfolios (ex post) are also given there. The situation depicted in Figures 3 and 4 is typical of most countries. In the majority of cases, the efficient frontier has moved "up and away" over time. Both the variance (always) and the return (10 of 17) of the minimum variance portfolio have increased.

Between the fixed and flexible periods, the relevant comparison involves the slope of the efficient line $i_H M$, which is less after 1971 than before. In other words, given an optimal speculation, compensation for a higher level of risk was less in the flexible exchange period. Since interest rates were higher in nominal terms during recent years, the opposite conclusion is obtained for very low levels of exchange variance (see Figure 3).

Returns should be measured in real and not in nominal terms. Assuming the Fisherian relation, this can be accomplished by subtracting from all returns the (risk-free domestic) interest rate over the corresponding period. This implies that only the slope (price of risk) of the efficient line is relevant for comparison purposes, since the real intercept would only change with the real rate of interest.

In calculating the efficient frontiers, the primary reason for having used nominal rather than real returns was the necessity of concurrent observations. One country was eliminated because of insufficient data;[17] its inclusion would have caused a reduction in the total sample size of about 57 percent. Using real rates would have entailed a similar sample size reduction. Of course, to the extent of significant variability in rates of inflation and cross-correlations among rates of inflation, the calculated real efficient frontier might have been located elsewhere and have had a different shape. If this had been true, the slopes of the nominal efficient lines would have been altered. We do not believe, however, that any significant alteration has resulted because (a) the inflation rate variability is relatively low, and (b) the empirical results of Tables 2 and 5 for nominal and real returns, respectively, indicate only minor differences in the

---

[17]Brazil was eliminated from the computations because there were only 49 observations in the fixed rate period.

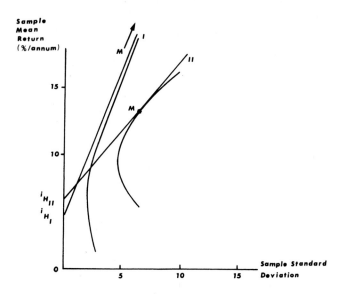

Figure 3
Empirical Efficient Frontiers for Belgium
under Fixed (I) and Flexible (II) Exchange Rates

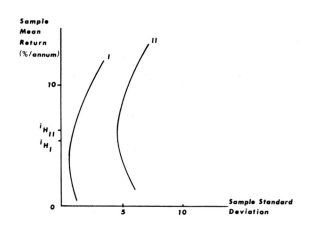

Figure 4
Empirical Efficient Frontiers for the U.S.
under Fixed (I) and Flexible (II) Exchange Rates

260

Table 6

Summary Statistics for Efficient Frontiers

(Monthly data, 1964 - 75)

Percent per annum

| Country of Origin | First period (1964-1971)[1] | | | | Second period (1971-75)[1] | | | |
| | Minimum Variance Portfolio Return | | Efficient Line | | Minimum Variance Portfolio Return | | Efficient Line | |
	Mean	Standard Deviation	Intercept	Slope	Mean	Standard Deviation	Intercept	Slope
Australia	4.4	.82	5.0	2.66	-1.1	27.0	6.7	1.15
Austria	4.0	1.07	4.4	2.61	8.8	6.4	5.5	1.13
Belgium	5.1	1.98	4.0	2.50	8.9	4.6	5.3	1.14
Canada	2.8	5.02	5.2	2.65	3.8	5.9	5.1	1.14
Denmark	5.0	1.81	7.1	2.71	6.4	6.2	8.2	1.13
France	2.4	12.9	6.0	2.63	3.1	15.2	8.4	1.13
Germany	4.1	6.82	4.7	2.62	3.7	8.5	7.4	1.09
Italy	3.8	1.93	3.9	2.62	13.8	9.2	5.6	1.13
Japan	4.0	2.03	8.6	3.18	- .7	13.0	7.9	1.14
Netherlands	4.3	1.96	4.6	2.63	3.0	7.7	4.4	1.13
Norway	4.8	.96	3.7	2.54	8.6	7.6	4.8	1.13
South Africa	5.2	.91	4.3	2.60	11.7	22.3	4.8	.93
Spain	5.7	1.22	5.1	2.52	3.8	11.1	5.7	1.14
Sweden	4.0	1.99	6.0	2.57	2.8	5.4	7.5	1.14
Switzerland	3.5	3.17	3.0	2.62	0	14.9	4.5	1.13
U. K.	5.1	1.16	6.3	2.74	9.6	15.7	8.1	1.13
U. S.	3.9	.62	5.0	3.05	6.6	4.8	6.0	1.14

[1]See Table 1 for data sources and sample dates.

distribution except for the means. The real returns are somewhat closer to Gaussian but we do not think this has significantly altered the computed efficient frontier.

Based on a mean-variance analysis alone, efficient frontiers shifted to the right after the debut of the flexible regime. However, the "price" of risk has declined. This is somewhat akin to a classical identification problem in microeconomics. Since the "quantity" of variance has increased and the "price" has decreased, the demand for variance must have increased, perhaps due to the other concurrent alterations in the world economic system. (Recall that variance is a "bad" so that its demand function is positively sloped.) But, supply also has shifted to the right (by an amount too small to offset the demand shift), so that the exact sizes of the two shifts cannot be identified. One obvious explanation for the increased demand for variance is the change in other distributional characteristics. A reduction in kurtosis, for example, might have induced such a change. Many other factors could have played a role as well, so no precise inference can be drawn. We only know that a given increase in portfolio variance is rewarded by a lower increase in real return under flexible rates. Thus, the cost to a hedger of reducing variance is lower now than before.

It is interesting to note that the premia required by the market vary over time but are quite similar among countries. In Table 6, the premia vary around 2.60 (percent of return per percent of total standard deviation in the first period), the extreme being 2.50 for Belgium and 3.18 for Japan. In the second period, it varies around 1.13 with little difference among countries (except 0.93 for South Africa).

IV. SUMMARY AND CONCLUSIONS

This paper contains empirical evidence regarding the risks associated with fluctuating exchange rates. In section II, the distributions of individual rates of change in exchange rates under the Bretton Woods regime and under the present flexible rate system are studied. The data show clearly that there is no such thing as a fixed rate. Rather, the choice of an international monetary system determines the shape of the distribution function of exchange rate changes. "Fixed rates" are characterized by many very small changes and a few large adjustments, whereas flexible rates are characterized by a sequence of intermediate-sized changes. With respect to the type of distribution, the Gaussian does not appear to provide a close representation of the data under either system. However, under the present flexible regime, the different parameters computed are closer to the values of a Gaussian distribution.

A major question is which regime would a risk-averse individual consider less risky. For individuals trading in a single currency, the question can be answered in principle by using the distribution functions of the individual currencies. A sample counterpart of first-order stochastic dominance has been used to discriminate between the two systems. No clear-cut result appears–neither system would have been unequivocably preferred by all risk-averse individuals. To measure the overall risk of the exchange market, a portfolio approach has been taken. Using the observed multivariate distribution, efficient frontiers have been computed for portfolios of foreign currencies as viewed by investors in each country. Once again, no clear answer appears valid for all risk-averse individuals. If lending and borrowing are taken into account, the efficient frontier in one period does not dominate the other period at all levels of risk.

In conclusion, the recent period (since 1971), which has been characterized by flexible exchange rates, has resulted in different time patterns of exchange rate changes. However, the resulting distribution of changes cannot be judged more (or less) risky than the earlier period's distribution (from 1957-1971). From this analysis alone, there can be no inference that a flexible rate system created more uncertainty, diminished foreign trade, or caused destabilizing speculation. Furthermore, the so-called fixed rate system was itself characterized by significant exchange risk but of a somewhat different distributional nature.

REFERENCES

1. Aliber, R.Z., "Speculation in the Flexible Exchange: The European Experience in the 1920's," Yale Economic Essays, (Spring 1972).

2. _____ , "Monetary Independence under Floating Exchange Rates," The Journal of Finance, XXX, No. 2, (May 1975), 365-376.

3. Cramer, H. Mathematical Methods of Statistics. Princeton: Princeton University Press, 1945.

4. Fama, E.F., "Efficient Capital Markets: A Review of Theory and Empirical Work," The Journal of Finance, XXV, No. 2, (May 1970), 383-417.

5. Fama, E.F., and Roll, R., "Some Properties of Symmetric Stable Distributions," Journal of the American Statistical Association, 63, No. 323, (September 1968), 817-836.

6. _____ , "Parameter Estimates for Symmetric Stable Distributions," Journal of the American Statistical Association, 66, No. 334, (June 1971), 331-338.

7. Farber, A.L., "A Note on the Optimal Level of Forward Exchange Transactions," working paper, Université Libre de Bruxelles, (September 1975).

8. Farrell, M.J., "Profitable Speculation," Economica, XXXIII, No. 130, (May 1966), 183-193.

9. Friedman, M., "The Case for Flexible Exchange Rates," in Essays in Positive Economics. Chicago: The University of Chicago Press, 1953.

10. Hadar, J., and Russell, W.R., "Rules for Ordering Uncertain Prospects," American Economic Review, LIX, No. 1, (March 1969), 25-34.

11. Hanoch, G., and Levy, H., "The Efficiency Analysis of Choices Involving Risk," Review of Economic Studies, XXXVI, No. 107, (July 1969), 335-346.

12. Levy, H., and Sarnat, M. Investment and Portfolio Analysis, New York: John Wiley and Sons, Inc., 1972.

13. Lintner, J., "The Valuation of Risk Assets and the Selection of Risky Investments in Stock Portfolios and Capital Budgets," Review of Economics and Statistics, XLVII, No. 1, (February 1965), 13-37.

14. Markowitz, H.M. Portfolio Selection: Efficient Diversification of Investments. New York: John Wiley and Sons, Inc., 1959.

15. Merton, R.C., "An Analytic Derivation of the Efficient Portfolio Frontier," Journal of Financial and Quantitative Analysis, VII, No. 4, (September 1972), 1851-1872.

16. Nurske, R. International Currency Experience. Geneva: League of Nations, 1944.

17. Roll, R.W., "A Critique of the Asset Pricing Theory's Tests," C.E.S.A. working paper, (April 1976).

18. Solnik, B.H. European Capital Markets. Lexington, Mass.: Lexington Books, 1973.

19. Sharpe, W.F., "Capital Asset Prices: A Theory of Market Equilibrium Under Conditions of Risk," Journal of Finance, XIX, No. 3, (September 1964), 425-442.

20. Stern, R.M. The Balance of Payments. Chicago: Aldine, 1973.

21. Yeager, L.B. International Monetary Relations. New York: Harper and Row, 1966.

22. Whitman, M. v.N.,"The Payments Adjustment Process and the Exchange Rate Regime: What Have We Learned?" American Economic Review, LXV, No. 2, (May 1975), 133-146.

SOCIAL WELFARE UNDER FIXED AND FLEXIBLE EXCHANGE RATES: A COMMENT ON THE FARBER, ROLL AND SOLNIK PAPER

Jerome L. Stein*

Brown University

Economists have long been concerned with the welfare arguments in favor of, or opposed to, a floating exchange rate regime. Two specific objections have been raised against free rates: speculation tends to "destablize" exchange markets; and exchange risk would be increased under floating rates, thereby impeding international trade and investment. The major aim of the paper by Farber, Roll and Solnik is to shed light on the validity of these objections and to determine which regime, free or stabilized exchange rates, a risk-averse investor would prefer. Section II of their paper examines the distribution functions of exchange rate fluctuations–a record is presented of what happened to each individual currency. Section III examines the risk-return relation for portfolios of currencies. First, I summarize their results. Then, I discuss what bearing their findings have on the question: Which exchange regime has been more desirable socially? Finally, I sketch a method of determining whether welfare was increased by adopting flexible rates.

I. SUMMARY OF THE RESULTS

Their basic random variable R(t) is the percentage change in S(t), the dollar price of a unit of foreign currency.

$$R(t) \equiv \frac{S(t)}{S(t-1)} - 1.$$

They examine the distribution of R(t) during the fixed exchange rate period prior to March 1971 and during the subsequent free period. Their results can be summarized as follows.

(1) "One fact which is immediately evident is that the two periods displayed quite different distributions in almost every attribute. . . .If the two distributions were random Gaussian samples, these mean returns would be different at any commonly used significance level."

(2) "Of the 17 countries. . . [o]nly Spain can be considered the exception to the rule that standard deviation increased with floating rates."

*Professor of Economics, Eastman Professor of Political Economy. I am indebted to G. H. Borts for his criticisms of an earlier draft.

(3) "In every case but one, the kurtosis was larger under fixed rates. . . .Intuitively, this means that the fixed rate period was characterized by larger probabilities of extreme changes. . . .Instead of a sequence of small changes under flexible rates, fixed rates bring a sequence of even smaller changes interspersed with extremely large changes." [Emphasis in the original.]

(4) ". . .the general impression is that the data are not very well described by a Gaussian process. . . .Given the apparent nonnormality of the empirical observations, the sample standard deviation may be a poor measure of dispersion. . . . In fact, the coefficient of variation. . .is smaller during the [free rate] period for 15 of 17 countries with monthly data. . . ." [Emphasis in the original.]

(5) They then consider stochastic dominance and ask whether an investor would prefer one distribution to another. It seems that for Italy the distribution of returns during the fixed period dominates. For Canada, Spain, and Brazil, the distribution of returns during the free period dominates. For the other countries, no judgment can be made. Since Canada was on a free rate even prior to 1971, the conclusion is that neither distribution dominates the other.

The authors also calculate what they designate a ". . .relative real rate of windfall return (above and beyond the real rate of domestic interest). . .":

$$(1) \quad r(t+1) \equiv \frac{S(t+1)}{S(t)} \frac{[1 + i_F(t)]}{[1 + i_H(t)]} - 1,$$

where i is the nominal rate, F refers to the foreign country, and H refers to the home country. This is the net uncovered yield from a long position in spot foreign exchange. It is a comparison of the yield on foreign assets relative to the yield on domestic assets of a similar type. A dollar will purchase $1/S(t)$ of foreign exchange which will be worth$[1 + i_F(t)] /S(t)$ at the end of the period, in terms of foreign exchange. It will be sold for dollars at price $S(t+1)$; hence, the investor will have $\frac{S(t+1)}{S(t)} [1 + i_F(t)]$ dollars. The return on a domestic asset is $1 + i_H(t)$. It follows that the net uncovered yield from a long position in foreign exchange is given by equation (1); but there is nothing "real" about it.

At times the authors work with (2), which they derive from (1), by assuming that the spot-forward relation is given by the interest parity formula.

$$(2) \quad r(t+1) \equiv \frac{S(t+1)}{F(t)} - 1,$$

where F(t) is the price of forward exchange. Equation (2) is the uncovered yield from a long position in forward exchange, since no funds are tied up in a forward contract. A dollar buys $1/F(t)$ of forward exchange which is later sold for $S(t+1)/F(t)$ dollars, giving a return of $r(t+1)$.

Consequently, equations (1) and (2) are simply rates of return from long positions in spot and forward exchange, respectively. Equation (2) was used for Belgium, Canada, France, Germany, Great Britain, Netherlands, and Switzerland. Equation (1) was used for the others.

Two conclusions are drawn concerning the distribution of $r(t+1)$, the net uncovered yield on spot or forward foreign exchange.

(6)   "Except for. . .(Canada and Italy), the mean return $[r(t+1)]$ was positive and between 1 and 2 times its standard error during the period of flexible rates." In 15 out of 17 cases, the absolute value of the mean $r(t+1)$ was higher in the free period. Standard deviations are higher during the free exchange period, in 16 out of 17 cases. Brazil is the exception.

(7)   "The stochastic dominance statistics have changed little. They still indicate that there is no uniform preference for one period or the other, except for the same three countries: Brazil and Spain for which the flexible rate period would have been preferred; and Italy with a fixed rate period preference."

For the two subperiods, they computed the ex post efficiency frontier in the mean standard deviation space on a portfolio of foreign currencies held by investors in each country. Consider a portfolio with the minimum variance. In 10 out of 17 cases, the risk was higher and so was the mean return in the free exchange period. The efficient line describes the return-risk combination derived from a portfolio of risky assets and a perfectly safe asset. ". . .[T]he slope of the efficient line. . .is less after 1971 than before. In other words, given an optimal speculation, compensation for a higher level of risk was less in the flexible exchange period."

II. EVALUATION

The issues which motivated this study were the following. Was welfare increased by changing to a free rate system? Did the freeing of the exchange rate lead to a more efficient flow of goods and services? Does speculation "destabilize" free exchange markets? The relation between these questions and the conclusion of their paper that, ". . .compensation for a higher level of risk was less in the flexible exchange period. . ." was not explained.The authors' choice of variable in the portfolio analysis is highly arbitrary.

Importing and exporting firms have many assets and liabilities, some denominated in domestic and others in foreign currency. What is the economic logic of examining the mean-variance properties of one subset of the balance sheet -- those items denominated in foreign currency? Why are the authors not interested in the earnings per share generated by a firm under alternative exchange rate regimes?

The reader is led to believe that the variability of the exchange rate, or rate of return on an uncovered position in foreign exchange, is economically significant and socially undesirable. Given the same mean of r(t), a rise in the standard deviation is supposedly undesirable because the efficient locus of a portfolio of foreign currencies rotates in the direction of more risk. This orientation does not seem to be justified on economic grounds. Suppose that a country, such as Great Britain in 1925, stabilizes the exchange rate at an overvalued level. To offset a potential gold outflow, deflationary policies are followed. The unemployment rate rises; actual output is below potential output; but the exchange rate is preserved. If the rate were free, and domestic policies were geared to maintaining full employment, the variance of the exchange rate would be much higher. Suppose that the mean of r(t) were zero, but its variance was quite high during the free period. Farber, Roll and Solnik would say that investors in foreign currency would be faced with less uncertainty in the fixed rate case, and would therefore prefer that distribution of r(t) to the one prevailing in the free rate case. It is not at all apparent what the economic significance of that point of view is.

The economy is operating inside the production possibility curve; output is unnecessarily sacrificed and the unemployment rate is needlessly high. Is there any question that the fixed rate leads to a worse situation for society?

If it were possible to correct for the exogenous disturbances impinging upon the economy, it would have made more sense to examine the returns and risks attached to equity in the firms than to focus upon the returns and risks attached to a portfolio of foreign currencies. The relevant variable for an investor is the earnings per share plus the capital gain, not the return on a particular subset of assets or liabilities. In both the free and the fixed period, the return on a unit of foreign currency r(t) could be zero, with a higher variance in the free period. But, the earnings per share of the firm would be very much higher in the free period, in the example of Great Britain used above. Utility is defined in terms of the characteristics of the earnings per share in the firms, not as the characteristics of the return on an uncovered position in foreign exchange. The distribution of earnings per share depends upon the means and the variance-covariance matrix of all types of assets and liabilities, domestic as well as foreign. For this reason, I am at a loss to interpret the economic significance and welfare implications of the authors' portfolio analysis.

270

It is often claimed that the existence of a forward market eliminates exchange risk and, hence, it is believed, the uncertainty cannot inhibit the international flows of goods and services. This is a misleading conception. As far as the firm is concerned, the uncertainty concerning future exchange rates can be eliminated without a forward market. The foreign exchange can be purchased spot at the time that the import commitment is made. Or, as soon as the sale is arranged, the claim to foreign exchange can be discounted; and the foreign exchange can be sold spot. The existence of a forward market is a convenient, but hardly a fundamentally different, way of avoiding risk. The fundamental question is whether it is better for the economy if the government generates the short-term capital flows or if the private sector fulfills this function. In the next section, I sketch a method which can be used to answer this question.

III. A METHOD OF DETERMINING WHETHER WELFARE WAS INCREASED BY ADOPTING FLEXIBLE EXCHANGE RATES

The economically significant question concerning the optimal exchange market is whether the government should fix the exchange rate at a level which will clear the foreign exchange market over a long period of time, or whether the exchange rate should float.

In my study of the optimum foreign exchange market,[1] I used a cardinal utility function of absorptions (consumption plus investment) over a set of n periods. The object was to find the time path of exchange rates which maximized social utility subject to a constraint and several relations. First, the constraint was that the country should neither accumulate nor decumulate claims against foreigners over the entire set of n periods. This means that, over the entire n periods, there should be balance of payments equilibrium. Second, absorption was assumed to depend upon real output and the price of foreign exchange. Third, real output was assumed to depend upon exogenous disturbances and the price of foreign exchange.

It was shown that the optimum foreign exchange market depends upon the structure of the economy and the nature of the disturbance. A free exchange market tends to be more desirable than a stabilized market if the disturbance affects income and the balance of payments in the same direction. As a result, the exchange rate generates countercyclical movements in aggregate demand and thereby raises social utility. If, however, the disturbance

---

[1] Stein (1963), 384-402.

affects income and the balance of payments in opposite directions, then a market stabilized at the equilibrium rate of exchange will tend to be more desirable. Essentially, I was led to focus upon the covariance between the price of foreign exchange and the ratio of income to capacity output. If the covariance is negative, then a free exchange market is preferable to a market stabilized at the long-run equilibrium rate. When income rises relative to capacity, the price of foreign exchange declines and excess aggregate demand is reduced. If the covariance is positive, the free exchange market would provide a positive feedback to aggregate demand. A market stabilized at the long-run equilibrium rate is to be preferred.

Tower and Courtney[2] and Turnovsky[3] developed my analysis. Drawing upon these three papers, I sketch an algorithm which can be used to compare the recent free foreign exchange market experience with the prior experience with stabilized rates.

In any model of an open economy, we are able to solve for the level of real income in terms of exogenous variables, policy variables, and (the endogenous) price of foreign exchange. Let real income Y be a function of exogenous disturbances U, government policies X, and the price of foreign exchange P. Then a reduced form equation for Y is given by:

(3) $Y = F(U,X,P)$.

Use the convention that $F_U > 0$, $F_X > 0$. If the idle resource effect is dominant,[4] $F_P > 0$ – a rise in the price of foreign exchange tends to raise real income. Expand the F function around the means of the variables and derive:

(4) $y = au + bx + cp$,

where lower case letters (y,u,x,p) are deviations of (Y,U,X,P) from their respective means;[5] and (a,b,c) are positive.

---

[2]Tower and Courtney (1974).

[3]Turnovsky (1976).

[4]Stein (1963), p. 387.

[5]All variables could be deflated per unit of effective labor.

Suppose that we value stability of real income because the social utility function is concave. Then we would like the exchange rate system to reduce the variance of y resulting from variations in the exogenous variables. The variance of y, denoted by $\sigma^2(y)$, is:

(5) $\quad \sigma^2(y) = a^2\sigma^2(u) + b^2\sigma^2(x) + c^2\sigma^2(p) + 2ab\sigma(u,x)$

$\qquad\qquad + 2ac\sigma(u,p) + 2bc\sigma(x,p),$

where $\sigma(i,j)$ denotes the covariance between variable i and j.

In a stabilized exchange market (denoted by S), the price of foreign exchange is a constant. As a result, the variance of real income $\sigma_S^2(y)$ is:

(6) $\quad \sigma_S^2(y) = a^2\sigma^2(u) + b^2\sigma^2(x) + 2ab\sigma(u,x).$

The difference between the variance of real income in a free exchange market, denoted by $\sigma_F^2(y)$ and $\sigma_S^2(y)$, is given by subtracting equation (6) from (5).

(7) $\quad \sigma_F^2(y) - \sigma_S^2(y) = c^2\sigma^2(p) + 2c[a\sigma(u,p) + b\sigma(p,x)].$

It is often convenient to express equation (7) in terms of product moment correlation coefficients:

$$r(i,j) = \frac{\sigma(i,j)}{\sigma(i)\,\sigma(j)}.$$

Then,

(8) $\quad \sigma_F^2(y) - \sigma_S^2(y) = c^2\sigma^2(p) + 2c\sigma(p)[ar(u,p)\sigma(u) + br(x,p)\sigma(x)]$

$\qquad\qquad = c\sigma(p)[c\sigma(p) + 2ar(u,p)\sigma(u) + 2br(x,p)\sigma(x)].$

Which exchange market is preferable will depend upon the nature of the disturbances, described by r(u,p), and on the policies followed, described by r(x,p).

Consider several examples of how equation (8) can be used to evaluate the pre-1971 experience relative to the recent free market experience.

Suppose that the government policies undertaken are completely independent of what is happening in the foreign exchange market:

POLICY $\quad r(p,x) = 0.$

273

Substitute policy $r(p,x) = 0$ into equation (8) and derive:

$$(9) \quad \sigma_F^2(y) - \sigma_S^2(y) = c\sigma(p) [c\sigma(p) + 2ar(u,p) \sigma(u)].$$

In this example, a free exchange market is socially more desirable than a stabilized market if:

$$(10) \quad r(u,p) <$$

If the disturbance is such that the balance of payments tends to move in the same direction as real income, then the price of foreign exchange will tend to move in a direction opposite to the movement of income--$r(u,p) < 0$. For example, if the disturbance is a shift in the foreign demand for our exports, then $r(u,p)$ is negative. The decline in the price of foreign exchange exerts a negative feedback upon income; and it is a stabilizing device. For the variance of real income resulting from this disturbance to be less under free rates, equation (10) must be satisfied.

Suppose that $r(u,p) > 0$, such that the price of foreign exchange rises when there is a disturbance to real income. For example, if the disturbance were primarily domestic and the rise in income led to a deterioration in the balance of payments, then $r(u,p)$ is positive. Then, as long as the government policy is independent of what is happening in the foreign exchange market, $r(p,x) = 0$, equation (10) cannot be satisfied. This means that, in light of the disturbance u, the free exchange market leads to a lower utility than would a market stabilized at the equilibrium rate of exchange.

On a purely theoretical level, there exists a policy response which would permit the free exchange market to produce a smaller real income variance than would occur with stabilized rates in response to any disturbance.[6] This can be seen by solving for $r(p,x)$, which would make equation (8) negative.

If there is a sufficiently large negative correlation between the policy response and the price of foreign exchange, defined by equation (11), then the free exchange market can lead to a lower variance of income when $r(u,p)$ is positive. This means that the use of the "correct" policy can make the free market more efficient, even when the disturbance u leads to a positive feedback in the foreign exchange market.

$$(11) \quad r(p,x) < -\frac{1}{b\sigma(x)}[\frac{c\sigma(p)}{2} + ar(u,p)\sigma(u)] \; => \sigma_F^2(y) - \sigma_S^2(y) < 0.$$

---

[6] I am not claiming that rationality can be expected, on a priori grounds, even from benevolent policy-makers.

274

There is no sense in comparing the actual variance of real income during the pre-1971 period with that found in the subsequent free rate period, because the disturbances, (σ^2 (u), r (p,u)), were different. What is interesting and important is to know whether the free exchange rate system helped, or hindered, the economy in adjusting to these shocks. The way to do that is to estimate the function r(u,p), which characterizes the disturbance, and the function r(p,x), which characterizes the policy responses. Then, we can ask whether $\sigma^2_F(y)$ would have been less than $\sigma^2_S(y)$, if the functions were r(u,p), r(p,x), given the historical disturbances σ^2 (u). Some ingenuity will be required to estimate an index of disturbances U, but that should not be beyond the abilities of economists.

The approach that I have sketched seems more capable than does the portfolio analysis of Farber, Roll and Solnik of answering the question: Was welfare increased by changing to a free rate system? However, in the words of Chairman Mao: Let a hundred flowers bloom.

REFERENCES

1. Stein, J. L., "The Optimum Foreign Exchange Market," American Economic Review, LIII, No. 3, (June 1963), 384-402.

2. Tower, E., and Courtney, M., "Exchange Rate Flexibility and Macro-Economic Stability," Review of Economics and Statistics, LVI, No.2, (May 1974), 215-224.

3. Turnovsky, S.J., "The Relative Stability of Alternative Exchange Rate Systems in the Presence of Random Disturbances," Journal of Money, Credit and Banking, VIII, No. 1, (February 1976), 29-50.

EURODOLLARS, PETRODOLLARS,
AND WORLD LIQUIDITY AND INFLATION

Richard James Sweeney

and

Thomas D. Willett *
U. S. Treasury

I. INTRODUCTION

In the three years since the "oil shock" of October 1973, the international financial markets have by and large functioned well. The dire predictions heard in 1974--of financial chaos, widespread bank collapses, and inability to recycle petrodollars—were clearly overstated.[1] While it remains prudent to watch for future signs of instability in world financial markets, concern now seems rightly •to have shifted to the role of these markets, particularly the Euro currencies markets, in the present virulent inflation. There is concern that the Euro markets have perhaps been too successful in handling the financial strains of the oil situation to the extent that the resulting expansion of official and private international liquidity may contribute significantly to another round of world-wide inflation.

In 1974, the OPEC nations accumulated approximately $55 billion in official reserves. Aided by substantial borrowing in the Euro markets, the oil importing countries in aggregate maintained a roughly·unchanged level of reserves.[2] Thus the accumulation of foreign exchange holdings by the oil exporters resulted primarily from an expansion rather than redistribution of the level of international reserves.

Further, substantial portions of the OPEC reserve accumulations have been placed in the Euro markets, raising fears of inflation on two grounds. First, the so-called Euro-currency multiplier may cause expansion in private holding of Euro currencies; some argue that such holdings contribute to inflation as would simple increases in national money supplies. Second, reserves deposited in the Euro markets have often been thought to contribute to an expansion

*This paper represents the personal views of the authors and does not necessarily reflect the position of the U. S. Treasury. The authors thank Donald W. Curtis, John Rutledge, and Edward Yardeni for helpful comments, as well as the participants at the Conference.

[1]For a discussion of the international financial aspects of the oil price increase, see Willett (1975).

[2]See the International Monetary Fund Annual Report, (1975).

of official reserves, which is not desirable from the standpoint of the overall operation of the international monetary system. For this reason, the central banks of the major industrial countries agreed in 1971 not to place additional reserves in the Euro markets.

The dual role of Euro currencies in inflation–as an addition to domestic money and credit supplies and as an addition to international liquidity–has been treated in a number of aggregative studies of world inflation. One purpose of this paper is to analyze the theoretical foundations and empirical limitations of such studies and to suggest how, in many instances, such studies have been seriously flawed by the uncritical application of analogies from domestic monetary theory to international monetary behavior.

All of the complex and far-reaching theoretical and empirical issues connected with this topic cannot be resolved in a single paper. Instead, we hope to highlight some of the key questions that must be answered and to indicate a number of ways in which some widely held world views are open to serious question. One of the most important of these is the tendency to add the growth in the size of the Euro currency market to the growth of national money supplies on a one-to-one basis in the analysis of world inflationary pressures. Another is the assumption of a world quantity theory in which causation runs from expansion of international reserves to consequent equiproportionate increases in national money supplies and price levels.

We argue that, in constructing world monetary aggregates, only a tiny fraction of the gross size of the Euro currency market should be added to national monetary aggregates; and that on average this portion of the Euro currency market behaves more like broad aggregates, such as M4 and M5, than like narrow aggregates, such as M1 or even M2. While the gross size of the Euro currency market is almost as large as M1 for the U. S., we argue that, for this purpose, a much more relevant comparison is the roughly $30 billion in Euro currency holdings of nonresident nonbanks versus the over $1 trillion value of M5 for the U. S. alone.

Section II considers the major ways in which the Euro markets could have an inflationary impact through their influence on private liquidity. Sections III, IV, and V discuss the analytical usefulness, and pitfalls, of various measures of the size of the Euro currency markets and of world money supply concepts, and the extent to which Euro currency holdings should enter such an aggregate. Section VI discusses some of the major theoretical issues concerning relationships between official reserve creation and international inflation, and section VII analyses some of the recent aggregate empirical studies on this subject. Section VIII concludes the paper with a brief discussion of some of the main policy issues concerning the Euro currency markets.

II. EURO CURRENCIES, PRIVATE LIQUIDITY, AND INFLATION

Though there are reasons for believing the Euro markets have contributed to inflationary pressures, these considerations, as we shall argue below, do not necessarily imply that this contribution has been very significant quantitatively, or that a measure of the Euro markets' size should simply be added to monetary aggregates to determine worldwide inflationary pressures.

As an element in the relatively high degree of integration of international financial markets and the substantial international mobility of capital, the Euro markets may have contributed to world inflation (particularly under pegged exchange rates) by making it more difficult for individual countries to run prudent, noninflationary monetary policy.[3] Furthermore, the Euro markets may have led to an increase in the measured velocity of, for example, M1 or M2 in at least two different ways. First, the existence of the Euro markets and their improved facilities for borrowing may have reduced the demands for various national monies by reducing "precautionary" demand for money balances. This would cause an increase in velocity and hence in prices, unless offset by a tightening of monetary policy. But it should be emphasized that this would generate only a one-time increase in the price level. Ongoing inflation from this source would require successive shifts in the money demand function.

A second possibility is that some part of the Euro aggregates may play the same role as national money supplies. The failure to count these Euro items appropriately in national monetary statistics would show up as an increase in measured velocity as calculated relative to the domestic money stock, and hence as an increase in prices. However, if the Euro component of the sum of the national stock plus the appropriate Euro measure were constant relative to the domestic money supply, there should be no continuing change in measured velocity and hence no added inflation, though the price level would be higher as a result.

In the last example, failure to include the relevant Euro items in the statistical series on the money stock would increase measured velocity. If the relative size of the domestic and Euro influences varies over time, velocity will also change. This suggests that failure to measure the money stock properly would result in variations in velocity that are significantly related to changes in the composition of the proper aggregate. Thus, monetary policy that concentrated only on the domestic component might be offset to some extent by inverse movements in the neglected Euro items, which would show up as un-

---

[3]We should note that the Euro markets were a substantial conduit for capital movements. Though they achieved this role by being the least-cost method of movement in many cases, it is not clear that their cost savings were so great that mobility would have been substantially impaired in their absence. See Willett (1976).

fortunate counterpolicy changes in velocity. Consequently, if this is a serious problem, we should expect to observe such an inverse relationship statistically.

However, as Willett (1976) has shown, calculations of the relevant velocities and ratios of domestic to Euro assets display none of the systematic variations of velocity, or increases in velocity, that might have been expected from these two possibilities. For major industrial countries, he calculated aggregate series of M1 and M2 in U. S. dollars; the size of the Euro currency market (as measured by both the Bank for International Settlements (BIS) net concept and the banks' liabilities to the nonresident nonbank concept, discussed below); and several relevant velocity measures. These data were not adjusted to remove the influences of the many factors beyond the Euro markets, and hence are not a definitive test. But, we feel that they strongly suggest that the Euro currency market has not been one of the major causes of world inflation.[4]

III. CONCEPTS OF EURO MARKET SIZE AND THEIR RELATION TO NATIONAL MONETARY AGGREGATES

The difficulty of selecting the proper Euro items and of gathering the data to perform the tests suggests the possibility that national monetary aggregates may frequently miss important items. Both the structure of the Euro markets and the system of collection of available statistics result in entire classes of Euro items failing to enter any calculations of national aggregate monetary or credit series. Of the gross size of the Euro markets reported by the BIS–approximately $220 billion worth of all currencies at the end of 1974[5] – some $180 billion is reported as net, in the sense that if bank A has deposits of $100 with bank B (in a different country), and B has deposits of $50 with A, the net deposit reported is $50. Neither the gross $100 nor net $50 deposits of bank A show up in any of that country's monetary series as conventionally measured. (The BIS gross–and hence net–measure does net out all interbank Euro deposits within the same country. If, in London, bank A deposits $100 with B, and B $100 with C, and finally C $100 with A, all of this is excluded. An individual's $100 deposit with a U. K. bank is also excluded.)

It is, as well, not apparent that even the BIS net size is particularly relevant. If, for example, A and C are banks in different (reporting) countries and C borrows $100 denominated in a foreign currency from A, this amount

---

[4]We had originally planned to undertake additional empirical work attempting to hold constant the other major factors influencing the demand for money functions. A brief review of the empirical literature suggested such widely differing results both in terms of specifications and apparent empirical conclusions that we concluded that, short of a major project, such an attempt would not be likely to yield worthwhile results. We are particularly indebted to Edward Yardeni who aided in the review of this body of literature.

[5]See the BIS Annual Report for 1975, covering 1974, pp. 129-30. On these accounting considerations, see Mayer (1976).

shows up in the BIS measure of net size of the Euro markets. The size of the Euro markets as given by Euro bank liabilities vis-à-vis nonresident nonbanks is far below the net size reported by the BIS; in 1974, it was on the order of $31 billion for the reporting "inner 8" countries,[6] which excludes the "outside areas" of Japan, the Bahamas, Singapore, and other non-Europe Euro centers.

It would be foolish to argue that gross interbank Euro deposits are irrelevant. After all, such deposits are freely entered into and are presumably made on rational, wealth-maximizing grounds; their significance seems similar to correspondent relationships, use of the Federal funds market, and other such domestic activities. Thus, a regulation requiring the gross size to equal the net (as reported by the BIS) by forbidding interbank deposits would have an economic effect--presumably harmful.

A primary rationale for this investigation of Euro claims is to determine which categories may have a significant influence on economic activity and should be included in consideration of national or world money supplies, but which still might be missed in national statistics. From this viewpoint, the effect of interbank deposits on banking activity that influences economic aggregates is captured presumably in the national money statistics. That is, the macro influence of interbank loans is not primarily direct but rather through encouraging monetary expansion. Such interbank loans should be excluded from the relevant money supply on much the same grounds that Federal funds and bank deposits with the Federal Reserve System are excluded.

Thus, adding the growth in the size of the whole Eurodollar market (even measured on the net BIS basis) to the growth of national money supplies on a one-to-one basis substantially overstates growth in private world monetary aggregates; greater domestic expansionary pressures resulting from the international borrowing and lending of banks would already have shown up in national monetary statistics. What would be missed in aggregate national monetary statistics would be the foreign liquid holdings of domestic nonbanking institutions. With respect to the Eurodollar market, the relevant portion for this purpose is Euro bank liabilities vis-à-vis nonresident nonbanks.

The gross size of the Euro market is not comparable to the usual monetary series. Rather, the situation is more analagous to the provision of forward cover in which gross transactions may be 20 times larger than net

---

[6]BIS (1975), p. 131. The "inner 8" are Belgium, France, Germany, Italy, Netherlands, Sweden, Switzerland, and the United Kingdom. Comparison of the gross figures for the inner 8 and the outside area suggests the total net figure may be 30 to 50 percent higher than reported for the inner 8. Morgan Guarantee kindly provided us with their estimates of foreign currency liabilities to nonbank, nonresidents for December 1974 for the nonreporting "outside" countries: Bahamas/Cayman, $4.0; Canada, $4.5; Japan, $3.0; Singapore, $1.6. Thus, the world figure is about $44 billion, which is a little over 40 percent larger than the text's figure. (We note that Morgan's estimated gross size of the market for December 1974 is $360 billion, which is again larger than the BIS figure, including as it does estimates of the outside area; also the BIS gross figure excludes all interbank redepositing in the same country while Morgan does not.)

transactions. In the Euro markets, the net size of the market when <u>all</u> deposits held by financial institutions are excluded approximates more closely the relevant monetary series in which, as is usual, nonbank private holdings of certain classes of financial assets are included.

Comparison with usual domestic practice suggests that, as of the end of 1974, only $31 billion of the more than $220 billion of BIS gross Euro deposits should actually be considered.[7] (See Chart 1 for a comparison of the gross size of the market and liabilities to nonresident nonbanks.)

Furthermore, at least some of these funds may be deposited by oil exporting countries,[8] and thus can be expected to be felt much more through the international reserve mechanism discussed in sections VI and VII than through the private liquidity mechanism discussed in sections II through V.

Having isolated this Euro item of perhaps $30 billion, the problem arises of how to allocate this amount across countries to determine its inflationary impact; it is not currently captured in national statistics. At one extreme, it may be true that (a) ownership of these deposits, (b) location of the banks, and (c) currency of denomination are all irrelevant for the inflationary impact (given there is one) on each individual country and worldwide. Consequently, the net figure might simply be added to each country's appropriate series -- but not necessarily on a one-to-one basis or with the same weight in every country.

It seems to us that this treatment would be most logical in a world in which a simple summation of national money supplies plus the relevant Euro items would give the best monetary explanation of inflation for each individual country, that is, where some world money supply concept is the best explanation of both individual country and worldwide inflation. We discuss below some of our doubts on this procedure. It should be noted here that if the individual country's money supply has at least a short-run independent influence on the domestic economy (beyond its contribution to the world money supply), we should expect that the proper treatment of Euro items is to

---

[7] This figure is reported in BIS <u>Annual Reports</u> as "External positions of reporting European banks in dollars and other foreign currencies" as <u>liabilities</u> vis-à-vis <u>nonbanks</u>. Thus, it excludes each of these banks' liabilities in foreign currencies to residents of the same country. It might seem that such a "position vis-à-vis residents," for which a partial series is provided as a "memorandum item," should be added to the figure in the text. However, many of the inner 8 countries <u>already</u> include the foreign currency denominated liabilities of their banks to their residents in their series on the various money supply statistics. Thus, as Promisel (1974) reports, Germany, Italy, and France all include such figures in their M1 series, while the U.K. includes them in M3 but not in M1. As we indicate below, it is not clear that aggregating, for example, M2 for a country with its nonbank residents' holdings of Euro assets is meaningful. Nevertheless, <u>if</u> some wide definition of money is used, and nonbank Euro assets are to be included, then those issued by banks to residents are <u>already</u> included for many countries.

[8] See BIS (1975), p. 130, which puts new deposits of the oil exporting countries at $24 billion for 1974.

Chart 1

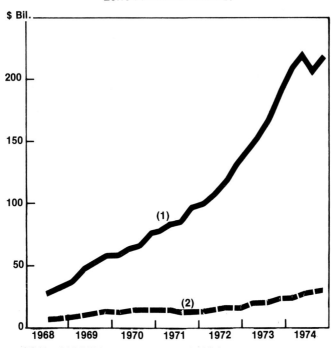

EUROCURRENCY MARKET

(1) Total Liabilities (gross size), of which
(2) Total Liabilities Vis-A-Vis Non-Resident Non-Banks

Source: *Bank for International Settlements Annual Report, 1975.*

283

allocate them to individual countries on the basis of their residents' ownership of the items. We strongly suspect that for all but the smallest and most open economies, individual country monetary conditions do have an effect beyond simply contributing to the world money supply.[9]

A final consideration is to ask to what extent Euro items are comparable to components of the usual domestic monetary series. Cooper (1974) notes that Euro deposits can be as small as $1,000 and as short-term as overnight. This is misleading, however, as the vast bulk of the market deals with units of $100,000 or more. Furthermore, consideration of the Maturity Analysis in Table 1 shows that for the U. K., the only area presenting such statistics on maturity distribution, only 20 percent of the Euro liabilities were of eight days duration or less, and less that 15 percent of the assets were so short. Perhaps, more importantly, it is only in times of great credit stringency that minimum transactions fall below $100,000--even then $20,000 is more likely than $1,000-- as these highly competitive, low margin markets depend on large volume transactions. Thus, these Euro deposits are much closer to U. S. certificates of deposit (CD s) over $100,000 than they are to the time or savings deposits included in M2 or M3. It follows that such Euro deposits are more likely candidates for aggregation in M4 and M5 concepts (which include CDs of over $100,000) than in M1 - M3. Note, too, that Euro deposits may be as good or better substitutes for U. S. Treasury bills as for CDs; thus the same arguments for adding Euro deposits to M4 or M5 would hold for at least testing whether Treasury bills should be added with or in place of these deposits.

IV. PROBLEMS OF INCLUDING EURO MARKET FIGURES IN WORLD MONEY SUPPLY CONCEPTS

A number of recent studies have used various versions of a "world money supply" to explain international inflation and aggregate economic activity. Several have considered the role of Euro currencies in such a money supply and, no doubt, others will. We wish to point out some of the conceptual problems involved when Euro currencies are used in this way, and then to discuss general problems of using world money supply series.

Separate and different definitions of world money are provided by Heller (1976), Laffer (1975), Meiselman (1975), and others[10] in their work on

---

[9] Some supporting evidence for this view is offered in Logue and Sweeney (1975).

[10] See Heller (1976); Laffer (1975); Meiselman (1975); Brittain and Sri-Kumar (1975), (note that Meiselman's piece is also based on City Bank data); and Logue and Sweeney (1975). For a discussion that moves beyond the reduced form relationships considered in the above works, using instead a world money supply concept, see Gray (1975). We have also seen investor newsletters that have used world money supply series, some even including the gross size of the Euro markets. For other recent papers in the area, see Parkin and Zis (1976).

Table 1

Maturity Analysis of Liabilities and Claims in Non-Sterling
Currencies in the United Kingdom, September 1973

(In millions of pounds sterling)

	Less than 8 days[1]	8 days to less than 1 month	1 month to less than 3 months	3 months to less than 6 months	6 months to less than 1 year	1 year to less than 3 years	3 years and over	Total
Vis-à-vis[2]								
Liabilities								
Other U.K. banks	2,369	2,756	3,551	3,326	1,387	371	286	14,046
Other U.K. residents	690	164	225	107	76	31	90	1,383
Banks abroad	4,988	5,615	7,799	5,967	2,345	668	885	28,267
Other nonresidents	1,425	1,116	1,411	984	576	164	292	5,968
Total	9,472	9,651	12,986	10,384	4,384	1,234	1,533	49,664
Assets								
Other U.K. banks	2,426	2,732	3,552	3,397	1,356	369	257	14,089
Other U.K. residents	213	447	772	743	271	354	798	3,598
Banks abroad	3,775	4,803	5,785	4,458	1,836	689	919	22,265
Other nonresidents	985	1,361	2,219	1,775	615	984	1,883	9,822
Total	7,399	9,343	12,328	10,373	4,078	2,396	3,857	49,774
Net Position								
Other U.K. banks	+57[+1,234][3]	-24	+1	+71	-31	-2	-29	+43
Other U.K. residents	-477	+283	+547	+636	+195	+323	+708	+2,215
Banks abroad	-1,213	-812	-2,014	-1,509	-509	+21	+34	-6,002
Other nonresidents	-440	+245	+808	+791	+39	+820	+1,591	+3,854
Total	-2,073 [-896][3]	-308	-658	-11	-306	+1,162	+2,304	+110

Source: Bank of England Quarterly Bulletin (March 1974).

[1]Includes sight deposits.

[2]The Bank of England also provides a breakdown, not given here, by type of reporting banks: British banks, Commonwealth banks, American banks, Japanese banks, other foreign banks, and consortium banks.

[3]Banks' holdings of London dollar certificates of deposit are included according to maturity dates. Figures in brackets show the effect of treating all such holdings of certificates as immediately realizable assets.

international inflation. Laffer's use is particularly interesting because of the difficulties that arise, in our opinion, in the way he includes Euro claims in his series, and because it represents one strand of reasoning used to advocate controls of these markets.

Not all analysts who have used them are totally sympathetic to world money supply concepts. For example, in an empirical study that is quite critical of some of the uses of world money concepts, Logue and Sweeney (1975) examined 16 OECD countries individually and defined a world money for each country as the sum of the 15 others' M1 money supplies valued in terms of the home currency.

Laffer (1975) defines world money as the sum of the M1 money supplies in 15 major industrial countries in which each observation in each series is converted into dollar values (using the then current exchange rate) plus the "net" size[11] of the Euro dollar market. He then argues to the effect that variations in this world money have effects on the world price level (in dollars) analogous to those in a monetarist theory of a closed economy. (We have also seen an unpublished set of world money supply figures defined as the sum of the M1s for the U. S., Europe (non-Communist, developed), and Japan plus the gross size of the dollar and nondollar Euro markets.)

We have grave reservations both about the uncritical use of "world money" concepts and in particular about the inclusion of Euro-currencies in such a series. We consider the latter problem first.

There are significant analytical problems in such an aggregation. First, Euro dollars are by no means a close substitute for cash and demand deposits in any of these countries. They are more akin to CDs with maturities of from one to 90 or more days, usually of denominations of $100,000 or more. It is reasonable to include them only in some very broad monetary aggregate in which their close substitutes, U. S. CDs (of over $100,000) and perhaps Treasury bills, are also used. Laffer presents no evidence of why this peculiar definition makes sense, but we are prepared to argue that even if this series gave better statistical results than aggregate series based on M1 or M2 figures alone, such results would merely be spurious correlation in an analytical hodgepodge.

Furthermore, even if Laffer had aggregated broad concepts such as M4 or M5, the figures he uses for the Euro markets vastly overstate their size when compared to national entries in M4 and M5. For example, Laffer apparently is using the net figures of the BIS -- some $180 billion in all Euro currencies

---

[11]As we argue below, this "net" size is, as reported by the BIS, not the relevant series on claims by nonbanks against Euro banks. Even this latter series is hardly comparable to M1.

for the eight reporting countries in 1974.[12] But, according to the available statistics, these deposits represent net assets of the nonbank sector of only about $31 billion.[13] For comparison, note that in 1973 the world money supply calculated by Willett (1976) gives M1 of $417.99 billion, and M2 of $1630.14 billion. The $31 billion that Laffer might reasonably include is thus less than 5 percent of the size of a world money supply based on M1s, and less than 2 percent when compared to M2-M5 world aggregates. For example, at the end of 1974, U. S. M5 alone was over $1 trillion. Furthermore, the size of Euro banks' dollar liabilities against nonbank nonresidents grew, between December 1970 and December 1974, from $11.2 billion to $23.1 billion. (For all Euro currencies the comparable figures are from $13.7 billion to $31.1 billion.) This increase of $12.1 billion simply cannot bear the weight of being a major cause of world inflation, as Laffer would have it. During this period, the U. S. M1 rose by more than $70 billion, from $214 billion (seasonally adjusted), and monetary growth was even faster in the rest of the world considered in such aggregates. It need not be elaborated that the use (in constructing world money supply figures) of the gross figures for the Euro markets is even more misleading than Laffer's use of the BIS net figure.

Thus, it seems to us that Laffer grossly overstates the effect of the Euro markets on world inflation. However, the argument that these markets have had no effect is clearly invalid _if_ the Euro markets are considered only for inclusion in some broad concept such as M4 or M5. It is frequently argued that Euro claims are not money; and to this it is frequently added that they are to a large extent the product of credit substitution and not credit creation. If, however, it is decided that some concept such as M4 or M5 is the "best" definition of money, or one of several which appear to give important independent information (presumably because of greater empirical success), then it seems that nonbank claims on Euro banks might well be considered for inclusion in this series; or, more generally, the foreign claims of nonbanks of the relevant degree of liquidity should be included.

To a large extent, Euro market activity has been a free market response to government attempts to alter credit market outcomes. We should not be surprised that U. S. regulations placing maximum rates on time deposits and CDs caused depositors to withdraw funds from U. S. institutions and switch them to

---

[12]See BIS (1975). Laffer includes only the Eurodollar portion of the market; he gives no reasons for excluding, for example, Euro-DMs.

[13]See BIS (1975), p. 131.

Euro banks, which in turn relent them to U. S. borrowers, thus enabling U. S. savers to frustrate government regulation. The same story can be told for other countries' restrictions.

The moral is that a good share of nonbank Euro claims are merely credit substitution. That the estimated size of the nonbank claims is on the order of only $30 billion should undercut claims that the Euro markets have played dominant direct roles in world inflation. Rather, their role was primarily to preserve international capital mobility, acting, in effect, as an endogenous increase in mobility to offset official effort to reduce it.

V. OTHER PROBLEMS IN THE CONSTRUCTION AND USE OF WORLD MONEY SUPPLY SERIES

We now turn to consideration of some of the problems that arise from using international monetary aggregates in small models and reduced form equations.[14]

While we concentrate in this section on some of the difficulties associated with such aggregation, we should note that there are also some clear rewards. In an open economy, monetary expansion is likely to result not only in increases in domestic prices and output but also in increased imports (particularly under fixed rates), and, to this extent, simple quantity theory-type results will not be found. However, to the extent that aggregation reduces the openness of the area considered, better results should be expected. For example, in the fixed rate period, Triffin and Grubel examined the EEC countries and found that their aggregate money supply produced better quantity theory results for the whole area than were found for individual country money supplies and GNPs.[15]

We find this sort of result quite plausible for short-run relationships; the nominal GNP of Belgium treated on a quarterly basis as a function of alternative money supply concepts is an example. Germany's and other EEC countries' demands for goods will be influenced by their money supplies and

---

[14]We take as given the standard issues and viewpoints on the question of using small models and/or reduced forms versus large structural models. There have been, for example, a number of articles on these questions in the Review of the St. Louis Federal Reserve Bank.

[15]Triffin and Grubel (1962). While such aggregation can thus "solve" some problems, it can as well introduce conceptual econometric problems of empirical importance. Note that, for the U. S. at least, it is reasonable to take the money supply (M) as exogenous in regressions on nominal income (Y)–though many deny this is so–and thus the assumption of classical regression theory, that the regressor is exogenous, is met. A key contribution of the monetary theory of the balance of payments is to reemphasize that, at most, only one country's M can be exogenous under fixed rates. Logue and Sweeney (1975) argue that this one country was the U. S., though other countries had substantial short-run independence. Thus, in the Triffin-Grubel results, the Ms for the individual countries were not truly exogenous, and (in the Logue-Sweeney view) neither was the aggregate, at least in the long run. Whether this makes a significant empirical difference is not known, but it is conceptually discoverable from the new literature on "causality" (where causality is equivalent to exogeneity); see Granger (1969), Sims (1972), and Feige and Pearce (1976).

will have significant impacts on Belgium. Over longer periods, however, under fixed exchange rates and hence with lack of long-run monetary independence, all EEC money supplies should move together. Thus, the aggregate EEC money supply should not be expected a priori to perform much better as an explanatory variable than the Belgium money supply, since the two tend to move in phase over yearly or biennial periods.

However, the policy implications of the estimated relationships are obscured in both the quarterly and yearly cases by inability to impute a causal role to the independent variable in the estimated equation. We expect the same long-run relationship between Belgium's GNP and money supply whether the "true" independent variable is the Belgium money supply, German money supply, U. S. money supply, or the structural parameters of a number of governments' reaction functions. Similarly, short-run relationships using world money concepts are merely a substitute for a structural model in which causality might be inferred and policy implications derived. Calling for the curtailment of world money growth gives no guidance on how to achieve this; attempting to curtail Belgium's monetary expansion as a partial step may well be futile and misguided.

To conclude, we shall discuss two particular world money supply concepts which have been advanced, and their use. First, we discuss Laffer's (1975) treatment as representative of the genre that merely adds up various money supplies, expressed in some given monetary unit. Secondly, we examine Heller's (1976) analysis which uses the IMF data series based on a geometric average of growth rates of currencies each expressed in terms of domestic currency.

The belief that quantity theory results tend to hold at least approximately in the long run, that purchasing power parity relationships tend to hold at least approximately in the long run, and that persistent inflation requires persistent monetary expansion leads one to expect a good long-run, average relationship between the world money supply expressed in U. S. dollars and U. S. prices. But, this relationship is consistent with a large number of hypotheses about the cause of dollar price inflation, and the correct policy prescription is quite different for different causes.

To demonstrate, we note that the same type of long-run relationship is to be expected between the world money supply expressed in German marks and German prices, and between the world money supply expressed in Belgian francs and Belgian prices.

For example, one hypothesis regarding the 1960s inflation under fixed exchange rates held that the U. S. unilaterally determined its money supply and thus its prices, and that all other Western money supplies and prices fell into line.[16] If this were so, a doubling of the U. S. money supply would lead to the doubling of U. S. prices, and the doubling of foreign prices and money supplies. Thus, the doubling of U. S. prices is associated with a doubling of the world money supply. Rather, the cause was U. S. monetary expansion, and the correct policy prescription for reducing such inflation is U. S. monetary restraint.

To take another possible case, we suppose that U. S. policymakers react primarily to foreign monetary events. If Europe and Japan become more expansionary, the U. S. falls into line; then, a doubling of the Europe/Japan money supply is likely, accompanied by a doubling of the Europe/Japan price level, the U. S. money supply, and dollar prices. The policy prescription here would be to try to encourage greater European and Japanese monetary restraint; failing this, U. S. restraint would exercise only a temporary influence on inflation.

Even in this second case, expansion outside the U. S. might be due to generalized desires in Europe and Japan to expand their money supplies "too rapidly," or it might be due to some dominant country's expansion. In the former case, it makes sense to encourage Belgium, as one of the several European countries, either to expand less rapidly or to let its exchange rate depreciate. If, however, EEC expansion were led primarily by Germany, with Belgium and other countries following, the policy prescription is to persuade Germany to exercise monetary restraint.

We will not try to sort out complex issues involved here. We merely wish to show that discriminating among these and many other hypotheses is not easy. This illustrates our point that high, positive correlations between the world money supply expressed in terms of a country's currency and that country's price level give little guidance for policy.

Laffer (1975) argues that exchange rate changes can alter the value of the world money supply expressed in dollars. While the rules of arithmetic ensure the accuracy of this statement, its validity does not support Laffer's preference for fixed exchange rates. For example, suppose exchange rates are fixed and every country but Belgium doubles its money supply. If Belgium is not to abandon fixed rates, it will be forced to double its money supply, and will therefore share in the doubling of world prices. If, alternatively, Belgium had allowed its exchange rate to appreciate to offset foreign monetary expansion and inflation, Belgium would, in the long run, suffer no inflation and the change in Belgium's exchange rate would have offset the expansion in other money supplies to keep the world money supply constant in Belgian francs. To suggest

---

[16] A lucid exposition of this view is given by Haberler (1974). Logue and Sweeney (1975) provide at least some evidence for this view.

another experiment: if the U. S. doubles its money supply and holds it there, other money supplies must double under fixed rates; or, if other money supplies are fixed, the U. S. dollar would depreciate on a free market. In either case, the U. S. price level doubles and the world money supply doubles in dollar terms. But, if rates are flexible and other countries resist U. S. expansion, foreign prices do not change. Thus, Laffer's correlations can be expected to have success without throwing light on either policy or causation, and without supporting the case for fixed exchange rates.[17]

Heller's (1976) analysis may be criticized on somewhat different grounds. His study attempts to explain international inflation as the result of increases in international reserves. The structure of his argument is quite reasonable – international reserves influence worldwide monetary expansion which (at least partially) causes inflation. We discuss the relationship between reserve creation and monetary expansion in the next section. We note here that any relationship between world monetary expansion and worldwide inflation is subject to the caveats expressed above. But, in addition to these warnings, we find severe technical defects in the IMF statistical series Heller uses.

It seems to us that the problem of explaining worldwide inflation on a highly aggregative level–if it can be done--is one of finding a few key international level aggregate variables that explain inflation in each individual country; this seems to be Heller's intention also. However, he uses two IMF data series that are, in our opinion, quite inappropriate for these purposes. The current IMF series on the world money supply is based on the geometric average of each member's rate of monetary growth on an M1 basis, without adjusting for exchange rate changes. Further, world prices are a geometric average of the rate of inflation in each country's prices measured in domestic currency. An aggregate relationship between the two concepts is quite consistent in a world view in which, for all practical purposes, each economy can be treated as a closed economy. In such a case, we should find that, for country j over the long run:

$$(1) \quad \frac{\dot{P}_j}{P_j} = \frac{\dot{M}_j}{M_j} - a_j \, ,$$

[17]Laffer has not presented his statistical results. However, Logue and Sweeney (1975) report passable results in explaining the level of nominal U. S. GNP on the basis of their world money supply of 15 OECD countries converted to dollars (in each period at the then current exchange rates). However, they find significantly better statistical results by using this world money supply and the U. S. M1 series as separate independent variables, from which they draw the conclusion that the U. S., like the other countries they examine, has some monetary control over its economy but is also subject to outside monetary influences.

where P_j and M_j are the price level and money supply measured in domestic currency; a_j is constant; and the dot indicates a time derivative. a_j should equal the real rate of growth of the economy and in actual estimation we would expect a lagged version to be used. Equation (1) then says that the inflation rate in j equals the rate of monetary growth less the real growth rate. Weighting such equations for all j by w_j, the country's share of worldwide GNP, gives

$$(2) \quad w_j \frac{\dot{P}_j}{P_j} = w_j \frac{\dot{M}_j}{M_j} - w_j a_j \ ;$$

and summing over j gives

$$(3) \quad \Sigma w_j \frac{\dot{P}_j}{P_j} = \Sigma w_j \frac{\dot{M}_j}{M_j} - \Sigma w_j a_j \ ,$$

which is the equation Heller uses (in lagged form).[18] If (1) gives a good fit for all j, so should (3). But, knowing that (3) works well sheds no light on how (1) works.

Conversely, suppose that world money is important in determining a country's inflation rate. From elementary considerations of the theory of flexible exchange rates, we would expect that monetary expansion abroad would influence the domestic economy to the extent that exchange rates do not vary to offset such expansion.

Thus, we might want to test for country i (a lagged version of):

$$(4) \quad \frac{\dot{P}_i}{P_i} = a_i + b_i \frac{\dot{M}_i}{M_i} + c_i \sum_{j \neq i} \left(\frac{\dot{M}_j}{M_j} + \frac{\dot{E}_j}{E_j} \right),$$

where a_i, b_i, and c_i are constants; E_j is the value of the unit of j's currency in terms of i's. Therefore, $\Sigma M_j E_j$ is the value of the rest of the world's money in terms of i's currency, and

---

[18]In fact, the IMF series are geometric rather than simple weighted averages. Our points, however, remain valid.

$$\Sigma \left(\frac{\dot{M}_j}{M_j} + \frac{\dot{E}_j}{E_j} \right)$$

is the percentage rate of change of this value. If the IMF world money supply concept can successfully explain $\dot{P}_i/P_i$, it would do so with

$$(5) \qquad \frac{\dot{P}_i}{P_i} = a_i + b_i \frac{\dot{M}_i}{M_i} + c_i \sum_{j \neq i} w_j \frac{\dot{M}_j}{M_j},$$

where (5) equals (4) minus $c_i \Sigma \dot{E}_j/E_j$; that is, (5) would seem to be simply a misspecification of (4). Further, across countries, b_i and c_i would be constrained by

$$\Sigma_i w_i \frac{\dot{P}_i}{P_i} = \Sigma_i w_i a_i + \Sigma_i w_i b_i \frac{\dot{M}_i}{M_i} + \sum_{i=1} w_i c_i \sum_{j \neq i} w_j \frac{\dot{M}_j}{M_j}$$

$$= \Sigma_i w_i a_i + \Sigma_i w_i \frac{\dot{M}_i}{M_j}.$$

Such a constraint seems not to have any rationale or useful purpose. Furthermore, we would not be surprised to find (3) working well even if (4) or (5) worked poorly for each country.

In general, then, it is often quite difficult to infer causal relationships from studies based on world money supply concepts. While such concepts can be useful, they must be employed in a critical and discriminating way, with careful qualifications made concerning the meanings of any observed relationship. Further, as we show below, the possible problems are increased when international reserves are also considered.

VI. THEORETICAL ISSUES IN ANALYZING THE INFLATIONARY EFFECTS OF OFFICIAL INTERNATIONAL LIQUIDITY CREATION

A frequently encountered view postulates a virtual one-to-one relationship between increases in the growth of international reserves and increases in world inflation. This theory says, in effect, that a world quantity theory of money operates with respect to international reserves in such a way that, if international reserves are doubled, then world prices will also be doubled.[19] Such a view ascribes the major responsibility for the high rates of world inflation in recent years to the rapid expansion of international reserves and argues that one should be quite concerned about further increases in official reserves such as have been occurring through the operation of the Euro currency markets.

This view overlooks the fact that there is not the same kind of behavioral relationship between expansions of national holdings of international reserves and increases in national spending as that between increases in national monetary supplies and increases in private spending. Undoubtedly, a rapid expansion of international reserves would lead to some increase in the rate of world inflation, as some countries would have greater freedom to follow more expansionary domestic policies. But, reserve increases need not induce national authorities to expand aggregate demand more than they otherwise would have. In order words, reserve expansion may reduce or remove balance of payments constraints on national spending, but they need not automatically induce countries to increase spending.[20]

In discussing the nature of countries' demands for reserves, a number of complexities must be dealt with which are either absent or relatively unimportant when considering aggregate domestic demand for money functions.[21] One of the most important of these is that national governments are much more concerned with domestic macroeconomic and exchange rate stability than are private individuals and firms. Thus, even though a country's authorities may

---

[19] In the following, we adopt the analytical convenience of abstracting from real economic growth. Rephrasing the argument to take account of real economic growth is straightforward.

[20] For further discussion, see Sweeney and Willett (1976); and Williamson's treatment of this topic in his survey article (1973), particularly his discussion of the "international quantity theory," pp. 708ff.

[21] The usefulness and limitations of various analogies between domestic and international liquidity were considered in a number of the papers and discussions at the 1970 IMF Conference on International Reserves. See also the recent survey papers by Grubel (1971), Williamson (1973), and Cohen (1975). We discuss some of the issues further in the sections on international liquidity in Willett (forthcoming), and in Sweeney and Willett (forthcoming).

have higher reserve levels than they desire, they also consider the costs of reducing their reserve positions in terms of their objectives for exchange rate and macroeconomic stability. In effect, over a wide range, the cost of having a nonoptimal reserve level is small relative to the costs of adjusting the reserve level through changes in economic policies. Thus, one would expect much less systematic and strong relationships between divergencies between the demand for and supply of international reserves and government behavior than between the demand for and supply of domestic money balances and consequent domestic private spending decisions. This provides an underlying economic rationale for the position that reserves act more as a constraint than as a behavioral variable, and for analogies to the extreme Keynesian view of monetary policy as a string—you can restrain the economy by pulling on the string, but you cannot induce expansion by pushing on it.

There is also a presumption that profit or economic maximizing incentives have on average much less influence on the behavior of national governments than on private firms and individuals. There is a substantial body of literature on public choice theory and bureaucratic politics which argues that because of information costs, for example, even under a generally well functioning system of representative democracy, national officials in areas such as international finance and national defense are likely to have scope for discretionary behavior.[22] In this context, it would not be surprising to see the operations of a Galbraith-type dependence effect which would be consistent with the amended Mrs. Machlup's wardrobe theory of the demand for international reserves.[23] For reasons of national power and diplomacy, and their own prestige, national officials might desire higher levels of international reserves, and place particular emphasis on avoiding substantial declines in reserve positions than would be suggested by models of optimal macroeconomic policy which focus on aggregate national economic efficiency alone. Contrary to some of the statements in the literature, this type of reserve behavior need not be irrational, or evidence of nonmaximizing behavior. National officials can rationally follow more complex utility functions than are generally treated in formal economic models of the demand for international reserves.

Such behavior could impart a substantial ratchet effect to national demands for international reserves. In other words, as reserves accumulate,

---

[22]See, for instance, Tower and Willett (1972); and also Amacher, Tollison, and Willett (1976), and references cited therein to the earlier literature by Buchanan, Downs, etc.

[23]See Machlup (1966).

national officials become accustomed to higher levels of real reserves and their demand function shifts upward. This is a point which appears not to have been fully appreciated in the debate on the effects of "reserve sinks" on the long-run inflationary impact of reserve increases which took place at the 1970 IMF Conference on International Reserves.[24] At this conference, considerable attention was directed to possible differences between domestic and international liquidity behavior. A number of participants emphasized that there frequently would not be short-run responses to reserve accumulations by countries already in strong reserve positions, and that responses can take forms other than adjustment of macroeconomic policies, such as controls. There was disagreement, however, over the longer run effects on inflation if adjustments in exchange rates and controls are ruled out, even in the expectation that reserves act primarily as a constraint on national behavior and that, as a consequence, countries in strong reserve positions may behave as "reserve sinks" or "international liquidity traps." Richard N. Cooper argued that reserve increases would cause ". . .proportionately higher rates of inflation. . .only. . . if no country behaved as an international 'liquidity trap.'"[25] But, Harry G. Johnson argued that this conclusion ". . .relied on too short a perspective of policy; in the long run an increase in reserves passes around via deficits and surpluses, and all affected national authorities alter their priorities; thus in the long run there can be no international 'liquidity traps' . . . ."[26] Jurg Niehans agreed with Johnson, arguing that, ". . .in the long run, the same countries do not persist as 'reserve sinks,' and the price level can be expected to respond to the reserve situation. This response. . .may only be observable with a very long lag,. . .[as long as ten or fifteen years]."[27] We agree with Johnson and Niehans that the assumption that reserves behave only as a constraint combined with the observation that one or more countries has excess reserves is sufficient to break the link between reserves and domestic inflation only in the short run. The longer the period considered, the more likely it is that initial reserve sinks will at some time run payments deficits larger than in the absence of the initial accumulation of reserves. Over the very long term, this process may give the result of an equiproportionate relationship between reserves and inflation even

---

[24]IMF (1970).

[25]IMF (1970), p. 92.

[26]IMF (1970), p. 92.

[27]IMF (1970), p. 152.

though an excess of supply over demand for reserves never directly motivates higher national spending.

We would like to emphasize, however, that, as we have shown,[28] this long-run result requires the absence of any dependence effect between the supply of and demand for reserves. In a world in which policymakers behave according to the Mrs. Machlup's wardrobe theory of seeking to avoid reserve declines, reserve accumulations will ratchet upwards the demand for reserves. Indeed, in a strong version of the wardrobe theory, the "reserve constraint" might ratchet up by the full amount of any accumulation, and national officials would immediately feel themselves under reserve pressure whenever the country went into deficit. Under such circumstances, reserve accumulations are fully and permanently sterilized. If a reserve sink is defined to include any sort of wardrobe-type dependence effect rather than just a simple constraint theory of reserve behavior, then Cooper's view is correct, that the existence of a single reserve sink would be sufficient to give less than full proportionality even in the long run.

This extreme version of wardrobe-type behavior is unlikely to occur very often. A reserve accumulation which is reversed rather quickly is unlikely to ratchet up the demand for reserves by very much. But, we would expect a large number, rather than just a few, countries to display some elements of wardrobe-type behavior. This leads us to expect that on average reserve increases will be accompanied by a higher average world price level, but that the lags involved would be quite long and variable; the long-run effects would normally be substantially less than proportionate; and, that the actual distribution of the increases could have major effects both on the time pattern of adjustments and the ultimate price change.

Another important consideration to emphasize concerns the ways countries react to divergencies between the demand for and supply of reserves. In the usual presentation of what Williamson (1973) has labelled the "international quantity theory" of the relationship between international reserves and world inflation, it is assumed that countries respond to an excess demand for or supply of reserves by changing aggregate demand policies (expanding domestic aggregate demand to eliminate an excess supply of reserves and reducing it in times of excess demand). In practice, however, as noted above, balance of payments adjustments frequently take the form of exchange rate adjustments or administrative measures such as exchange controls. Thus, even if countries generally react strongly to changes in excess demands for and supplies of reserves, there need be little relation between the level of

---

[28] Sweeney and Willett (in preparation).

297

international reserves and the average of national price levels.

Views on the likely types of reactions to excess demands for reserves may strongly influence views as to desirable policy with respect to international liquidity. Consider the expansion of official reserve holdings following the OPEC oil price increase. Official views of the international liquidity developments of 1974-75 were much influenced by the concern that many countries might react to their larger excess demands for reserves by resorting to trade restrictions and controls, rather than by allowing their exchange rates to float down and/or by adopting tighter domestic fináncial policies. Coupled with recognition that virtually all of the increases in gross international reserves were accruing to the oil exporting countries, it seems quite fortunate that stringent official efforts were not made to limit increases in the growth of measured international reserves. If total reserves had been held constant and the reserve accumulations of the OPEC countries had had to come primarily at the expense of reduction in other countries' reserves, it is probable that the initial predictions of severe international financial difficulties and spread of beggar-thy-neighbor balance of payments restrictions might have come true. It is quite likely that, if the expansion of international reserves had been substantially less following the oil price increases, the result would have been considerable additional costs to the world economy in terms of balance of payments restrictions and international financial strains, without much of a concomitant reduction in inflationary pressures.

VII. CRITIQUE OF SOME RECENT AGGREGATE EMPIRICAL STUDIES OF INFLATION AND INTERNATIONAL RESERVES

Despite the preceding theoretical reasons for doubting that an international quantity theory between official reserves and world inflation would hold, even if all national economies behaved according to the quantity theory, several recent empirical studies have suggested that aggregate relationships have behaved in recent years in a manner consistent with an international quantity theory. We review below several of these studies and conclude that the evidence they contain does not offer strong support for the strict international quantity theory. The basic difficulty is that focusing on the behavior of aggregate indices of global reserves, money supplies, and prices can indicate false relationships which do not obtain when the individual underlying relationships are examined.

A clear example of this is given in the studies by Goldstein (1974) and Meiselman (1975) which focused on the high correlation in the aggregate between the rapid accumulation of international reserves by industrial countries during 1970-72, and the rapid acceleration of growth in national money supplies over the same period. With respect to these aggregate relationships, both

Goldstein and Meiselman conclude that the reserve increase was the primary cause of monetary expansion. When one looks at these relationships on a country-by-country basis, however, there is little systematic relationship across countries between increases in reserves over this period and increases in monetary expansion, as shown by Willett (1976). Across the group, there is no significant rank correlation between the amount of reserve accumulation over the 1970-72 period and either the rate of monetary expansion or the absolute or percentage increases in the rate of monetary expansion.

Recent articles by Heller (1976) and Keran (1975) provide highly aggregative but quite different approaches to explaining world prices on the basis of world reserves. Using regression analysis, Keran found an equiproportionate relationship between increases in international reserves and world prices, while Heller found a strong relationship the magnitude of which varied depending on the equation estimated.

We believe one must be wary of accepting regression results showing a significant one-to-one relationship between inflation and reserves. As noted above, such a relationship is not strongly predicted by theory. With Dennis E. Logue, we examined the level of total nominal economic activity of 16 OECD countries as a function of the sum of their official reserves during the fixed rate period, and found that by suitable choice of length of lags and degree of polynomial, an Almon lag relationship could be found which gives a sum of lagged coefficients consistent with a unit-elastic relationship of nominal activity to official reserves. However, different lags did not give such a relationship and the equation was sometimes sensitive to minor changes. Hence, we concluded, the unit-elastic hypothesis could not be flatly rejected in the sense of having failed every test, but neither were the results very robust. This experience, then, makes us dubious of reported relationships (unit-elastic and otherwise) between reserves and prices. We turn now to a specific critique of the Heller (1976) and Keran (1975) studies.

Heller draws a line of causation from changes in world reserves to changes in the world money supply, and from changes in the world money supply to changes in the world price level. He uses the IMF series on the worldwide rate of change of official reserves in dollars to try to explain a weighted average of changes in countries' prices in domestic currency. This imputes an element of exchange illusion to the system, as is also true when reserves are used to explain the IMF's average of money supply changes as measured in each country's domestic currency.

Heller explains the link between world reserves and the world money supply by relying on direct links for each country between its reserve inflows and its monetary expansion. In such a world, for country j we would expect a fairly decent relationship of the form:

$$(6) \quad \frac{\dot{M}_{j,t}}{M_{j,t}} = A_j + \sum_{i=0}^{\infty} b_{j,t-i} \left(\frac{\dot{R}_{j,t-i}}{R_{j,t-i}} + \frac{\dot{E}_{j,t-i}}{E_{j,t-i}} \right) ,$$

where $M_{j,t}$ is j's money supply at time t, measured in units of its own currency; $R_{j,t-i}$ is the dollar value of j's reserves at time t-i ; $E_{j,t-i}$ is the number of units of j's currency required to buy one dollar; and a dot indicates a time derivative. Such an equation would be consistent with the explanation of individual countries' money supplies and prices on the basis of reserve flows if $\Sigma b_{j,t-i}$ is statistically significant. Given a proportionate relationship between money supply and prices, (6) would give an equiproportionate link between prices and reserves if $\Sigma b_{j,t-i}$ is not statistically different from unity. A positive A_j allows for increases in technical efficiency in financial markets (the ability to borrow reserves can substitute for owning them), and in the use of reserves.

Equation (6) explicitly recognizes that the influence of the dollar value of j's reserve on monetary expansion in j depends on j's exchange rate vis-à-vis the U. S. Put another way, j will presumably be more expansionary, given its dollar reserve position over time, if its exchange rate is depreciating; conversely, j can expand without losing reserves if it allows its rates to depreciate.

Now suppose we aggregate (6)'s relationship to the world level. Weighting (6) by j's share in the world's GNP gives

$$(7) \quad w_j \frac{\dot{M}_{j,t}}{M_{j,t}} = w_j A_j + w_j \Sigma b_{j,t-i} \left(\frac{\dot{R}_{j,t-i}}{R_{j,t-i}} + \frac{\dot{E}_{j,t-i}}{E_{j,t-i}} \right) ;$$

and summing across countries gives

$$(8) \quad \Sigma_j w_j \frac{\dot{M}_{j,t}}{M_{j,t}} = \Sigma_j w_j A_j + \left(\Sigma_j w_j \Sigma b_{j,t-i} \frac{\dot{R}_{j,t-i}}{R_{j,t-i}} \right)$$

$$+ \left(\Sigma_j w_j \Sigma b_{j,t-i} \frac{\dot{E}_{j,t-i}}{E_{j,t-i}} \right) .$$

It can be considered that Heller is testing the hypothesis of a one-to-one relationship between inflation and reserve growth, in which case we would expect $\Sigma \, b_{j,t-i}$ to be about equal to unity for all countries. From the w_j definition, $\Sigma_j w_j = 1$. We would then expect:

$$(9) \quad \Sigma_j \; w_j \; \frac{\dot{M}_{j,t}}{M_{j,t}} = \Sigma_j \; w_j \; A_j + \overset{\infty}{\underset{i=0}{\Sigma}} \; c_{t-i} \; \frac{\dot{R}_{t-i}}{R_{t-i}} + \overset{\infty}{\underset{i=0}{\Sigma}} \; c_{t-i} \; \frac{\dot{E}_{t-i}}{E_{t-i}} \; ,$$

where R_{t-i} is now the dollar value of <u>world</u> reserves at time $t-i$; E_{t-i} is the average (or here GNP-weighted) world exchange rate in terms of dollars; and $\Sigma \, c_{t-i}$ is approximately equal to unity. However, the equation actually used when trying to explain the IMF series on money supplies as dependent on reserve growth is

$$(10) \quad \Sigma_j \; w_j \; \frac{\dot{M}_{j,t}}{M_{j,t}} = \Sigma_j \; w_j \; A_j + \Sigma \; c_{t-i} \; \frac{\dot{R}_{t-i}}{R_{t-i}} \; .$$

It seems to us that while (9) properly handles exchange rates, (10) explicitly assumes total exchange rate illusion. On yearly data, Heller finds estimates of $\Sigma \, c_{t-i}$ that are significantly less than unity. However, this can hardly be a valid test, since he has omitted the exchange rate variable.

Further, we are highly suspicious of this type of aggregate procedure as a test of whether individual countries' reserve flows explain their monetary expansion and inflation. Given the view that reserves are related to world money through individual countries' reactions, the relationship of fundamental interest is equation (6) for the individual countries. While obtaining valid results across countries for (6) would lead us to expect fair results for (8) and (9), we would not be satisfied until results for (6) were also reported. But, good or poor results for (8) or (9) would hardly alter our prior convictions about (6), and results for (10) have even less weight.

We wish to emphasize that we do not believe that (6) must hold for individual countries in order for inflation to have a one-to-one relationship to reserve growth. That position rests on the premises that (a) no subset of countries can act consistently as a world reserve sink, and (b) reserve inflows do not create ratchet effects that alter the underlying country demands for reserves. We feel condition (a) is likely to be valid, at least for a period of a few decades. If (b) holds, we should not be surprised at world quantity theory results that are characterized by very different country behavior in different country episodes. In one instance, country X may resist reserve flows adamantly but in the end fruitlessly, while in another, X may yield to or even anticipate the first inflows. Thus, we do not think equation (6) need hold very well for any single country in circumstances where equation (9) would be expected to work well. What we do believe is that equation (9) rather than (10) is a better test of the hypothesis, as (10) imposes stringent exchange rate illusion.

As a final comment on Heller's study, we wish to note a certain instability among his empirical results. He reports (pp. 78, 72, 80, respectively):

$$(11) \quad P_t = -2.72 + .89 \ M_{t-2}$$
$$ (1.39) \quad (.16)$$

$$\bar{R}^2 = .58, \ D.W. = 1.63 \ ;$$

$$(12) \quad M_t = 7.71 + .17 \ R^{\$}_{t-1}$$
$$ (.67) \quad (.05)$$

$$\bar{R}^2 = .54, \ D.W. = 2.14 \ ;$$

and,

$$(13) \quad P_t = 3.43 + .07 \ R^{\$}_{t-2} + .17 \ R^{\$}_{t-3} + .17 \ R^{\$}_{t-4}$$
$$ (.64) \quad (.03) \qquad (.04) \qquad (.07)$$

$$\bar{R}^2 = .89, \ D.W. = 2.36,$$

where M_t, P_t, and R_t are the IMF growth rate indices discussed above; the data has been altered to remove serial correlation; the figures in parentheses are standard errors; and insignificant variables are omitted. From equation (11), a 1 percent increase in the rate of world monetary expansion, as measured by the IMF series, will (with a lag) increase the world inflation rate by approximately 1 percent. From (12), an increase of world reserve growth by 1 percent will raise world monetary growth by about two-tenths of 1 percent, and combining this result with (11) will raise the world inflation rate by about two-tenths of 1 percent. But, equation (13) argues that a persistent increase in reserve growth of 1 percent will raise world inflation by about four-tenths of 1 percent. Such markedly differing results do not inspire confidence in either. Furthermore, he also reports (p. 81, Table 8) a sum of lagged coefficients almost exactly equal to unity. It is this sort of instability of coefficients for world aggregate relationships using reserves that we question.

Keran's (1975) world money supply series does not have the difficulties we discussed above with respect to the IMF series. He defined "world money" as the sum of the dollar value of developed countries' international reserves (a potentially misleading definition). He then examines the empirical relationship between percentage changes in these reserves and percentage changes in the average of the dollar value of countries' export price (unit value) indices. His procedure is based on the view that reserve changes influence government behavior in the same way that changes in money balances influence private individuals and companies, but he offers no rebuttal to the several analyses which have shown that this analogy does not hold. He finds a significant relationship ($R^2 = .57$) and a coefficient for the effect of reserve growth on inflation that is not significantly different from unity; an increase in the rate of growth of reserves brings a corresponding increase in world export price inflation.

He then argues that domestic inflation is influenced by the domestic money supply (as in the usual closed economy case) and by the world money supply (by which he means reserves) through the empirical relationship described above. For example, he finds that the addition of the rate of growth of world reserves to an equation explaining U. S. CPI inflation on the basis of U. S. monetary expansion will improve the R^2 (from .53 to .90); improve the D. W. (from .58 to 2.24); and give significant coefficients for each variable. However, the coefficient for U. S. monetary growth, 1.8, is statistically significantly different from 1 but not from 2, meaning that a 1 percent increase in the rate of domestic expansion will give an approximate 2 percent increase in CPI inflation.

This difficulty is compounded by Keran's implicit assumption that, while reserves influence U. S. inflation, they do not influence U. S. nominal income. Since the growth of nominal income equals the rate of real growth plus CPI inflation, it follows that an increase in reserve growth will raise inflation and cause real growth to fall in an offsetting way. Keran does not mention this implication or indicate the mechanism to bring it about. Further, he finds that the growth rate of nominal income depends on the rate of U. S. monetary expansion, with the coefficient not statistically different from unity. Therefore, an increase in U. S. monetary expansion by 1 percent causes nominal growth to rise by 1 percent, while, as was shown in the previous discussion, inflation rises by 2 percent–and hence real growth falls by 1 percent.

Heller's and Keran's aggregate equations have strong statistical properties and find a significant correlation between increases in international reserves and world prices (though, in fact, the various elasticity estimates range from approximately .2 to unity). Nevertheless, careful examination of the specific formulation of the estimating equations and of some of the types of disaggregate relationships implied by the behavior of a true international quantity theory based on international reserves suggests that the aggregate correlation may be largely spurious and that the empirical case for an international reserve quantity theory remains unproved.

VIII. POLICIES TOWARD THE EUROCURRENCY MARKETS

Interest in proposals for regulation of the Euro markets appears to have been increasing.[29] In part, this is motivated by dissatisfaction with the effects of international capital mobility in general on the ability of countries to conduct independent monetary policies at constant exchange rates, and by the arguments that Euro markets play a significant role in inflation and are "undisciplined" creators of international liquidity.

A detailed, quantitative weighing of costs and benefits of Euro market regulation is beyond the scope of this paper, but we believe there is a very strong qualitative case against regulation.[30] (We should make clear that we are discussing international regulations such as uniform reserve requirements and quantitative ceilings, not national regulations which affect transactions between the country in question and the Eurocurrency markets.) We do not believe that uncontrolled liquidity creation through expansion of the Eurocurrency markets has been a major cause of world inflation in the past decade. Nor do we believe that the proposals for a modest increase in international regulation and control of the Eurocurrency markets and the establishment of international open market operations would be very effective in achieving the objectives of their advocates. International regulation could run the danger of seriously weakening the effectiveness of the Euro markets as an international financial shock absorber-- the role played in the petrodollar case. It could also lessen the competition that international financial markets provide to the oligopolistic national markets.

Furthermore, reserve requirements would do little to aid international financial stability through strengthening Eurocurrency banks. Required reserves are not available for use. The greater safety that depositors in the U. S. now enjoy has little to do with required reserves, but more to do with the Fed's lender-of-last-resort role, and with deposit insurance.

---

[29] See, for instance, Hayes (1975).

[30] For discussion of international regulation and control of the Eurocurrency markets, see, for instance, Carli, et al., (1973); Machlup (1972); Ossola (1973); Savona (1974); and Stem (1976).

Beyond the difficulty of achieving an agreement to impose an effective initial reserve requirement (if, for example, the Bahamas and Singapore did not agree to the regulations, a substantial part of the Eurocurrency market would likely relocate there), there is the difficulty that the requirements would have to be varied over time if they were to have more than a one-time effect on aggregate demand. This would require even more complex international agreements if the objective of securing greater effective international control over world monetary conditions were to be achieved, as opposed to merely inhibiting the growth of the market. While coordinated open market operations might have symbolic value, they would have to be undertaken on a truly massive scale if they were to have a marked impact on liquidity conditions in the major industrial countries.

Coordinated international policies toward the Eurocurrency markets may appear as a way of achieving greater harmonization of national monetary policies by the back door. Apart from its symbolic value, such an approach, in our opinion, would be effective only if national actions (or the activities of a supra national authority) were coordinated on a large scale, agreement on which would be as politically difficult to achieve as on direct national policy harmonization. (As to the desirability, apart from the political feasibility, of monetary policy harmonization, we will only indicate that, as is illustrated in the literature on optimum currency areas,[31] there are both important costs and benefits to such harmonization, and there is no unique answer for all countries with respect to optimal harmonization.)

Interest in regulation of the Eurocurrency market is partly attributable to the belief that it is the size of the Euro market that causes difficulties for governments in implementing their financial policies. However, the high mobility of capital and the integration of international capital markets are the real sources of difficulty.

There is no doubt that high capital mobility reduces the scope for independent government policy. The Euro markets have been a conduit for substantial world capital movements, and it is therefore tempting to urge their regulation. But it is not clear that, even if the Euro currency market were regulated out of existence, international capital mobility would be significantly lowered. The ease of international capital movements would be somewhat reduced at least initially, but it seems unlikely that such efforts would be sufficiently large so as to alter fundamentally the degree of capital mobility facing national financial authorities.

---

[31] See, for instance, Tower and Willett (1976).

305

Concern has also been expressed that the ability of national governments to borrow from the Eurocurrency and international financial markets offers governments an escape route from financial discipline. In our view, however, such borrowing has been an important source of international financial stability, in the face of the shocks of the oil price increases and consequent international financial flows, rather than a destabilizing influence.

Indeed, there is an important discipline imposed on borrowers by the operation of the market which limits the ability of governments to abuse this source of finance. Rapidly increased borrowing by any particular entity causes the market to reevaluate the borrower's creditworthiness. "Over-borrowing" incurs the penalty of increased borrowing costs and, at the extreme, inability to find new lenders. There is no presumption that such discipline will be optimal at all times, but neither has this process, in our opinion, been productive of serious inefficiencies. On balance, we believe that, rather than representing an escape from financial discipline, the private international financial markets have provided a healthy discipline. Hence, we are wary of actions which might destroy or seriously impair the operations of the Eurocurrency markets and the ability of governments as well as individuals to lend to and borrow from them.

REFERENCES

1. Amacher, R., Tollison, R.D., and Willett, T.D., "Risk Avoidance and Political Advertising: Neglected Issues in the Literature on Budget Size in a Democracy," in The Economic Approach to Public Policy, (eds. R. Amacher, R.D. Tollison, and T.D. Willett), Ithaca: Cornell University Press, 1976.

2. Bank for International Settlements, Annual Report for 1975, Basle, (1975).

3. Brittain, B., and Sri-Kumar, C., "Monetary Balance of Payments Theory: Implications and Tests," New York City Bank, 1975.

4. Carli, G., et al., "A Debate on the Eurodollar Market," Quaderni di Ricerche, No. 11, Ente per gli studi monetari, bancari e finanziari "Luigi Einaudi," 1972.

5. Cohen, B.J., "International Reserves and Liquidity," in International Trade and Finance, (ed. P. Kenen), Cambridge: Cambridge University Press, 1975.

6. Cooper, R.N., "Implications of the Eurodollar for Monetary Policy and the U.S. Balance of Payments Deficit," in National Monetary Policies and the International Financial System, (ed. R. Aliber), Chicago: University of Chicago Press, 1974.

7. Feige, E.L., and Pearce, D.K., "Economically Rational Expectations: Are Innovations in the Rate of Inflation Independent of Innovations in Measures of Monetary and Fiscal Policy?" Journal of Political Economy, 84, No. 3, (June 1976), 499-522.

8. Goldstein, H., "Monetary Policy Under Fixed and Floating Rates," National Westminster Bank, Quarterly Review, (November 1974), 15-27.

9. Granger, C.W.J., "Investigating Causal Relations by Econometric Models and Cross-spectral Methods," Econometrica, 37, No. 3, (July 1969), 424-438.

307

10. Gray, M.R., "A Small Econometric Model of the World Economy," paper presented at the Konstanz Conference on Monetary Theory and Policy, June 1975.

11. Grubel, H.G., "The Demand for International Reserves: A Critical Review of the Literature," Journal of Economic Literature, IX, No. 4, (December 1971), 1148-1166.

12. Haberler, G., "International Aspects of U.S. Inflation," in A New Look at Inflation, (P. Cagan, et al.), Washington, D.C.: American Enterprise Institute, 1974.

13. Hayes, A., "Emerging Arrangements in International Payments: Per Jacobsson Lecture," Washington, D.C., September 1975.

14. Heller, H.R., "International Reserves and Worldwide Inflation," IMF Staff Papers, 23, No. 1, (March 1976), 61-87.

15. International Monetary Fund (IMF). Seminar on Questions Relating to International Needs and Availabilites, Washington, D.C.: International Monetary Fund, 1970.

16. _____. Annual Report, 1975, Washington, D.C., 33-40.

17. Keran, M.K., "Towards an Explanation of Simultaneous Inflation-Recession," San Francisco Federal Reserve Bank, Business Review, (Spring 1975), 18-30.

18. Laffer, A.B., "Global Money Growth and Inflation," Wall Street Journal, September 23, 1975.

19. Logue, D.E., and Sweeney, R.J., "Aspects of International Monetary Influences," U.S. Treasury, OASIA research discussion paper, 1975.

20. Machlup, F., "The Need for Monetary Reserves," Banca Nazionale del Lavoro, Quarterly Review, No. 78, (September 1966), 175-222.

21. Machlup, F., "The Eurodollar System and Its Control," in <u>International Monetary Problems</u>, conference sponsored by the American Enterprise Institute for Public Policy Research,Washington, D.C.: American Enterprise Institute, 1972.

22. Mayer, H.W., "The BIS Concept of the Eurocurrency Market," <u>Euromoney</u>, (May 1976), 60-66.

23. Meiselman, D.I., "Worldwide Inflation: A Monetarist View," in <u>The Phenomenon of Worldwide Inflation</u>, (eds. D.I. Meiselman and A.B. Laffer), Washington, D.C.: American Enterprise Institute, 1975.

24. Ossola, R., "Central Bank Intervention and Eurocurrency Markets," Banca Nazionale del Lavoro, <u>Quarterly Review</u>, No. 104, (March 1973), 29-45.

25. Parkin, M., and Zis, G. (eds.) <u>Inflation in the World Economy</u>. Toronto: University of Toronto Press, 1976.

26. Promisel, L., "The Definition of the Stock of Money in Open Economies," Board of Governors of the Federal Reserve System, 1974.

27. Savona, P., "Controlling the Euromarkets," Banca Nazionale del Lavoro, <u>Quarterly Review</u>, No. 109, (June 1974), 167-174.

28. Sims, C.A., "Money, Income, and Causality," <u>American Economic Review</u>, LXII, No. 4, (September 1972), 540-552.

29. Stem, C., "The Eurocurrency System," in <u>Eurocurrencies and the International Monetary System</u>, (eds. D.E. Logue, J. Makin, and C. Stem), Washington, D.C.: American Enterprise Institute, 1976.

30. Sweeney, R.J., and Willett, T.D., "The International Transmission of Inflation: Mechanisms, Issues and Evidence," <u>Kredit und Kapital</u>, Special Supplement on Bank Money, Credit and Inflation in Open Economies, 1976.

31. _____ , "Alternative Theories of the Demand for International Reserves and Their Implications for World Inflation," (in preparation).

32. Sweeney, R.J., and Willett, T.D. (eds.) Studies on Economic Inter-
    dependence and International Monetary Stability. Washington, D.C.:
    American Enterprise Institute, (forthcoming).

33. Tower, E., and Willett, T.D., "More on Official Versus Market Financing
    of Payments Deficits and the Optimal Pricing of International
    Reserves," Kyklos, XXV, Fasc. 3, (1972), 537-552.

34. _____ , "The Theory of Optimum Currency Areas and Exchange-
    Rate Flexibility," Special Papers in International Economics, No.
    11, Princeton, N.J.: International Finance Section, Princeton University
    Press, May 1976.

35. Triffin, R., and Grubel, H.G., "The Adjustment Mechanism to Differential
    Rates of Monetary Expansion Among Countries of the European Econ-
    omic Community," Review of Economics and Statistics, LXIV, No. 4,
    (November 1962), 486-491.

36. Willett, T.D., "The Oil Transfer Problem and International Economic
    Stability," in Essays in International Finance, No. 113, Princeton,
    N.J.: International Finance Section, Princeton University Press, 1975.

37. _____ , "The Eurocurrency Market, Exchange-Rate Systems, and
    National Financial Policies," in Eurocurrencies and the International
    Monetary System, (eds. D.E. Logue, J. Makin, and C. Stem),
    Washington, D.C.: American Enterprise Institute, 1976.

38. _____ . Exchange-Rate Flexibility and Reform of the International
    Monetary System. Washington, D.C.: American Enterprise Institute,
    (forthcoming).

39. Williamson, J., "International Liquidity: A Survey," Economic Journal,
    83, No. 331, (September 1973), 685-746.

EURODOLLARS, PETRODOLLARS,
AND WORLD LIQUIDITY AND INFLATION:
A COMMENT

Dale W. Henderson*
Board of Governors of the Federal Reserve System

This comment is divided into four sections. The first section is a summary and elaboration of the thorough discussion by Sweeney and Willett (S-W) of how to treat Eurocurrency deposits when constructing monetary aggregates. The second is an analysis of the contention that central bank deposits of international reserves in the Eurodollar market have led to additional official reserve accumulation. The third is a brief discussion of some features of two suggested methods for controlling the Eurocurrency markets. The last is a comment on the S-W criticisms of Heller's (1976) study of the relationship between changes in international reserves and world inflation.

<u>Eurocurrency Deposits and World and National Monetary Aggregates</u>
The rapid growth of the Eurocurrency markets has generated much discussion concerning the treatment of Eurocurrency deposits in the construction of world or national monetary aggregates. Attention is devoted to the construction of monetary aggregates primarily because many analysts contend that some monetary aggregate should be used as an intermediate target for monetary policy. The logic of the intermediate target approach to monetary policymaking and procedures for implementing it have received much attention.[1] To be useful as an intermediate target, a monetary aggregate must have a reliable relationship to the variables which are the ultimate targets of monetary policy and must be subject to close control through the instruments of monetary policy. The choice of an intermediate target, whether it be a monetary aggregate or some other kind of variable, must be based to a large extent on empirical investigation. However, it is widely agreed that certain simple rules should be employed to reduce the number of alternative monetary aggregates considered as possible intermediate target variables. It is in this spirit that S-W conduct their discussion of which Eurocurrency deposits should be included in which monetary aggregates.

*The analysis and conclusions of this paper should not be interpreted as representing the views of the Board of Governors of the Federal Reserve System or of any other member of its staff. In writing the second section of this comment, I have benefited from discussions with Jeffrey Shafer, who independently arrived at conclusions similar to mine.

[1] See, for example, Federal Reserve Bank of Boston (1969 and 1973).

S-W suggest two relatively noncontroversial rules to employ in deciding how to treat a particular type of bank deposit when constructing a monetary aggregate for use as an intermediate target. First, a deposit should be included only if it is a liability to a nonbank. Second, a deposit should be included if, and only if, other deposits with the same general characteristics are included.

They then present some facts about Eurocurrency deposits which relate to the use of these rules in deciding how to treat Eurocurrency deposits when constructing monetary aggregates. First, no more than one-fifth of the total volume of Eurodollar deposits are liabilities to nonbanks.[2] Second, the usual minimum size of Eurodollar deposits is $100,000. Third, what sketchy data are available suggest that more than three-quarters of Eurocurrency deposits have maturities of more than eight days.[3]

These facts provide a basis for deciding how to treat Eurocurrency deposits in the construction of world monetary aggregates. Only those deposits owed to nonbanks should be included. If all similar nonbank deposits are to be treated alike, Eurocurrency deposits should only be included in very broad monetary aggregates which contain other larger denomination, longer maturity deposits. In the U.S., for example, large certificates of deposits which closely resemble the typical Eurocurrency deposit are included in M4 and M5, but not in M1, M2, or M3. Nonbank Eurocurrency deposits constitute a very small fraction of world aggregates comparable to M4 and M5 and, despite their rapid growth, account for only a very small part of the growth in these world aggregates. If data were available, the uncommon, small denomination, and very short maturity Eurocurrency deposits owed to nonbanks could be separated out and included in world aggregates comparable to M2 and M3.

The facts about Eurocurrency deposits are much less helpful in deciding how to treat these deposits when constructing national monetary aggregates for open economies. It seems clear that Eurocurrency deposits should only be included in broad monetary aggregates, although some countries now include Eurocurrency deposits owned by residents in narrow aggregates.[4] It is difficult to proceed further using simple rules as a guide in the case of an open economy. Indeed, difficulties in applying simple rules in the construction of national

---

[2] In their footnote 6 S-W report that Morgan Guaranty estimates that the gross amount of Eurocurrency deposits was $360 billion, and that the amount of Eurocurrency deposits owed to nonbank nonresidents was $44 billion in December 1974. S-W do not report on estimates of the amount of Eurocurrency deposits owed to nonbank residents, but adding these deposits almost certainly would not raise the total amount of deposits owed to nonbanks above $72 billion.

[3] See Table 1 in S-W.

[4] Promisel (1974) reports that Germany, Italy, and France include Eurocurrency deposits owned by nonbank residents in M1, and that the U.K. includes such deposits in M3.

monetary aggregates for open economies would exist even in the absence of Eurocurrency deposits. Nonbank deposits with given maturity and size characteristics can be classified exhaustively either by the country of residence of the owner, or by currency of denomination, or by the country of the issuing bank. While it might seem logical to choose one of these exhaustive classifications as a rule in constructing national monetary aggregates for an open economy, there is at least one other very appealing rule--include only deposits owned by residents and denominated in domestic currency. It is likely that further theorizing will suggest that some of these rules are likely to be better guides than others, but a number of possibilities will remain. Empirical work of the sort which has been used in deciding between alternative suggested intermediate targets will then be needed.[5] There is, of course, a possibility that no monetary aggregate or other proposed intermediate target variable will perform well enough empirically to justify the use of the intermediate target approach to monetary policymaking in open economies.

Central Bank Deposits in the Eurocurrency Markets

S-W mention, without endorsing, the familiar contention that when central banks deposit their reserves in the Eurocurrency markets, or offer special inducements to domestic commercial banks to make deposits in these markets, they set in motion forces which lead to further official reserve accumulation. To analyze this contention, it is convenient to suppose that a European central bank has just acquired a demand deposit in a New York commerical bank as a result of intervention made necessary by some shock to financial market equilibrium. Consider three alternatives available to the central bank: (1) holding the demand deposit; (2) purchasing a U.S. Treasury bill in the open market; or (3) acquiring a Eurodollar deposit.[6] The first alternative results in no further reserve accumulation, but is unattractive because interest earnings are forgone; therefore, a central bank would usually choose alternative two or alternative three. Now, following either of these alternatives leads to further reserve accumulation by the European central bank because under either alternative interest rates on dollar denominated assets are bid down. However, it is not at all clear why acquiring a Eurodollar deposit should lead to a larger reserve accumulation than purchasing a Treasury bill. If Eurodollar deposits and/or

---

[5]Several studies which are representative of the state of the art in the empirical comparision of alternative suggested intermediate target variables are included in Federal Reserve Bank of New York (1974). For an evaluation of this type of empirical study, see Friedman (forthcoming).

[6]There are, in fact, other alternatives open to the European central bank such as acquiring a deposit at the New York Federal Reserve Bank or acquiring SDRs, but these alternatives are not relevant here.

Eurodollar loans are very good substitutes for Treasury bills in the portfolios of a significant subgroup of market participants, then the effects of pursuing either alternative are the same.[7] Furthermore, if, as some contend, Eurodollar banks hold demand deposits at U.S. commercial banks equal to a small, but stable, fraction of their Eurodollar deposit liabilities as precautionary balances, the additional reserve accumulation will be less if the central bank acquires a Eurodollar deposit because of the induced demand for U.S. high-powered money. It may well be that, when compared to the most relevant alternative, central bank deposits in the Eurodollar market lead to less additional reserve accumulation.

When allowance is made for restrictions on the outflow of capital from the U.S. such as the capital controls which existed before January 1974, the conclusions above are altered. In the limiting case in which the U.S. money market is completely segmented from the Eurodollar market and European money markets, a central bank purchase of a Treasury bill and the resulting downward pressure on the Treasury bill rate do not lead to any substitution between U.S. dollar assets and Eurodollar or foreign currency assets; there is then no additional reserve accumulation by the European central bank. Central bank acquisition of a Eurodollar deposit leads to a decline in the Eurodollar rate and to substitution between Eurodollars and foreign currency assets, so the European central bank accumulates additional reserves. While U.S. capital controls did not completely insulate the U.S. money market, they appear to have impeded capital outflow somewhat since Eurodollar rates were at times significantly above U.S. money market rates. Thus, the concern over the effects of central bank deposits in the Eurodollar market, which first arose in the early 1970s, was justifiable as long as U.S. capital controls were in effect.

Some Effects of Two Suggested Methods for Controlling the Eurocurrency Markets

S-W make a case against the use of open market operations and reserve requirements as methods for controlling the Eurocurrency markets. While their arguments are rather convincing, S-W do not discuss the nature and effects of these two methods of control in much detail.

Although it has often been suggested that open market operations could be used to control the Eurocurrency markets, there has not been much discussion of how these operations could be carried out or of what their effects

---

[7]It is assumed here that the Eurodollar loan rate differs from the Eurodollar deposit rate by a small, constant markup.

would be. One possible type of open market operation is a swap of U.S. Treasury bills for Eurodollar deposits.[8] The ingredients of an analysis of what would happen if a central bank sold U.S. Treasury bills and deposited the proceeds in the Eurodollar market have been presented above. If Treasury bills and Eurodollar deposits and/or Eurodollar loans are very good substitutes in the market portfolios of a significant subgroup of market participants, there will be only a slight rise in the Treasury bill rate and a slight decline in Eurodollar deposit and loan rates. The average level of dollar interest rates will remain roughly unchanged or will rise slightly if Eurodollar banks hold precautionary balances at U.S. commercial banks.

Another, more effective, type of open market operation is the switch by a foreign central bank between deposits at U.S. commercial banks and Eurodollar deposits. If a central bank draws down its deposit at a U.S. commercial bank and acquires a Eurodollar deposit, the demand for U.S. high-powered money is reduced, and Eurodollar deposit and loan rates and the general level of dollar interest rates will fall. The scope for expansionary open market operations of this type is limited by the size of central bank deposits at U.S. commercial banks; the scope for contractionary open market operations is limited by the size of central bank Eurodollar deposits.[9]

It has also been suggested that Eurocurrency deposits should be subjected to reserve requirements. Some insight regarding the effects of introducing reserve requirements can be obtained from a highly simplified two country (U.S. and Europe), two currency (dollar and Europa) model of international financial markets under fixed exchange rates which incorporates banking sectors.[10] Banks in both countries consider loans and securities regardless of the currency of denomination to be perfect substitutes, so the interest rate on dollar obligations is always equal to the interest rate on Europa obligations. Banks in the U.S. have as liabilities dollar-denominated demand deposits and time deposits. Banks in Europe have as liabilities Europa-denominated demand and time deposits and dollar-denominated time deposits (Eurodollar deposits). No interest is paid on demand deposits. Time deposit interest rates are equal to one minus the relevant reserve requirement times the difference between the loan-security rate and a constant intermediation cost expressed in percentage terms.

---

[8]Swaps of securities denominated in, say, pounds for Eurodollar deposits would have quite different effects. This type of open market operation, which is probably better thought of as a type of exchange market intervention, is not considered here.

[9]A central bank could also switch between deposits at the New York Federal Reserve Bank and Eurodollar deposits. This type of operation would be more effective than the one described in this text.

[10]With minor modifications, the model can be used to analyze the effects of introducing a reserve requirement on Eurodollar deposits when the exchange rate is allowed to float.

European banks regard dollar and Europa time deposits as perfect substitutes, and differences between the rates paid on these deposits arise only because of differences in reserve requirements. The public in each country holds demand deposits denominated in home currency, U.S. dollar time deposits, Eurodollar time deposits, Europa time deposits, securities, and loans. Publics in both countries regard all assets as strict gross substitutes. In each country, high-powered money is the only liability of the central bank and is matched on the asset side by securities denominated in domestic currency, and by foreign assets such as gold or securities denominated in foreign currency. Equilibrium occurs when the demand for high-powered money equals the supply of high-powered money in each country. These two equations determine the loan-security interest rate and the U.S. stock of reserves.

Placing a reserve requirement on Eurodollar deposits lowers the interest rate that European banks are willing to pay on Eurodollar deposits for a given loan-security rate. Demand for U.S. high-powered money is increased because the public shifts out of Eurodollars into U.S. dollar demand and time deposits. Demand for European high-powered money rises for two reasons. First, the public shifts out of Eurodollars into Europa demand and time deposits. Second, banks are now required to hold reserves against Eurodollar deposits. Given these increases in demand for high-powered money, the loan-security rate must rise. The U.S. gains (loses) reserves if the increase in demand for U.S. high-powered money is greater (less) than the increase in the demand for European high-powered money at the initial loan-security rate. Of course, the demand for U.S. high-powered money is likely to rise more if U.S. dollar demand and time deposits are better substitutes than Europa demand and time deposits for Eurodollar deposits.

On the Sweeney-Willett Critique of Heller

Sweeney and Willett present several criticisms of Heller (1976) which attempts to measure the impact of the rate of change of world reserves on a geometric average of rates of national money growth and, through money growth, on a geometric average of national inflation rates. Their primary criticism is well taken. They present arguments which suggest that there is probably no reliable relationship between changes in international reserves and changes in national monetary policies, and report that they found no significant rank correlation between reserve accumulation and rates of money growth across countries in the period 1970-72. The S-W view is supported by other researchers such as Parkin, Richards and Zis (1975) who find no significant correlation between changes in world reserves and changes in world central bank domestic assets for the period 1961-1971.

316

Several of the other criticisms are less sound. First, S-W seem to suggest that Heller argues that the relationship between changes in reserves and changes in prices should be unit elastic. Heller never makes this argument. He does claim (1976, p. 78) that his results support the view that the relationship between changes in a geometric average of money growth rates and a geometric average of inflation rates is approximately unit elastic. Second, S-W contend that differences in implications among some of Heller's tests suggest "a certain instability among his empirical results." Though it is a matter of opinion, few observers are likely to agree with S-W that the differences in implications between the pair of Heller's tests, summarized in equations (11), (12), and (13) in S-W, suggest instability. However, in a third test, Heller employs an unconstrained regression of a geometric average of national inflation rates on changes in world reserves led four periods and lagged four periods, and finds that the sum of the coefficients on lagged reserves is approximately equal to one. The results of this regression seem to conflict with the results of the other tests. However, since this regression is not directly comparable with the other regressions and since Heller does not include all of the summary statistics for this regression, it is not possible to determine whether or not the third test casts serious doubt on the results of the other two tests. Third, S-W contend that Heller's regressions embody "an element of exchange illusion" since he uses changes in world reserves measured in dollars or SDRs. S-W make the unconvincing argument that monetary authorities respond to changes in international reserves measured in domestic currency if they respond to reserve changes at all. Surely, if the monetary authorities have a reserve target, it is set in terms of foreign currency, and changes in monetary policy result from deviations between that target and actual reserves measured in foreign currency. It is no doubt true, as S-W suggest, that the monetary policy response to a given change in reserves measured in foreign currency is different when the exchange rate is allowed to change. However, simply switching to a domestic currency measure of reserve changes is not a satisfactory way of dealing with this potentially important complication.

REFERENCES

1. Federal Reserve Bank of Boston. Controlling Monetary Aggregates. Boston: Federal Reserve Bank of Boston, 1969.

2. _____ . Controlling Monetary Aggregates II: The Implementation. Boston: Federal Reserve Bank of Boston, 1973.

3. Federal Reserve Bank of New York. Monetary Aggregates and Monetary Policy. New York: Federal Reserve Bank of New York, 1974.

4. Friedman, B., "Empirical Issues in Monetary Policy: A Review of the New York Fed Papers," Journal of Monetary Economics, (forthcoming).

5. Heller, H.R., "International Reserves and Worldwide Inflation," IMF Staff Papers, 23, No. 1, (March 1976), 61-87.

6. Parkin, M., Richards, I., and Zis, G., "The Determination and Control of the World Money Supply Under Fixed Exchange Rates 1961-1971," The Manchester School of Economic and Social Studies, 43, No. 3, (September 1975), 293-316.

7. Promisel, L., "The Definition of the Stock of Money in Open Economies," Board of Governors of the Federal Reserve System, mimeo, 1974.